Twayne's English Authors Series

Sylvia E. Bowman, *Editor*

INDIANA UNIVERSITY

John Morley

John Morley

By EDWARD ALEXANDER

University of Washington

Twayne Publishers, Inc. :: New York

Library of Congress Catalog Card Number 70–187618

F11

For Sadie and Harry Alexander

Preface

In this study of John Morley as a man of letters I have tried to convey an accurate impression of the nature and importance of his ethical and political ideas, his historical studies of the French Enlightenment, and his literary criticism. I hope that the reader will discover in this book the reasons why, as Basil Willey wrote in 1956, Morley "deserves to be recognized and revalued by any historian or student of Victorian literature and ideas . . . he was one of the most influential critics of his time, sharing the literary and intellectual dictatorship only, perhaps, with Leslie Stephen and Matthew Arnold."

I have restricted this work to that part of Morley's career and to those aspects of his work which are of importance to students of literature and ideas. For this reason, Morley's political biographies and much else which he wrote after 1883, when he entered politics, are not discussed. I have, however, tried in my first chapter to describe his political career and to relate it to the literary career which preceded it. Those who are inclined to think the literary career important solely as a preamble to the political career would do well to remember that Morley was already forty-five years old when he was first elected to Parliament and to give some thought to the misgivings he expressed in an unpublished letter to Thomas Huxley written a month before his election: "You are right about the mire of politics; but I have floundered into this mess somehow, and I don't see my way out of it just yet. I used to think that I could perhaps improve politics: so far, it looks as if politics has rather *dis*-improved me" (Letter of January 22, 1883, in Huxley Papers. 23.77).

I have incurred several debts, which I am happy to acknowledge, in the course of writing this book. First, I am indebted to the books on John Morley by Professor Warren D. Staebler and by Miss Frances W. Knickerbocker; to Professor Walter E. Houghton for information about Morley's papers; to Mr. David I. Masson of the Brotherton Collection, Leeds University, for allowing me to examine Morley's letters to Edmund Gosse; and to Mrs. Jeanne Pingree of the Imperial College of Science and Technology for allowing me to consult the Huxley Papers. Passages from the Huxley Papers are reproduced by the kind permission of the Governing Body of Imperial College. I am also indebted to the Agnes H. Anderson Section of the Graduate School Research Fund of the University of Washington for granting funds to cover the expense of typing the manuscript of this book. For help and suggestions of various kinds I am indebted to Morton Alexander, Professor Frederick M. Garber of the State University of New York at Binghamton, Professors Malcolm Brown, David Fowler, Jacob Korg and Leonard Neufeldt of the University of Washington, and Professor G. Robert Stange of Tufts University.

Finally, I should like to thank my wife, Leah Alexander, for cheerfully relieving me of many of the tasks involved in the making of this book.

EDWARD ALEXANDER

University of Washington
Seattle, Washington

Contents

Chronology

1838   John Morley born December 24, Blackburn, Lancashire.

1852   Enters University College, London.

1855   Moves to Cheltenham College, a new public school.

1856   Enters Lincoln College, Oxford, with intention of becoming an Evangelical clergyman.

1859   Leaves Oxford with a Pass degree after quarreling with his father over his loss of religious faith.

1860   Goes to work as a journalist in London.

1865   Makes the acquaintance of John Stuart Mill; publishes *Modern Characteristics*.

1866   Makes the acquaintance of George Eliot and George Henry Lewes. At end of year is appointed editor of *The Fortnightly Review*.

1867   *Edmund Burke: A Historical Study*, and *Studies in Conduct*.

1868   Visits America; meets R. W. Emerson and W. Whitman. Is unsuccessful in attempt to win a parliamentary seat from Blackburn.

1871   Publishes first volume of *Critical Miscellanies*.

1872   *Voltaire*.

1873   *Rousseau* and *The Struggle for National Education*.

1874   *On Compromise*.

1876   Visits Italy.

1877   Travels in Austria. Plans "English Men of Letters Series."

1878   *Diderot and the Encyclopaedists*.

1879   *Burke* in "English Men of Letters Series."

1880   Assumes editorship of *Pall Mall Gazette*. Tries unsuccessfully to win parliamentary seat from Westminster. Joins Joseph Chamberlain in urging conciliation and land reform for Ireland.

1881   *The Life of Richard Cobden*.

1882   Resigns editorship of *Fortnightly*.
1883   Elected to Parliament as Liberal member for Newcastle. Resigns editorship of *Pall Mall Gazette*. Assumes editorship of *Macmillan's Magazine*.
1886   Serves briefly as chief secretary for Ireland.
1889   *Walpole* (in "Twelve English Statesmen Series").
1891   *Studies in Literature*.
1892   Begins a second term, lasting three years, as chief secretary for Ireland.
1895   Removed from office; resumes private citizenship.
1900   *Oliver Cromwell*.
1903   *The Life of William Ewart Gladstone*.
1904   Visits America at invitation of Andrew Carnegie; meets Elihu Root and Theodore Roosevelt.
1905   Appointed secretary of state for India.
1908   Enters House of Lords as Viscount Morley.
1910   Resigns Indian secretaryship; appointed lord president of the Council.
1914   Resigns from cabinet in protest against England's intention to enter the war.
1917   *Recollections*.
1923   Morley died at Wimbledon on September 23.
1928   *Memorandum on Resignation* posthumously published.

CHAPTER 1

The Man of Letters as Statesman

This treatment of politics with one's thought, or with one's imagination, or with one's soul, in place of the common treatment of them with one's Philistinism and with one's passions, is the only thing which can reconcile . . . any serious person to politics, with their inevitable wear, waste, and sore trial to all that is best in one.
—Matthew Arnold, Letter of 1864

I am . . . reduced to wondering whether I shall ever be able to resume those quiet studies which are so prodigiously better for the mind itself than the tiresome labour of chipping off little bits of one's thoughts of a size to be swallowed by a set of diminutive practical politicians incapable of digesting them. One ought to be very sure of being able to do something in politics that cannot be as well done by others, to justify one for the sacrifice of time and energies that might be employed on higher work.
—John Stuart Mill, Letter of 1865

THE career of John Morley dramatized the Victorian conviction that literature is a criticism of life by testing it against the actualities of modern politics. Morley shared with the great Victorians the belief that literature is immediately connected with life and that worth-while criticism of literature inevitably becomes criticism of philosophy, religion, and politics as well. But

13

Morley, unlike Thomas Carlyle, John Ruskin, and Matthew Arnold, put this belief to the rigorous test of a long public career in politics, and the chief interest of his life lies in its embodiment of the conflict between the ideals of Victorian liberalism and the realities of modern political life. When Morley resigned from the British Cabinet in August, 1914 (just before the war began), Winston Churchill—who was to play so crucial a role in the terrible world then being born—saw in Morley's predicament "the horrible impact of the Great War upon the statesman who above all others then alive represented the Victorian age" and described the action as symbolic proof that "the old world of culture and quality, of hierarchies and traditions, of values and decorum, . . . was doomed." [1]

The primary concern of this study is Morley's literary work and not his life; and the value of his best work as a man of letters exists independently of his career as a statesman. Yet we must remember that he was engrossed in politics even before he became a politician and that, when we are dealing with an author who saw his life's work as the translation of literary and philosophical ideas into political forms, knowledge of the writer's life may make a considerable contribution to the understanding and to the criticism of his work.

I *Life to 1883*

John Morley was born December 24, 1838, in Blackburn, Lancashire, the son of a surgeon of good reputation. He spent the first twenty years of his life in this manufacturing center, and he always retained a kind of loyalty to its stiff Evangelical character as well as to its industrial spirit. In September, 1899, decades after he had left the world of Blackburn, he was able to mollify a hostile, jingoistic audience in Manchester by reminding them that he was "a Lancashire man."

Although Morley's father was a communicant of the Church of England, he reared his son in the atmosphere of nonconformist Wesleyan Evangelicalism in which he had himself spent his youth. Thus John Morley, like many of the great Victorian writers —Thomas Macaulay, John Ruskin, John Newman, George Eliot, and Robert Browning—was brought up under the aegis of that somber, introspective, and Bible-centered form of Christianity which is so often supposed to be hostile to the arts. He attended a school in Blackburn which "abounded in the unadulterated milk of the Independent word, and perhaps accounted for nonconformist affinities in some of the politics of days to come." [2] In fact, Morley understates the case, for his loyalty to a Protestantism in whose religious foundations he no longer believed remained a powerful influence on his social and political thought.

Morley entered Lincoln College, Oxford, in 1856 with the intention of becoming an Evangelical clergyman. His father, apparently aware of the fact that in 1726 John Wesley had been nominated a fellow of Lincoln by a rector named John Morley, arranged for his son to occupy what had once been Wesley's rooms. But even the most conscientious arrangement of circumstances was no substitute for conviction; for, during the very terms he was lodged in Wesley's rooms, Morley was losing his youthful Methodism. At the beginning of his third year at Oxford, he revealed to his father that his religious views would not permit him conscientiously to enter Holy Orders; his father, in consequence, cut off his allowance, and young Morley had to leave Oxford in 1859, at the end of his third year, with a Pass degree. There is undoubtedly a personal recollection latent in Morley's severe judgment in *On Compromise* of clergymen who "vow almost before they have crossed the threshold of manhood that they will search no more. They virtually swear that they will to the end of their days believe what they believe then, before they have had time either to think, or to know the thoughts of others. They take oaths, in other words, to lead mutilated lives." [3]

Morley's formative period at Oxford coincided with the last years of the clergy's official hold on university education. Oxford was still, as Matthew Arnold described it in 1865, in the Preface to *Essays in Criticism,* the "home of lost causes, and forsaken beliefs, and unpopular names, and impossible loyalties!" It clung to the old forms of dogmatic and ecclesiastical religion, staunchly resisted the new spirit of scientific inquiry, and set itself firmly against democracy. But between the rigidities of Oxford and the fermenting mind of the best thinkers of the period lay a great divide. John Henry Newman, the leader of the Oxford Movement, the upholder of the dogmatic principle in all areas of life, and a determined foe of popular political movements, was himself compelled to admit in 1864 that "the Liberalism which gives a colour to society now, is very different from the character of thought

which bore the name thirty or forty years ago. Now it is scarcely a
party; it is the educated lay world." [4]

Liberalism manifested itself in various ways during Morley's
years at Oxford. The empirical school of philosophy that had found
its most articulate recent spokesman in Mill battled against intuitionism in its various forms. The year 1859, Morley's last one at Oxford, saw the publication of J. S. Mill's *On Liberty* and Charles
Darwin's *Origin of Species;* and in the following year a group of
scholars, many of them ordained clergymen, brought liberal
thought and scientific criticism to bear on the Scriptures in the
book *Essays and Reviews,* a plea for the liberalization of religion.
The Church of England tried two of the clerical authors in a
church court, convicted them of heresy—one of their sins being
the refusal to believe in eternal damnation—and suspended them
from their posts (though the decision was eventually overturned
in the House of Lords). In 1862—two years after Morley's religious quarrel with his father had forced him to leave Oxford—
John William Colenso, bishop of the African see of Natal, published *The Pentateuch Critically Examined,* in which he stated
that the Mosaic narrative of the Pentateuch, "whatever value it
may have, *is not historically true."* He was peremptorily excom-
municated by the colonial bishop and barred from his own cathe-
dral as a heathen. In court, where William Gladstone was attor-
ney for the conservative faction, Colenso's excommunication was
reversed and his salary continued; but he remained a pariah in
"respectable" society.

Such raw assaults by conservative ecclesiastical force upon human reason helped to undermine Morley's faith. On the one hand,
he saw not only the leaders of thought but even the popular mind
ready "to extend an excited welcome to explanations whether of
species or social phenomena by general laws, at the expense of
special providence." On the other, he saw ecclesiastical power unable to comprehend and unwilling to recognize an age of transition. The situation seemed to him to require a suspension of faith
in the old creeds and a willingness to experiment with new ones.
He described the spiritual state of England during his youth as
one of "much empty profession of barren orthodoxy, and, beneath
all, a vague disquiet, a breaking up of ancient social and natural
bonds, and a blind groping toward some more cosmopolitan creed

and some deeper satisfaction for the emotional needs of mankind." [5]

After having his university career abruptly terminated and after reading law for a time, Morley tried to make his way in London through journalism. From 1860–67 he read for, and contributed to, the publishing house of Macmillan; he was a reviewer and reporter for the *Leader,* edited by George Henry Lewes, and for the *Star* and *Times;* he temporarily edited the *Library Gazette;* and he reviewed books and wrote articles (exclusively on nonpolitical subjects) for the *Saturday Review.* He collected and reprinted what he considered to be the best of his *Saturday Review* articles in two anonymous volumes—*Modern Characteristics* (1865) and *Studies in Conduct* (1867)—the second of which he withdrew from sale shortly after its appearance. The majority of these essays—there are exceptions—are of a light, social, merely suggestive nature that is sufficiently indicated by their titles: in *Modern Characteristics,* we have "False Steps," "Quarrels," "Social Salamanders," "Clever Men's Wives," "The Theory of Life from Below-Stairs," "Praise and Blame"; in *Studies in Conduct,* "Small Hypocrisies," "Social Troglodytes," "The Philosophy of Sour Grapes," "Favorite Authors," "Drawing-Room Critics," "Town and Country."

In 1867, Morley assumed the editorship of the *Fortnightly Review* and retained it until the summer of 1882 when he turned in earnest to a political career. The journal had been founded in 1865 in order to be, in the words of one of its tutelary spirits, Anthony Trollope, both good in its literature, and "strictly impartial and absolutely honest." In pursuit of the latter aim, it adhered to the then revolutionary policy of having its authors sign their articles. When Morley appeared to be interviewed for the job, Trollope doggedly adhered to the magazine's policy that people should make their views known: "Glaring as if in fury through his spectacles, and roaring like a Bull of Bashan, he asked the young applicant 'Now, do you believe in the divinity of our beloved Lord and Savior Jesus Christ?' " [6] Morley was not the man to duck such questions or to conceal his agnosticism; and it is a tribute to Trollope's tolerance that he hired the young man despite his heresies.

As editor of the *Fortnightly,* Morley's aim was, in his own

words, "the diffusion and encouragement of rationalistic standards
in things spiritual and temporal alike." [7] The journal was
avowedly liberal in spirit, but the many-sidedness of its idea of
liberalism may be seen in the variety and diversity of its most
distinguished contributors: Arnold, A. C. Swinburne, George
Meredith, D. G. Rossetti, Walter Bagehot, Thomas Huxley, Walter Pater, G. H. Lewes (its first editor), Frederic Harrison, A. V.
Dicey, Leslie Stephen, Mark Pattison, F. W. H. Myers. But my
discussion of the character, influence, and achievements of the
Fortnightly Review under Morley's management is reserved for
the following chapter.

In 1867, Morley also published his first important book, *Edmund Burke: A Historical Study.* The book was critical rather
than biographical (Morley published a biography of Burke in
1879), and "historical" in the sense that it was concerned with
Burke only insofar as he originated, helped, opposed, or represented certain progressive historical forces. Morley wanted to
show, somewhat as J. S. Mill had done with Samuel Coleridge,
that one might admit that Burke had taken the wrong side in the
controversy over the French Revolution and that he had been
blind to all of its positive contributions, yet recognize that his
writings conveyed "a wiser, deeper, broader, and more permanent
view of the elements of social stability, of its priceless value, of its
power over the happiness of men, than it was possible for his
adversaries . . . to arrive at in the midst of the storm and convulsions that enveloped them." [8] Burke's conclusions might be
wrong, but his methods and principles were invaluable.

A fact of the first importance for Morley is that Burke could
have supported the American Revolution but have violently opposed the French one. There was no inconsistency here, for Burke
had preceded the nineteenth-century Utilitarians in perceiving
"the profound speculative truth that politics is not a science of
abstract ideas, but an empirical art." He had grasped, in advance
if his contemporaries, the doctrine of political relativism—the
doctrine that, in Burke's own words, "nothing universal can be
rationally affirmed on any moral or political subject." England's
attitude towards the American colonies was based (officially) on
the metaphysical conception of *right,* a notion Burke despised.
Convinced that it was as sovereign in the colonies as at home, the
English government saw nothing to justify delay in enforcing this

abstract right. But Burke argued that there was no such thing as an abstract right divorced from expediency and convenience. He asserted what Morley calls "the utilitarian truth, that the statesman is concerned, not at all with the rights of the government, but altogether with the interests and happiness of the governed. . . ." [9] So convinced was Burke of the danger of Englishmen's becoming enamored of the idea of abstract rights that he believed American independence the price that had to be paid for maintaining free government *in England.* It was from Burke that Morley learned to look upon the American Revolution as in some sense a conservative one; and, when he himself entered public life, he referred to Burke's writings on the conflict with America as "the most perfect manual in our literature, or in any literature, for one who approaches the study of public affairs, whether for knowledge or for practice." [10]

Morley did not, of course, adopt Burke's opinions about all aspects of the French Revolution; but it was the influence of Burke which enabled him to see why the application of the doctrines of the rights of man had succeeded in America, yet had failed in France. Americans had had experimental knowledge of the principles of government as well as a doctrine of rights; in France, as Burke had shown, all maxims of action were deduced from a priori principles. Burke, however blind to the positive aspects of the French Revolution, had clearly apprehended the danger of its intellectual method. Nothing could be more dangerous than abruptly to sever the mass of men from the collective experience of the human race and expect them to base their actions on reason alone.

Morley learned from Burke that, "although no rule of conduct or spring of action ought to endure which does not repose in sound reason, yet this naked reason is in itself a less effective means of influencing action, than when it exists as one part of a fabric of ancient and endeared association." [11] Burke, to be sure, tended to mistake ancient and endeared association, or "prejudices" as he frankly called them, for reasons; but this error was no cause to neglect the truth of human nature which Burke did grasp. It is a truth, Morley would always argue, that had been remembered during the Reformation and the English and American revolutions; but it was unhappily forgotten in France. Burke's influence over Morley was a lasting one. But, whereas Burke had deduced an antidemocratic political theory from an empirical and Utilitarian philosophy, Morley was to show his eclecticism and flexibility by building a very democratic politics upon the same philosophical premises. (Morley's enduring affection for Burke may also have had something to do with the fact that Burke was a man who, like Morley himself, had deserted letters for politics.)

In 1868, Morley visited America. He had been among the few English men of letters—Mill was another—to espouse the Northern cause in the Civil War and to see in its triumph a confirmation of liberalism. On this first visit, he met such Northern generals as U. S. Grant and William Sherman, and he made the acquaintance of Walt Whitman. Unlike many of his countrymen who had visited America in the period, he was not generous with criticism and advice: "I was wise enough in 1868 to leave the country without venturing, with such meteoric short notice, . . . on a single original idea as to the institutions of the American Union, their durability, or the sort of pattern they were destined to supply for democracy in Europe." [12]

In the same year, and again in 1880, Morley made unsuccessful attempts to win a parliamentary seat from his home town of Blackburn. In the general election of 1880, however, the Liberals won the House of Commons, Gladstone was installed as prime minister, and Morley in the *Fortnightly Review* could hail the results as a rejection of Tory imperialism. He had by this time been editing and contributing to the *Fortnightly Review* for thirteen years, during which time he had also published his French studies, two books on Burke, and the Millite tract *On Compromise*. Yet always the political man was latent in the man of letters. Thomas Hardy once said that if only Morley had let politics alone, he might have been the Gibbon of his age. But Morley's desertion —if it is properly to be called that—of literature for politics was always implicit even in his purely literary work. From the start he was attracted to "the long list of writers who have shown that to take an active part in public affairs and mix in society give a peculiar life, reality, and force to both scholarship and speculation." [13] In 1871, he told Frederic Harrison that his obstinate preference of action to literature (a preference Harrison had articulately expressed a few years before in his criticism of Matthew Arnold's doctrine of culture) was leading him away "from the organ where power resides at this moment." [14]

It seems likely that Morley turned to politics when he had done all that he believed he ever could do for the cause of reform through literature and journalism; for Morley did not, in later life, believe that he had made a great sacrifice or had mutilated himself in any way by turning from literature to political action. His choice had not, after all, been so momentous as that of such literary-political predecessors as Macaulay, Alexis de Tocqueville, Edward Bulwer, or Benjamin Disraeli. Naturally, he "would rather have written the *Decline and Fall* than have been Mr. Pitt"; but his decision involved merely "the more modest selection between an outdoor publicist on the one hand, and member of the House of Commons on the other, with all the advantages of a wider and closer field of political observation, and all the chances of influence this position carries with it."

In the spring of 1883, running as a Liberal, he was elected from Newcastle-on-Tyne to the House of Commons, where he was to serve for twenty-five years. The man who had begun in the world of literature by repudiating conventions was launched on a career whose first working principle is compliance with convention.[15] But, before we can examine the conflict between Morley's intellectual ideals and the circumstances of his political career, we must analyze his intellectual development in the period before he entered the political arena.

II *Intellectual Influences*

Morley called John Stuart Mill his intellectual father; and Mill was certainly the most potent and most lasting influence upon his mind and temper. "Ideas," Morley once wrote, "are not everything in a teacher, vital though they may be. Mill's merit was the extension of them in spirit and letter to social and political issues. . . ."[16] Morley's career may usefully be viewed as the attempt to translate the precepts of Mill's liberalism into practice. In fact, Morley was just the kind of disciple, and paid exactly the kind of tribute, that Mill would most have appreciated. For what he found most inspiring in Mill was his quality of mind and method of inquiry rather than a particular set of doctrines (though he adopted many of these as well): "The edification lay in the processes that brought him to his conclusions—impersonal temper, tentative feeling of the way, acquiescence in the provisional when you could not reach certitude, instant readiness to weigh a new fact or a revised presentation of an old argument." [17]

Mill's method of reasoning was historical in the sense that it respected circumstances and was both flexible and relative. In his great essays on Jeremy Bentham and S. T. Coleridge, Mill had argued that the seeker after truth cannot bind himself to one sect or thesis but must, like history itself, admit that, for every thesis, there is an equally valid antithesis. Instead of riveting himself to what has long seemed a true position, he must be flexible enough to swing to the opposite position when a changed historical situation makes it the true and desirable one. But he must also take care that, in reaction against the weaknesses of a mode of philosophy, he does not forget its strengths. The thinker disciplined by a sense of history must work for the ultimate reconciliation of adversaries: Bentham and Coleridge; empiricism and intuitionism; radicalism and conservatism.[18]

In this flexible attitude toward history and ideas Morley recognized and responded to a remarkable flexibility of intelligence and health of spirit. He saw Mill's intellectual impressionableness as a kind of emotional sensibility which allowed its owner to live and to act without having certainty. He was charmed by Mill's power of adaptation because it seemed to grow out of a personal fortitude and also because it was so wonderfully persuasive.[19] It enabled Mill to appeal, in a modest and impersonal way, to his reader's love of finding and embracing truth for himself rather than of having it handed to him by some authority external to himself. Setting for himself the enormous task of radically transforming, not merely the opinions of his countrymen, but the modes of thought and states of mind which had produced those opinions, Mill saw the need to temper courage with patience, modesty, and tolerance. According to Morley, Mill was "unrivalled in the difficult art of conciliating as much support as was possible and alienating as little sympathy as possible, for novel and extremely unpopular opinions"; his unique combination of boldness and tolerance had accomplished as much for the liberty of expressing unpopular opinions in England as had his direct plea for it in *On Liberty*.[20]

As a young man, Morley was attracted to Mill because, nearly alone among the thinkers of the time, he seemed to combine the social with the scientific impulse: the moral ardor for improvements in society, politics, and religion with the dispassionate and impartial temper supposed to be characteristic of the scientist. He was, in Morley's words, a miraculous "union of stern science with infinite aspiration, of rigorous sense of what is real and practicable with bright and luminous hope." [21] What was rarer still, Mill brought ideal and imaginative elements to bear upon society and politics; for he was a humanist as well as a liberal. He saw liberty not merely as an end in itself but as a means to the harmonious development of the individual: in the sphere of action, he recommended liberty yet exemplified duty; in the sphere of thought, he showed that a commitment to free and disinterested criticism was not inconsistent with strongly held convictions about what was right and wrong, useful and pernicious.

Mill wrote many essays and books on an astonishing variety of subjects, but in Morley's view all were united by the principle of devotion to the common good. Even Mill's purely philosophical works, like *A System of Logic,* and *An Examination of Sir William Hamilton's Philosophy,* were undertaken, according to Morley, because of his awareness that the differences between the philosophical school of Intuition and his own school of Experience and Association were not only differences on abstract questions but were at the root of the opposition between conservatism and liberalism; therefore, these works were of immense practical consequence.

In *A System of Logic* (the work by which Mill was best known in his century) and in Mill's criticism of the intuitional philosophy of Sir William Hamilton, Morley found the basis of what he called "a true positivism" in "the habit of seeking explanations of all phenomena in experience, and building up from the beginning the great positive principle that we can only know phenomena, and can only know them experientially." [22] Mill, unlike Auguste Comte, expounded a true Positivism because he did not try to erect systematic negation into a dogmatic and sectarian religion, and he did not suppose that the mere first application of empirical principles to the study of society was tantamount to establishing the final truths of sociology. In 1865, Mill had published *Auguste Comte and Positivism,* a brilliant and judicious balance of the truth and error in Comte's philosophy. The book certainly increased Morley's interest in Comte, one which was strong for many years.

But for Morley, as for most twentieth-century readers, Mill's

most important work was *On Liberty*. It was published during
Morley's last year at Oxford, and he never forgot its impact: "I do
not know whether then or at any other time so short a book ever
instantly produced so wide and so important an effect on contemporary thought as did Mill's *On Liberty* in that day of intellectual
and social fermentation (1859)." [23] Morley saw the book as primarily "a moral appeal to the individual man and woman, and
only secondarily to the legislator." [24] Impressed as he was by Mill's
plea for individual freedom of expression in speech and action,
Morley was still more attracted by the organic and vital idea of
human nature that informed the book. *On Liberty* was a protest
against the growing mechanism and uniformity of modern life; it
proclaimed that "human nature is not a machine to be built after a
model, and set to do exactly the work prescribed for it, but a tree,
which requires to grow and develop itself on all sides, according
to the tendency of the inward forces which make it a living
thing." [25] Because it articulated this ideal of human nature in relation to social and political issues, *On Liberty*, in Morley's view,
"added a cubit to man's stature." [26]

In addition to inheriting from Mill as much as can be inherited
of a man's spirit and method, Morley adopted many of his hero's
doctrines and opinions. He learned from Mill to look upon the
French Enlightenment as an analogue, with some qualifications,
of the Victorian age of criticism and transition.[27] He acquired
Mill's passionate admiration for the French statesman and economist Anne Robert Turgot and for Antoine Nicolas Condorcet,
chief French expounder of the doctrines of progress and perfectibility. He learned from Mill to abhor sectarianism—religious, political, and philosophical. He followed Mill in doing justice to
those conservative and historic sentiments in life which, prior to
Mill's modification of the liberal tradition, had been supposed the
exclusive property of the antiliberal politician. Even as a colonial
administrator, Morley could turn to the wisdom and experience of
Mill, even if not always for agreement. Mill had for years advo-
cated turning land over to the Irish peasants; and Morley, when
he became secretary of state for Ireland, adopted Mill's argument
that the land question was the fundamental Irish problem. Mill
had spent thirty-five years of his life as a chief conductor of correspondence in the East India Company, a branch of the government of India under the Crown. In 1905, nearly half a century

after the company had been disbanded, John Morley was appointed head of the government's India Office.

Morley once said, echoing his master's remarks on Bentham and Coleridge, that Mill's influence on Morley's generation had been so pervasive that it determined, even among those who rejected Mill's principles, the very questions to be considered. Morley asked himself most of the great questions Mill had posed, and he often reached Mill's answers. Yet there were exceptions. He was out of sympathy with what he took to be the drift toward socialism of Mill's later writings and thought he saw a connection between it and what a posthumous publication revealed to be Mill's growing theism in later life; was there not, after all, a link between modern socialism and the "Communistic" spirit of the Primitive Church? Morley was plainly shocked by Mill's posthumously published essay "Theism," in which the man whom Gladstone had called "the Saint of Rationalism" argued that, in religious matters, belief in something not absolutely known to be false was not blamable and that intellectually untenable beliefs could sometimes be morally useful. Though it pained Morley to do so, he said the essay had made "a sort of intellectual scandal" and severely criticized it as "a laboured evasion of plain answers to plain questions." [28] He also criticized Mill's failure to weave Darwin's theory of evolution into the fabric of his thought,[29] a criticism in which Bertrand Russell has joined in the twentieth century.[30]

On the whole, however, Morley was Mill's fervent admirer and his truest disciple, if we judge discipleship by the similarity in spirit between master and follower. His admiration for the older man was personal as well as intellectual. When Morley first met Mill in 1865, he found that the modesty and self-effacement of the writer were truthful reflections of the man. He continued Mill's friend until the latter's death in 1873, and his recollections of his meetings with the great man are among the most informative and most moving glimpses we have of Mill.

Mill was without any serious competition for dominance over Morley's mind between 1867 and 1882, although, as we shall see later, Morley closely imitated Matthew Arnold in his literary criticism. Whatever other creeds may have contributed to Morley during this period, he was essentially, like Mill, a Utilitarian and a liberal. In 1869, he wrote, in defense of Utilitarianism: "If the true answer to a question now so often put be that mankind cannot live without a religion, it is certain that that religion, whether it be the Religion of Humanity, or some regenerate form of Christianity, or mere morality highly spiritualised and elevated, will assimilate for its central principle what is the central principle of the utilitarian or beneficential ethics—that he is the best man who finds his own highest happiness in promoting the happiness of as many other people as possible." [31]

To Morley, Utilitarianism was inseparable from liberalism. For him, liberalism meant respecting the worth and dignity of the individual, submitting all questions to human judgment rather than to religious authority, making laws with an eye more attentive to man's higher qualities than to his baser, tempering justice with mercy, and generally trying to put oneself into the skins of one's fellow men. The practical aims dictated by these principles—disestablishment of the Church of England, establishment of a system of free public education, and sponsorship of anti-imperialism —were pursued by Morley during his fifteen years as an editor of the Fortnightly Review.

Nevertheless, there were men besides Mill and forces besides Utilitarian liberalism that were forming Morley's mind in the years before he entered Parliament. In later life, he recalled that three men had "first placed chart and compass" in his hands, "both in respect of civil conscience for the day and definite thoughts of history, progress, perfectibility. . . ." [32] The first of these was Mill; the others were Frenchmen of the eighteenth century, Turgot and Condorcet. Both Frenchmen were intellectuals who had entered the realm of political action out of the disinterested desire to do good for their fellow men, to put intellect at the service of society; and for this reason alone they must have interested Morley. The fact that both men failed the great tests of their political lives did not lessen the attraction of their ideas for Morley.

Turgot, like Morley, declined the ecclesiastical career his father wished for him because he would not "enter into an engagement which would irrevocably bind him for the rest of his life, either always to hold exactly the same opinions, or else to continue to preach them publicly after he had ceased to hold them privately." He entered the law in 1761, was made intendant, or chief commissioner, of the Limousin district, where he worked great administrative, judicial, and economic reforms. In 1774, when

Louis XV died, Turgot, "one of the men to whom good government is a religion," [33] was brought into the new king's administration, at first serving briefly as head of the Department of Marine, and then becoming controller-general, the manager of national finance.

Turgot at once attempted to extend to the whole of France the reforms he had realized in the Limousin, beginning with the suppression of certain burdensome and discriminatory taxes. But the monarchy quickly showed itself incapable of reform from within; and the populace, whom Turgot had championed against the vested interests, opposed him because they had come to suspect anything which emanated from the government of the king. The people wrongly supposed—a point Morley often makes about the decades preceding the French Revolution—that they had long been suffering from despotism when in reality they had been enduring the evils of anarchy. Turgot's failure to overcome the resistance of vested interests or to win the support of popular bodies was aggravated by his unwillingness to be personally conciliatory toward absolutism and religious intolerance. After being in office for just over twenty months, he was dismissed in May, 1776, and returned to a private life of writing and study.

Turgot stood in Morley's mind as the originator of the modern idea of history and, therefore, as the necessary forerunner of the historical and sociological speculations both of Condorcet and Comte. In his Sorbonne discourse of December, 1750, on the "Successive Advances of the Human Mind," Turgot had argued that the cyclical movement of death and rebirth that characterized the natural world stood in sharp contrast to the novelty and variety introduced by the course of human history: *"All epochs are fastened together by a sequence of causes and effects, linking the condition of the world to all the conditions that have gone before it."* [34] Starting from this premise, Turgot discerned the operation of law rather than accident in the movement of history and in the growth of social institutions; a network of cause and effect united each age with every age that had preceded it. In applying the comparative method to social institutions, in seeing history broadly and comprehensively and under the aspect of law, Turgot was, Morley admits, heavily indebted to Montesquieu, whose *Spirit of the Laws* had appeared two years earlier in 1748.

But Turgot was more "positive" and "scientific" in interpreting the law of history as one of "ordered movement of growth or advance among societies." [35]

Turgot discovered the source of historical progress in that of the human mind. But he equated the progress of the mind with that of knowledge, and with this equation Morley is not entirely satisfied. Should not the idea of progress, he asks, include—indeed, emphasize—moral progress? "The leading of souls to do what is right and humane," Morley objects, "is always more urgent than mere instruction of the intelligence as to what exactly is the right and the humane." [36] He does not explain how one may inculcate morality in others without first knowing wherein morality consists, but his objection shows the extent to which Morley had been leavened by the Romantic movement and the conviction of Percy Bysshe Shelley and Thomas De Quincey that it was not man's wit but his will that needed to be transformed.[37]

The most faithful friend and disciple of Turgot was Condorcet, whose political career was more dramatic and more tragic than that of his master. For Condorcet, alone among the great philosophical precursors of the French Revolution, lived to see the revolution itself—and to be swept away by the force he had himself helped to create. Condorcet was an economist but also a passionate believer in the perfectibility of human nature and a man who valued knowledge exclusively as a means to social action. Morley considered him "the incarnation of the revolutionary spirit, as the revolutionary spirit existed in geometers and Encyclopaedists; at once too reasonable and too little reasonable; too precise and scientific and too vague; too rigorously logical on the one hand and too abundantly passionate on the other." [38]

When the Revolution of 1789 arrived, Condorcet expressed his chagrin that Voltaire, Turgot, and the others who had spiritually prepared the revolution by imbuing a whole people with the passion for reason, justice, and equality did not live to see their ideals realized; but he was soon to see the irony of his regret. His lifelong preference for political over intellectual activity was at last gratified. In the summer of 1789, with the king in virtual captivity in Paris, Condorcet espoused the Republican cause, which was not yet popular. In August, 1791, he was returned as a Parisian deputy to the legislative assembly and became one of its secretaries. But his speeches were ineffective because his probity kept

him from expressing the contradictory whims of the assembly
with any fervor or conviction. When the Convention was formed,
Condorcet was rejected by the electors of Paris but was elected
for the department of the Aisne. When the Convention decided
the fate of the king, he voted to find the king guilty of conspiring
against liberty, but he also voted for exile rather than for death as
the punishment.

On January 19, 1793, the Convention voted to execute the king.
Condorcet, believing as always that one may be calm in the midst
of frenzy and reasonable with madmen, proposed to mitigate the
effect of the decision upon European public opinion by announc-
ing along with it a whole series of humane reforms, including abo-
lition of the death penalty. But the Reign of Terror was about to
commence, and Condorcet was overruled. In June, he vigorously
opposed the new constitution, saying that the arrest of the Giron-
dins had deprived the national representation of any claim to le-
gitimacy. Within a few days of the passage of the constitution,
Condorcet was tried *in absentia,* found guilty of conspiring
against the unity and indivisibility of the republic, and ordered
arrested. He fled and remained in hiding for nine months, during
which time he composed, without the help of a single book, his
study of the progress of the human mind. At its completion, he
left his refuge and wandered for several days before being cap-
tured and imprisoned. On his first night in prison he died under
mysterious circumstances.

For Morley, the interest of Condorcet's great work—*Progrès de
l'Esprit Humain*—was inseparable from the circumstances of its
composition. Never was a man's faith in the progress of reason so
sorely tried as was Condorcet's; and Morley was one of the first to
see the full implications of the expressions "*faith* in reason" and
"*faith* in progress." Disappointed in his hopes for the realization of
his ideals in his lifetime, and cast out by those he had wished to
aid, Condorcet sought consolation in the knowledge that he
would be justified by a posterity of just and reasonable human
beings who had been restored to their natural rights and dignity.
Long before Carl Becker described the "heavenly city" of the
eighteenth-century philosophers,[39] Morley pointed out how the
doctrines of progress and perfectibility had become the articles of
faith of a religion of humanity, how the *philosophes* had shifted
the heavenly city of the Middle Ages to earthly foundations, and

how the new rational doctrines aroused a prayerful religious enthusiasm:

> It has long been the fashion among the followers of that reaction which Coleridge led and Carlyle has spread and popularised, to dwell exclusively on the coldness and hardness, the excess of scepticism and the defect of enthusiasm, that are supposed to have characterized the eighteenth century. . . . The truth is that, working in such natures as Condorcet's, the principles of the eighteenth century, its homage to reason and rational methods, its exaltation of the happiness of men . . . into the highest place, its passion for justice and law, its large illumination, all engendered a fervour as truly religious as that of Catholicism or of Calvinism at their best, while its sentiment was infinitely less interested and personal.[40]

Morley seems to have been about equally attached to Condorcet's generous aspiration to help mankind and to his "disciplined and scientific intelligence." The two qualities were combined in the philosophy of history that Condorcet expounded in *Progrès de l'Esprit Humain.* In his general idea of history, Condorcet was greatly influenced by Turgot. Continuing the train of thought started by his master, Condorcet argued that there was a law in the succession of social states and that this law could be discovered by examining the collective phenomena of past history. According to Morley, it was in the mind of Condorcet that "the notion of the scientific treatment of history and society took its earliest start." [41] What Condorcet accomplished was to unite the Physiocratic principle that there is a natural—in the sense of being advantageous to mankind—and scientific order in the conditions of each particular society with the historical theory of Montesquieu and of Turgot that one age is bound to another by a chain of causation.

Condorcet maintained that a social science might be erected on the very premises which supported the natural sciences: that the general laws regulating the phenomena of the universe are necessary and constant and that they will operate in the future as they have in the past. The premise of the uniformity of nature is transferred by Condorcet to the realm of history to justify the prediction of the future destiny of the human race on the basis of our knowledge of the laws which have operated in history. Condorcet sought in the past a "scientific" justification of his belief in man's splendid future.

Morley was greatly impressed by Condorcet's general view of the nature of society, whether static or in the process of movement; and he shared Condorcet's belief in progress. But Morley could not accept Condorcet's definition of progress and therefore rejected the particulars of Condorcet's historical laws and predictions. In Morley's view, Condorcet repeats the error of his master Turgot in equating progress with intellectual improvement and in ignoring questions of moral standards and ideals. (Morley himself always assumes, without any reason given, that moral progress is possible.) Beyond this, he disapproves of Condorcet's "unscientific" rage against religion and his consequent inability fairly to assess the contributions of religion to progress.

Condorcet saw future progress coming in three main areas: the destruction of inequality among nations; the progress of equality among the people of each nation; the perfection of man. Morley is aware of the merely conjectural nature of Condorcet's particular predictions of the future and of the overly sanguine expectation of their immediate realization. But for Condorcet to have been sanguine about the imminence of human perfection in the circumstances under which he wrote betokened a quality of generosity and of faith to which Morley could not but respond: "If, as some think, the world will gradually transform its fear or love of unknowable gods into a devout reverence for those who have stirred in men a sense of the dignity of their own nature and of its large and multitudinous possibilities, then will his name not fail of deep and perpetual recollection." [42]

The chief advocate, in the nineteenth century, of the usefulness of "deep and perpetual recollection" of the great benefactors of humanity was Auguste Comte, founder of the Religion of Humanity, of the Positive philosophy, and of sociology in its modern acceptation. Although Morley did not put Comte among Mill, Turgot, and Condorcet as one of those who first placed chart and compass in his hands, no analysis of the influences that were forming Morley's mind before he entered Parliament can be complete without some mention of Comte and of Positivism. Morley was first introduced to Comte's ideas at Oxford by his friend J. Cotter Morison, but it was not until he moved to London and became

friendly with such English Comtists as Frederic Harrison, George
Eliot, G. H. Lewes, and Richard Congreve that he imbibed the
zeal of the converts to the new religion. In 1871, he confessed to
Harrison that his whole idea of history and nearly all his particular ideas on subordinate points were Comte's yet insisted he was
"not Comtist but Positivist." In 1873, he could facetiously refer to
Comte, Harrison, Mill, and himself as "us people who have a religion." But, in the following year, his correspondence shows him
becoming skeptical about the religious side of Positivism and indicates that his friendship with Harrison is cooling. Later in life,
Morley admitted that at one time only his "anti-sectarian instinct"
and the influence of Mill had kept him from joining the "new
church" of the Comtists.[43] In 1876, he had become sufficiently detached to attempt a balanced estimate of Comte in an essay for
the *Encyclopaedia Britannica*.

The first premise of Comte's life and work was that the social
order cannot be transformed until all its theoretic conceptions
have been recast in the spirit of science and unified into a comprehensive system. In this doctrine Comte was the successor of
Turgot and of Condorcet, whom he called his "philosophic father." He saw two opposing movements at work in modern society: one was a movement to break up old institutions and beliefs
by dissolving the foundations on which they rested; the other, a
movement toward a new and reformed social state in which man's
moral and emotional cultivation will flourish. Comte saw the need
to dissolve the old system through philosophical analysis, but he
saw it in relation to the need to synthesize a new system that
should supply the foundation of the new society. Morley could
follow Comte in much of his work of destruction, but he hung
back from acquiescence in Comte's schemes for a new society and
a new religion. Frederic Harrison, impatient of Morley's skepticism, once wrote to him: "I wish you would turn your mind to
founding rather than destroying churches." [44]

The essence of Comte's philosophy, as set forth in his *Course of
Positive Philosophy* (1830–42), is the Law of the Three States.
According to it, every branch of knowledge passes successively
through three different stages, corresponding to the three different
ways in which the mind explains phenomena: the theological, the
metaphysical, and the positive. Knowledge is in the theological
state when it explains phenomena by the will of the object under

examination or by the will of a supernatural being; it is in the metaphysical state when explanation is sought in some abstract force residing in the object, yet existing independently of it; knowledge has reached the positive state when a phenomenon is explained by another phenomenon, by establishing a relation between some given fact and a more general fact, or law. The major aim of Comte's Positive philosophy was to advance the study of society into the third stage; social phenomena would be studied scientifically, and sociology would take its place alongside—in fact, above—physics, chemistry, physiology. Once the benign light of science had been extended to the study of society, all knowledge would have the character of positivity and—what was to prove a troublesome contention to many of Comte's followers—all ideas in every area of knowledge would be unified and homogeneous. With philosophical disagreement and contentiousness things of the past, society would reconstruct itself on the basis of a universally accepted philosophy.

In defining the nature and conditions of progress, Comte, in Morley's view, had gone beyond such theoretical predecessors as Turgot and Condorcet. For Comte not only found the main cause of social evolution in intellectual development; he saw too that "the improvement of the social organism can only be effected by a moral development. . . ." [45] Therefore, he celebrated social feeling or altruism—a word he coined—over self-love and egoism.

So far Morley could follow Comte, but no further. When Comte had laboriously traced the slow development of the natural and physical sciences from the theological through the metaphysical and finally into (and within) the positive stage, he leaped to the conclusion that, as Mill put it, "the mere institution of a positive science of sociology [was] tantamount to its completion." [46] All differences of opinion on the subject, he decided, had arisen from the fact that it was formerly studied in the theological and metaphysical modes. The time had at last arrived for the final truths of sociology to be formulated. Sociological phenomena no longer required to be analyzed but only to be synthesized. To give the new synthesis the force of authority, Comte set about transferring the worship, discipline, and intolerance of Roman Catholicism to a system in which the conception of God would be replaced by the abstract idea of Humanity, conceived as a personality. Comte's haste to synthesize and his indifference to intellectual freedom led

him to clothe his doctrine of reason and science in the incongru-
ous garb of dogmatism and idolatry.

Morley's final judgment of the religion of Positivism—as opposed to Comte's theories of history and knowledge—is that it is
"utilitarianism crowned by a fantastic decoration": namely, the
erection of Humanity into a Being requiring worship. What good,
after all, is accomplished by inventing this object of worship when
we do not yet know for certain what will do humanity most good?
Might not two equally fervent devotees of the Religion of Humanity conscientiously espouse the opposite sides of a question? If so,
Morley concludes, "the Comtists are no better off than other utilitarians in judging policy, events, conduct." [47] Nevertheless, Morley
had learned from Mill the art of extracting from a philosophy only
that which is valuable and of leaving the rest behind. Rejecting
Comte's system, he nevertheless was enabled by Comte to see the
great intellectual characteristic of his period as the transformation
of all the sciences into history—the triumph of the historical and
relative method of seeing the world as a place perpetually in
movement.

III *Political Career*

When Morley entered Parliament in the spring of 1883, it was
embroiled in squabbles over imperial policy—in South Africa, in
Egypt, in Ireland (the cause of half of the divisions in the session
of 1882). In the years prior to his entry into active political life,
Morley had taken a strong anti-imperialist position. He had attacked the notion that England could justify the imposition of its
rule on foreign lands by calling itself a "civilising power" and a
"Christian government": "When I come across such phrases in a
blue-book," he wrote in 1879, "I shudder; they always precede
a massacre." Not for nothing had he learned from Turgot, Condorcet, and Comte that there is a natural law of growth in
every society and that each must be judged relatively to its
conditions and state of development, not absolutely: "If you want
to civilise Cetewayo [a Zulu king], or to civilise so many of
his people as your Gatlings spare, you will not do it by breaking
up a system of society which, barbarous as it may seem, is still a
sort of polity. . . . Nature will not have her hand forced." [48]

Morley's first maxim of foreign policy was not to meddle in the
affairs of other people. He believed that, as he stated at the very

outset of his political career, "every entanglement abroad
is . . . a wicked interruption of social improvement at home,"
and that "backward" races should be left to themselves. If, however, British force had brought Britishers into necessary contact
with "these poor barbarians," then it was imperative that British
agents and representatives "should practice towards them the
same fairness, the same honesty, and the same vigorous good faith
which we exact from others towards us." [49] Morley's commitment
to the second article of his anti-imperialist creed was to be tested
sooner than he could have expected—and more severely than he
could have wished.

In his first years in Parliament, Morley was a popular Liberal
orator who tried to push his party towards the Radical (as opposed to the Whig) definition of liberalism. He urged colleagues
to listen to the complaints of workmen as well as the demands of
Liberal capitalists. "I believe," he wrote in 1883, "we shall have to
bring to bear the collective forces of the whole community,
shortly called the State, in order to remedy things against which
our social conscience is at last beginning to revolt." [50] A radical
liberalism also meant stringent criticism of the persistent refusal
of England to initiate land reform in Ireland and of the facility
with which the British government resorted to coercion in dealing
with Irishmen.

In the article "A New Policy for Ireland," in the *Pall Mall
Gazette* for April 3, 1882, Morley demanded the release of Irish
political prisoners; a thorough overhauling of the administrative
machinery of Dublin Castle (whence British rule emanated); abandonment of the bankrupt policy of coercion; and the replacement
of its author, the chief secretary for Ireland, William Forster, who
was the brother-in-law of Matthew Arnold and a leader of the
Whig faction of Morley's party.[51] In 1883, while campaigning in
Newcastle (which had a large Irish population), Morley rightly
reminded the electorate that he had been the most zealous English defender of the Irish cause. Once in Parliament, he repeatedly
urged recognition of "the natural desire of the Irish people to
legislate for themselves on matters of purely Irish concern." By
September, 1885, he had given up his old hope that England and
Ireland could coexist as parts of one empire and was insisting on
"some form of Home Rule" for Ireland.[52]

In January, 1886, Morley was asked by Gladstone, the new

prime minister, to become chief secretary for Ireland. He had
been in the House of Commons less than three years and had
never held office; yet he was now called to administer an Ireland
in turmoil. Queen Victoria allowed Morley and Joseph Chamberlain into the Cabinet, on the advice of Lord Salisbury, in order to
keep them from becoming martyrs; she was, besides, certain that
Morley, as a freethinker, "in fact a Jacobin," would scarcely make
a popular secretary of state for Catholic Ireland.[53] Morley's tenure
was, in any event, brief; for, in June, Gladstone's momentous
Home Rule Bill—which Morley had helped to draft—was rejected in the House of Commons, an election was held in July,
and Lord Salisbury formed a Conservative government that retained power for five years. But, even during his first brief term of
office, Morley's name had been tarnished by the fanaticism of
Irish politics. A wild rumor was spread through Protestant Belfast
that he had sent out extra police—promptly dubbed "Morley's
Murderers"—to massacre Protestants, and terrible rioting and vio-
lence ensued.

During the next six years Morley traveled throughout England
and Ireland expounding his views on Ireland and on the necessity
for an Irish parliament. Charles Parnell, the great Irish patriot
whom Morley had known well since about 1880, called him "perhaps the only Liberal in Parliament, whose record on the Irish
question has been consistent from first to last." [54] Morley saw his
role during this period as keeping the Liberal party firm to its
pledges, particularly those relating to Ireland.

In 1892, Gladstone and the Liberals returned to office. Morley,
in his own campaign, had appealed to the electorate "solely on the
ground of applying to the case of Ireland the principles of self-
government that are the secret of the strength and greatness of
the Empire." [55] He was returned to his post at Dublin Castle for a
second term, which was to last for three frustrating years. They
were inevitably frustrating because, in 1893, a new Home Rule
bill, drawn up by Morley—"about the best stay I have," Gladstone called him[56]—was defeated in the House of Lords after it
had passed in the Commons. By choosing to stay on in his post at
Dublin Castle, Morley was committing himself to carry out policies the principles of which he had consistently repudiated in his
campaign for Home Rule. It is hard to say why Morley made the

decision he did. The position of Irish secretary was generally thought to be, as one Irish leader put it, "the ugliest, dirtiest, and most dangerous . . . in the whole Government." [57] Yet even when Gladstone resigned in 1894 and Morley could have been secretary of state in the new Cabinet he ignored the pleadings of his wife, as well as his own weariness, and stayed in Ireland. He seems to have believed he owed this much to a cause which had been the main preoccupation of his life for over a decade. But we may ask whether he would not more effectively have aided the Irish cause by working, as a man of letters, to transform the English mind than by trying to guide political machinery of which he disapproved toward beneficent ends for which it was never intended.

Morley did achieve some reform in the English administration of Ireland. After much wrangling, for example, he succeeded in reducing the proportion of Protestant to Catholic magistrates in Ireland from four to one to two to one. But, generally, he was forced to negate demands which he considered just and to enforce laws he thought oppressive. On the one side, he had to deal with Englishmen who saw Irish degradation as the result of race rather than of history; on the other, he had to enforce the law in Ireland, yet be conciliatory enough to give the moderate Irish Nationalists a position they could defend against the Parnellite extremists. He satisfied neither the Conservative advocates of coercion nor the Radical advocates of independence. As one Irish newspaper put it, he had "completely failed to be either a Lincoln or a Bismarck." [58]

Morley was acutely aware of the charges of temporizing with evil that were brought against him:

Why had I not overturned Dublin Castle until not one brick remained upon another? Not a brick had stirred. Why had I not flung down the reins, rather than allow a single man of the Royal Irish Constabulary to go to an eviction? As if even Bismarck himself . . . could have refused to let police attend evictions, after the Queen's Bench had firmly warned him that if he did he would be attached for contempt in refusing force for executing decrees at night! And how could either of these two giants of history [Lincoln and Bismarck] pull down Dublin Castle, without at the same time sweeping away the mass of vested interests guarded by Statutes, Treasury Minutes, Orders in Council, and all the other bulwarks and bastions of the civil service? [59]

In truth, though often identified by himself and others as a Radical, genuine radicalism was beyond Morley's capacity to imagine.
But it is not so much his radicalism that we must call into question
as his decision to stay in office in Ireland after Home Rule had
been defeated. He was, after all, a man of letters as well as a
practical politician; and if he had not learned from Matthew Arnold—who had taught him much—that there are times when political ends are better realized by literary than by political effort,
he ought to have heeded the words he had once quoted from his
acknowledged master, Turgot, who had said of the race of practical politicians to which he belonged: "All our small benefits are
transitory, while the light that a man of letters is able to diffuse
must, sooner or later, destroy all the artificial evils of the human
race, and place it in a position to enjoy all the goods that nature
offers." [60]

In attending overmuch to Ireland, Morley had neglected Newcastle; and in the General Election of 1895 he was defeated. He
gave up his office and (with very little regret) left Ireland. But,
within a few months, he was invited to become a candidate for
the five Montrose burghs in Forfarshire, Scotland; elected in 1896,
he retained the seat for twelve years. Much of his effort in the
years immediately following his election and his departure from
Ireland was directed to opposing the British imperialism then
rampant. He openly criticized the actions in Egypt of Lord Kitch-
ener, the popular British field marshal who reconquered the
Sudan between 1896 and 1898 and became its governor-general.
In 1899, Morley braved angry imperialist jingoes in Manchester to
speak out against the war policy for South Africa.

The words he used to describe Britain's imperialist adventures
may be relevant even today and even in countries which take
themselves to be immune from Old World sins:

First, to push on into places where you have no business to be, and
where you had promised you would not go—second, your intrusion is
resented, and in these wilds resentment means resistance; third, you
instantly cry out that the people are rebels and their act is rebellion,
in spite of your own assurances that you had no intention of setting up
a permanent sovereignty over them; fourth, you send forces to stamp
out the rebellion; fifth, having spread bloodshed and confusion and
anarchy, you declare with hands uplifted to heaven, that moral reasons
force you to stay, for if you were to leave, this territory would be left

in a condition no civilized power would contemplate with equanimity and composure.[61]

In 1899, Morley began the awesome task of writing the biography of William Gladstone, which appeared "punctually," four years later, in October, 1903. The three-volume work is now a rich source of information about most of the major political questions of the Victorian period, from electoral reform and disestablishment of the Irish Church to imperialist expansion and the great battle over Home Rule for Ireland. As a biography, it is far more of a Victorian "monument"—with all the good and the bad which that implies—to its subject than are the "historical studies" of Burke and the French *philosophes*. Yet it does have a cohering, unifying principle in Morley's characterization of Gladstone.

Morley presents Gladstone as a complex union of powers and sympathies often thought to be antithetical. He depicts Gladstone as a man of action and as an idealist; a staunch adherent of "high abstract principle" and yet a politician who knew how greatly principles are modified by the circumstances of their application; a devotee of Burke and of Burke's antithesis, Rousseau; an eloquent public figure with a popular following that the queen herself envied, who had the instincts of a recluse; a man whose ideas on nearly every social and political subject progressed from toryism to liberalism at the same time that he remained perfectly stationary in his dogmatic High Church Christianity. But Morley also shows how the religious beliefs which seemed to many a contradiction of Gladstone's liberalism were really the mainspring of his life and the force which impelled and unified all his activities. "This, we can hardly repeat too often, is the fundamental fact of Mr. Gladstone's history. Political life was only part of his religious life. It was religion that prompted his literary life. It was religious motive that . . . stirred him and guided him in his whole conception of active social duty. . . ." Because he was so motivated, Gladstone always "strove for the lofty uplands where political and moral ideas meet." Morley cannot help expressing admiration (and often wonder) at Gladstone's consistent application of moral standards to politics; but equally he cannot help raising, again and again, the question of whether right and wrong can be determined by the same set of moral maxims in public life as in private. Morley had already begun to see, in his unhappy experi-

ence as Irish secretary, that the question could be "cardinal and
fundamental," not only for Gladstone, but for every statesman
who attempted to translate ideals into action.[62]

In 1904, Morley again visited America, this time—perhaps sig-
nificantly, in view of the fact that Morley was at this period frequently accused of indifference or downright hostility to the interests of labor—at the invitation of Andrew Carnegie. He arrived in
time to witness Theodore Roosevelt's landslide victory and was
later the president's guest at the White House. He also visited Dr.
Eliot of Harvard and his old friend Charles Norton. Everywhere,
Morley expressed generous admiration of the American system,[63]
though we may be sure he was somewhat chilled by often being
reminded that a declared freethinker like himself would have no
chance in American politics. After returning to England in 1905,
Morley found himself launched on a new phase of his political
career. Sir Henry Campbell-Bannerman, head of the new Liberal
government, appointed Morley secretary of state for India, an
office he held until 1910. Thus, the vocal anti-imperialist was once
again called on to administer a particularly troublesome section of
the empire.

Though Morley was not sufficiently disinterested in his anti-
imperialism to think that Hindus and Mohammedans could be as
deserving of Home Rule as Irish Catholics,[64] he did insist that the
spirit of English institutions must be applied to India, lest the
same disaster befall England there as had befallen her in Ireland.
"What are we in India for? Surely in order to implant . . . those
ideas of justice, law, humanity, which are the foundation of our
own civilisation?" He worked hard and effectively, and in the face
of bitter opposition, to give to India's legislative councils a more
representative character and to appoint an Indian member to the
Executive Council of the Viceroy, Lord Minto. He also set an
example by appointing two Indian members to his own council. It
took over three years to push through the needed legislation. But
in India, as in Ireland, he would not go beyond piecemeal reforms, and he disclaimed any "sort of ambition . . . to take a
part in any grand revolution during my time of responsibility
whether it be long or short." In India, as in Ireland, his idea of
reform was limited by what he thought necessary to draw the
teeth of native extremists while encouraging "moderates." [65]

The question of force, always the hardest for a conscientious

liberal to resolve in practice, constantly beset Morley in his administration of India. A colonial administrator committed to reform, he was faced in 1907 with violent disorder begun by Indian
agitators for independence from British rule. His solution was to
invoke a "Regulation of 1818" to justify the immediate arrest and
deportation of the supposed spreaders of sedition; in 1908, he
again had recourse to the same law. "It is an old and painful
story," he wrote in 1907. "Shortcomings in government lead to
outbreaks; outbreaks have to be put down; reformers have to bear
the blame, and their reforms are scotched; reaction triumphs; and
mischief goes on as before, only worse." [66] There can be no doubt
that Morley was greatly pained when forced to resort to arbitrary
measures; and his correspondence with his viceroy, Lord Minto, a
man only too ready to employ police power, shows Morley's extreme reluctance to do so.[67] We may criticize him, in an absolute
sense, for departures from liberalism; but, when he is placed in relation to his fellow colonial administrators and to liberals, past and
present, placed in similar predicaments, he shines forth as a man
of unusual integrity.

In 1908, Morley took yet another step which seemed to violate
the liberal principles he had professed for years: he moved to the
House of Lords as Viscount Morley. But there seems little doubt
that he did so simply to stay in his post as Indian secretary: "I
have had a pretty industrious life, and I shall do my work all the
better for the comparative leisure of the other place." [68] His enemies found his "inconsistency" in entering the House of Lords aggravated by his perfidy to his new colleagues when he supported
the movement, which culminated in 1911, to strip the upper house
of its powers over legislation. P. E. More, in an odious essay which
exemplifies the ugly side of the American movement called "New
Humanism," finds in Morley's action "a taint of ingratitude, of
unconscious duplicity one might say." [69] If one proves his gratitude to a bad institution by allowing its acceptance of himself to
persuade him that it is a good one, then Morley was guilty of
ingratitude to the House of Lords; but, since he never changed his
unfavorable view of the House of Lords and never concealed it, it
is hard to know where the "duplicity" lies. We ought rather to be
impressed once again by Morley's retention of liberal ideals in
circumstances where they rarely flourish.[70]

In November, 1910, Morley resigned as secretary of state for

India. He was tired; he thought that a new viceroy—Minto was being replaced—would work better with a new secretary in Whitehall; and he wanted a last chance at "literary self-collection." [71] He remained in the Cabinet as lord president of the Council, soon had to put in another six months at the India Office when his successor—Lord Crewe—fell ill, and then was charged with the important task of guiding through the House of Lords the bill designed greatly to reduce its power.

The third and last great crisis of Morley's political career came in July and August, 1914. Sir Edward Grey, the foreign secretary in the Herbert Asquith Cabinet to which Morley belonged, seemed bent on a policy of armed intervention on the side of France and Russia in the event of war with Germany and Austria. For once, Morley decided to stand firmly on principle rather than work, as he had in Ireland and India, with available machinery; he made an open break with what he considered a disastrous policy by resigning from the Cabinet. Though he resigned from the Cabinet on public grounds, he did not make his vindication a public matter or attempt to sway public opinion against the policy he had opposed. After the war began, he composed, on the basis of notes he had made at the height of the crisis, his *Memorandum on Resignation;* but he saw no use in publishing an *apologia* after the war was under way. As it turned out, the *Memorandum* was only published posthumously, in 1928, by his nephew Guy Morley.

Morley had always been a "little Englander" and a "peace-man" who was opposed to English imperialism and to intervention in foreign affairs; but these large, underlying principles are not much dwelt on in the *Memorandum.* Instead, Morley mentions only those arguments with which he tried to persuade Grey and other colleagues. First of all, he opposed Grey's view that German policy was essentially aggressive; "I have no German partialities," he rather disingenuously told Grey;[72] but he wanted tangible proof of Germany's aggressiveness. Then he alleged—as some very notorious characters have also done since his time—that Germany's defeat in war would make Russia the pre-eminent power in Europe. Beyond this danger lay the possibility that war would disrupt domestic order, especially industrial order, and aggravate the Irish Home Rule dilemma.

Morley was no absolute neutralist, and he apparently urged that English neutrality be made contingent upon Germany's not invading Belgium. But he also believed that the question of Belgian neutrality was merely being used by powerful English interests as an excuse for going to war; and, in any case, he did not think that, as a general rule, England's involvement in the quarrels of the Continent should go beyond "diplomatic energy and armed neutrality." [73]

Warren Staebler, in his generally acute and judicious study of Morley, has some harsh words for the man who, having twice in his political career slightly adjusted his principles to circumstances, would not do so a third time: "His decision to resign from the Cabinet rather than violate his principles was lofty and laudable. But it was only a subdued, departing gesture of the hand where a bold, challenging sweep of the arm was needed. Why did he not speak in Parliament condemning what he knew to be the growing intention of his colleagues to declare war? Why did he not make at least one attempt to stem the tide by exposing before the assembled Houses some of the ministerial duplicity he had discovered, and so prompt an investigation?" [74] If it is not sufficient answer to the charges implied by these questions that Morley at seventy-six could hardly have been capable of a heroic radicalism that was beyond him at fifty-four, perhaps it is best to say that Europe was entering an era of madness to which no man and no political philosophy, however sane, was entirely adequate. Morley, at least, proved more adequate than most. Asquith called him "the last survivor of the heroic age"; and Edmund Wilson, who has severely censured Bernard Shaw for supporting the war once it was under way, has praised Morley's conduct as the best answer to Shaw's asking what else he could have done. "He could have expressed his disapproval," says Wilson, "and shut up, as John Morley and others did." [75]

Morley was aware that the world had entered a new era, one "very unlike the times in which my lot was cast";[76] for it was an era which denied rather than confirmed the sanguine belief in progress which he had learned from Mill, Turgot, Condorcet, and Comte. "The old liberalism," he admitted in his memorandum on resignation, "had done its work, and the time had come for openly changing imperial landmarks, and extinguishing beacons that needed new luminants." [77] Yet he had little sympathy with the newer forms of radicalism. It was a symbolic moment when, in 1902, after a lecture at Toynbee Hall, he was much ruffled by the

close questioning of a man named "Jacob Richter," the German
alias used during his exile in London by V. I. Lenin.[78] By 1923, the
year of his death, Morley could comment bitterly on the contrast
between the promises and anticipations of world rulers at the
opening of World War I and the catastrophe which later over-
whelmed them as "the most savage irony in the history of civilisation." [79] But his bitterness did not mean disillusionment with his
own creed. Rather, he saw the moral and political debacle that
was symbolized by the Great War as a result of the repudiation of
the best ideals of nineteenth-century liberalism. The man of letters had not succeeded in transforming his world; but neither had
the world destroyed his faith in the reality of the mind and the
spirit: "Those who have felt life no stage-play, but a hard campaign with some lost battles, may still resist all spirit of general
insurgence in the evening of their day. The world's black catastrophe in your new age is hardly a proved and shining victory
over the principles and policies of the age before it." [80]

CHAPTER 2

The Politics of Disinterestedness:
The Fortnightly Review

What is at present the bane of criticism in this country? It is that practical considerations cling to it and stifle it. It subserves interests not its own. Our organs of criticism are organs of men and parties having practical ends to serve, and with them those practical ends are the first thing and the play of mind the second; so much play of mind as is compatible with the prosecution of those practical ends is all that is wanted. An organ like the *Revue des Deux Mondes*, having for its main function to understand and utter the best that is known and thought in the world, existing, it may be said, as just an organ for the free play of the mind, we have not.
—Matthew Arnold,
Essays in Criticism

I *Origin and Character of* Fortnightly Review

IN 1864, Matthew Arnold published in the *National Review* an essay treating "The Functions of Criticism" which deplored the corruption of criticism by the spirit of party and sect that prevailed in English periodicals. The free play of ideas was in England always subordinated to the interests of a party, and each periodical allowed only as much freedom of thought as suited the interests of the party it represented. The *Edinburgh Review* allowed as much freedom of discussion as was compatible with Whiggery; the *Quarterly*, as much as was compatible with Toryism; the *British Quarterly,* as much as was compatible with Dissent; the *Dublin,* as much as was compatible with English and Irish Catholicism; and so on down the line. "It must needs be," Arnold scolded, "that men should act in sects and parties, that each of these sects and parties should have its organ, and should make this organ subserve the interests of its action; but it would be well, too, that there should be a criticism, not the minister of these interests, not their enemy, but absolutely and entirely independent of them." The French were more fortunate in this respect, for they had the *Revue des Deux Mondes,* a magazine devoted to the freedom of thought and "having for its main function to understand and utter the best that is known and thought in the world." [1]

In the very next year, a group of English men of letters, led by Anthony Trollope, J. Cotter Morison, and Frederick Chapman, decided to carry out Arnold's suggestion by founding the *Fortnightly Review,* an avowed imitation of the *Revue des Deux Mondes.* Like its French model, it would include fiction, poetry, and discussions of literature, politics, and the arts. It would meet Arnold's demands by being independent of party and of sect and by following the revolutionary policy (never before tried with success in England) of having each contributor sign his work. As Trollope wrote in his *Autobiography:* "The matter on which we were all agreed was freedom of speech, combined with personal responsibility. We would be neither conservative nor liberal, neither religious nor free-thinking, neither popular nor exclusive;—but we would let any man who had a thing to say, and knew how to say it, speak freely. But he should always speak with the responsibility of his name attached." [2]

The founders of the review, acting under the influence of Trollope, chose George Henry Lewes as its first editor. George Lewes, now remembered chiefly as the man whose liaison with George Eliot was a major Victorian scandal, was in fact a distinguished man of letters (his biography of Goethe is even now in print), a zoologist, a fine critic of literature (especially of fiction and drama), and a militant liberal journalist. George Eliot contributed only to the first number of the review, but she helped Lewes by attracting many distinguished contributors to the new periodical.

The ideal of "freedom" espoused by the *Fortnightly* was genuinely new, for it would be a periodical that welcomed to its pages all shades of political and religious opinion. The contributors to the first issue included Walter Bagehot and Anthony Trollope, who might be termed conservatives, and Lewes, George Eliot, and Frederic Harrison, all liberals or radicals. But eventually (and perhaps inevitably) the *Fortnightly* became a liberal periodical—not because it had changed its "free" editorial policy but because precious few replies to liberal articles were forthcoming from the conservative side. (In his *Autobiography,* Mill complained that the great problem of the London Debating Society had been to recruit speakers to represent the conservative position.) Before long, and in large part because of Lewes's editorials urging electoral reform, the review became identified as a supporter of the Liberal party. Trollope, needless to say, was irritated, but not surprised:

That theory of eclecticism was altogether impracticable. It was as though a gentleman should go into the House of Commons determined to support no party, but to serve his country by individual utterances. Such gentlemen have gone into the House of Commons, but they have not served their country much. Of course the project broke down. Liberalism, free-thinking, and open inquiry will never object to appear in company with their opposites, because they have the conceit to think that they can quell those opposites; but the opposites will not appear in conjunction with liberalism, free-thinking, and open inquiry. As a natural consequence, our new publication became an organ of liberalism, free-thinking, and open inquiry.[3]

Lewes's tenure as editor was relatively brief, for ill health forced him to resign the post in December, 1866; but he had contributed much to the review, both as editor and as writer. While he was editor, he wrote more for the *Fortnightly* than any contributor, including Trollope. He serialized his *Principles of Success in Literature,* wrote on science and philosophy, and reviewed at least one book on a scientific or Classical subject in each issue. He proved that the policy of signature could attract first-rate writers of strong and independent views. But he did not leave the magazine in good financial condition, and at his departure the author-proprietors sold the copyright to their publishers, Chapman and Hall. Just before doing so, they changed the *Fortnightly* to a monthly publication in order to please magazine dealers and, perhaps, in order to provide the magazine with at least one genuinely English characteristic, an anomalous title.

The new owners chose John Morley as Lewes's successor. If the "independent" image of the *Fortnightly* had been tarnished under Lewes's editorship, when the magazine came more and more to resemble an organ of the advanced liberals, it threatened to vanish altogether under Morley's editorship, when the review acquired the reputation of being the organ of the English Positivists. We have already noticed, in the first chapter, how considerable was the influence of Comte and of his English followers upon Morley in the 1860's and early 1870's. But we have also noticed that his antisectarian instinct and the influence of Mill had kept him from ever joining the Comtist "church." Readers of the *Fortnightly*, however, could not be expected to make such fine distinctions. They knew that the *Fortnightly* often printed essays by English Positivists; that it persistently celebrated, in the Positivist manner, the universal application of the spirit of science; and they drew the logical conclusion that the magazine's editor was a member of the sect.

Yet Morley certainly did not allow such Comtist devotees as Lewes and Frederic Harrison to go unanswered by formidable opponents in the *Fortnightly*. From mid-1869 to mid-1870 the review became a meeting point for controversy between Positivists and anti-Positivists. Foremost among the latter was Thomas Henry Huxley, whose lecture "On the Physical Basis of Life," printed in the review, expounded a rigorous scientific materialism and denied all scientific value to the Comtist philosophy, which it tersely described as "Catholicism *minus* Christianity." [4] Richard Congreve, an ardent English disciple of Comte, immediately came to the defense of his master—only to provoke Huxley to another article in the June issue, charging Comte with insufficient knowledge of science and Congreve with insufficient knowledge of Comte.[5] J. E. Cairnes, the economist, was invited, in May, 1870, to defend his discipline—or social science—against the denigrations of Comte, who had omitted political economy from the hierarchy of the sciences because of what he held to be its irrational method. In general, then, if Morley did not keep the *Fortnightly* entirely neutral on the subject of Positivism, he went as far toward doing so as could reasonably be expected of one who was himself a Positivist. His own view was that the *Fortnightly* and the *Westminster* had been the only English reviews even to accord Positivism a fair treatment, and they were thus rectifying an imbalance in stressing its virtues. Fortunately, in any case, the *Fortnightly's* preoccupation with Positivism abated somewhat with the outbreak in 1870 of the Franco-German War.

Morley, writing many years after he had resigned the *Fortnightly's* editorship, said that its major achievement during his reign had been "the diffusion and encouragement of rationalistic standards in things spiritual and temporal alike." [6] Certainly, from the very outset of his editorship, he promoted the twin causes of science and rationalism. In his first year, he asked the scientist John Tyndall to assess J. B. Mozley's Bampton Lectures of 1865 "On Miracles." An excerpt from Tyndall's dismissal of theology's pretensions to scientific knowledge gives us some notion of the condescending, even arrogant, tone that characterized many *Fortnightly* utterances on this subject:

To the theologian with his wonderful theories of the "order of nature," I would in conclusion say, "Keep to the region—not, however, exclusively yours—which is properly known as the human heart; the region, I am willing to confess, of man's greatest nobleness and most sublime achievements. Cultivate this, if it be in you to do so; and it *may* be in you; for love and manhood are better than science, and they may render you three times less unworthy than many of those who possess ten times your natural knowledge. But unless you come to her as a learner, keep away from physical nature. Here in all frankness I would declare, that at present you are ill-informed, self-deluded, and likely to delude others." [7]

In matters of theological controversy and religious politics, the *Fortnightly* assumed the positions we might expect of a rationalist and liberal organ. It took the side of Bishop Colenso in his contention with the Church of England, and it came to the defense of such works of scientific and historical biblical criticism and reconstruction as D. F. Strauss's *Das Leben Jesu* (translated into English by George Eliot in 1846) and John Seely's *Ecce Homo* (1865), which Lord Shaftesbury described as having been "vomited from the jaws of Hell." The publication persistently attacked the Anglican priesthood and urged disestablishment of the state church. Even Morley, who was usually sparing of irony and gen-

erous to a fault when dealing with religion, could be both ironical
and uncharitable when dealing with the clergyman: "As the
oracle of the immortal gods, he is beyond question and beyond
argument. That societies of men should be happy on their own
terms he will not allow, if he can help it. . . . You speak to him
in the language of Policy; he answers with the phrases of Thau-
maturgy. You ask what the common weal demands: he tells you
something about the sacred fowls, or the thirty-nine articles,
about sacramental churches, or the aspect of the sacrificial en-
trails." [8] As for the Established Church, Morley held it to be a
class rather than a national institution, and he decried it as the foe
of social improvement and of disinterested scientific investigation.

In his *Recollections,* Morley insisted that, although the *Fortnightly* had been miscellaneous in its writers as well as its subjects, it had not lacked a unifying principle. This principle was, at
least during his editorship, "the spirit of Liberalism in its many-
sided sense." [9] In order to clarify the liberalism which unified the
Fortnightly Review, we should examine a few of those general-
ized statements of liberal principles and aims which Morley peri-
odically made in the *Fortnightly.* The first is "The Liberal Programme," published in September, 1867, just after the passage of
the Second Reform Bill; the second is a series of four articles,
beginning in April, 1874, entitled "On Compromise"; the last is
Morley's "Valedictory" of 1882 upon the occasion of his retirement
from the editorship of the *Fortnightly.* These three statements
should provide some notion of Morley's political preoccupations
at various stages of his fifteen-year editorship.

II   *"The Liberal Programme"*

On August 15, 1867, Disraeli and the Tories, sensing at last the
futility of continued resistance to democracy, and desirous of
gaining for themselves the credit for a momentous reform, proposed and got the House of Commons to pass the Reform Bill
(first proposed by the Radical John Bright fifteen years earlier)
which enfranchised the bulk of the English working classes and
committed the country irrevocably to democracy. In Morley's
view, set forth in the following month in the *Fortnightly,* the Second Reform Bill had transferred political power from a class to
the nation. Satisfaction was in order, but complacency was a danger. "The first campaign in the war of this generation against Priv-

ilege and Obstruction has been brought to a fairly successful close." [10] But the war was far from over, and the question remained whether and how the nation would use its newly acquired power.

The question, Morley continues, is not primarily a party one. The Tories, he charges, are plainly unprincipled. A year before they had vilified the working classes as dangerous and revolutionary, the ready tools of demagogues; but now that these working classes had the suffrage, Conservative *Realpolitik* transformed them into humble persons "amenable to the influence of position and intelligence." [11] But the Liberals are hardly deserving of any more sympathy than their rivals, for their last administration was perhaps the most incompetent and fumbling of governments within memory. In any case, "people are weary of the old divisions and the old issues and the old names, because they have lost all their meaning. Whig and Tory mean nothing, and point to nothing, and tell us nothing about the men who are so called." [12] In future, the only relevant political division will be between the Obstructionists and those adhering to what Morley calls the "National Party."

The Reform Bill, rightly considered, is a commitment by the English people to "a greatly enlarged conception of national life and activity." Following a line of argument remarkably similar to that which runs through Arnold's *Culture and Anarchy* (which also grew out of the political situation created by the Reform Bill and the first part of which had appeared in July), Morley says that democracy will strengthen rather than (as many had warned) weaken the idea of the state and of the scope of action of the executive. In a democracy, the executive "receives its life and motive power directly from the collective impulses of a whole people." The action of the state, formerly looked upon by the classes barred from political expression and power, as the instrument of a class, will in future be looked upon, and hopefully be, the action of the nation itself. Given the high ideal implied by a democratic executive, the great object in modern English politics must be "to stir these impulses for high national aims, to find the men capable of feeling and understanding them, and earnest in realising them at whatever cost to the sacro-sanctity of routine." [13] The Reform Act will only be successful if it helps bring such men into the House of Commons.

Morley now turns his attention to the state of the Liberal party. Again very much in the manner of Arnold, he chides the Liberals for their obsession with such petty, short-sighted aims as abolishing church rates and introducing the ballot. Why is it that Liberals devote so much energy to such practical questions and ignore the larger questions of principle which are crying for attention and settlement? The problems which, according to Morley, ought to be uppermost in the minds of Liberals, and of others as well, are education, poverty, religious domination of the universities; unequal and unintelligible laws; the consolidation of home territory; Ireland, and India. Yet Liberals have little or nothing to say of these matters; and, on the Irish situation in particular, they seem to be of the view that doing nothing about a dreadful problem is the best way of resolving it.

Morley admits that there are plenty of conscientious and able minds in public affairs. Only tradition keeps them from widening their presently very narrow ideas of the possible scope and activity of government. The fatalism inherent in this tradition of government inaction has saddled England with a political system that has not altered throughout a long period when social and economic conditions were being entirely transformed. As a result, the country abounds with anomalies and incongruities.

Departing temporarily from the more general view of the political situation, Morley says that the major existing impediment to all schemes of reform is the "Territorial" spirit. "At nearly every point it is the superstition or sinister interest of the territorial power which thwarts, restrains, and depresses the harmonious adjustment of laws and administration to the needs of the public well-being." [14] The land monopoly of English landlords in Ireland is the chief barrier to making that country a peaceable and justly governed part of the empire; it is the landowning squires in England who are the great foes of education for classes beneath their own and who oppose any improvement in the human resources of industry. In fact, the landowning spirit is as opposed to industrial development as it is to schemes for national education.

Without describing in detail just how the myriad evils brought about by the landowning interest are to be expunged, Morley implies that the spirit of the landowning class, like any merely class spirit, will be found incompatible with a truly democratic spirit because democracy unites all classes into a nation. Therefore, the main, immediate task of political leaders is to achieve social unity, to realize the ideal of a whole people working with a set of common convictions toward common goals. The Reform Act has given them the means to do this, but they themselves must supply the will.

The particular social and political policies which were established on the principles set forth in "The Liberal Programme" have been fully described and analyzed by Professor Edwin M. Everett in *The Party of Humanity*, his study of the *Fortnightly* from 1865 to 1874; therefore, they are only summarized briefly here. The *Fortnightly* was reformist, but definitely not revolutionary. Its ideal country was America, stable as well as democratic. It persistently and vehemently urged compulsory education and state support of the schools and set itself against church or sectarian influence in education. In conflicts between classes, the sympathies of the *Fortnightly* systematically went to the "multitude" —the only class, Morley called it in a forgetful moment, whose interests could never be antisocial. Frederic Harrison led several *Fortnightly* writers in the defense of trade unionism against its many enemies in the press and public, maintaining that unions were a positive force for the defense of the law, for the diffusion of education, and for the prevention of slavery. The review did not, however, arrive at a uniform set of views on economic questions, for liberals were already approaching the great divide that was to separate those wedded to "political economy" from those ready to experiment with Socialist forms.[15] (It may be noted, in this connection, that in 1871 the most illiberal of the new Socialists—Karl Marx—tried and failed to place an article in the *Fortnightly*.)

The Liberal party failed (as inevitably it had to) to live up to the principles of Morley's "Liberal Programme." By 1873, therefore, the *Fortnightly* was lending its name and giving its support to a severe attack by Joseph Chamberlain upon established Liberalism, upon Gladstone, and upon the Liberal party. Chamberlain espoused a radical program whose slogan was "Free Church, Free Land, Free Schools, and Free Labour."[16] Morley was at first uneasy at the very idea of an ambitious program with large, general (which was as much as to say un-English) aims; and he was also reluctant to confuse the education question with any other. He wondered too whether the Puritans, who favored freeing schools

from church domination, would be equally concerned with setting
workers free to organize against industrialists. Nevertheless, he
went along with Chamberlain, who rapidly began to replace Mill
as the chief "outside" influence upon the *Fortnightly Review*.
Morley was to promote Chamberlain's radical program throughout the rest of his tenure as editor.

But in 1874 Liberal and Radical hopes were dashed by a Conservative victory, which made Disraeli prime minister. Chamberlain himself was defeated in Sheffield by John Roebuck; his own
slogan of the four freedoms had not had the vote-getting power of
Roebuck's "The Briton's Bible and the Briton's Beer—our National Church and our National Beverage." [17] Harrison told Morley that the seemingly Socialist doctrines of Mill had frightened
the electorate away from radicalism for the time being. At any
rate, both men agreed that the conservatives' victory and their
ensuing reign would at least give Liberals a much-needed opportunity to take thought. Morley at once set about asking himself
the questions about the relation between principles and politics
that had been suggested by the recent defeats; and the result was
On Compromise,[18] a series of articles setting forth the ethical principles which underlay the social and political programs of Morley
and the *Fortnightly*.

Basil Willey has said that *On Compromise* is "a pure distillation
of the spirit of the *Fortnightly Review*" as well as Morley's "central pronouncement, and one of the central documents of the Victorian age, ranking with such works as Mill's *Liberty* . . . and
Arnold's *Culture and Anarchy*." [19] But the articles, the first of
which appeared in April, 1874, are also an intrinsically valuable
general defense of qualities of intellectual integrity and moral
courage that are as relevant to our own age as to Morley's.

III   On Compromise

The title of this work and our knowledge of the political career
which Morley was to follow can well mislead us as to its nature,
for *On Compromise* is a rigorous attack on compromise in general and on Victorian compromise in particular and also a plea for
de-emphasizing the "political" mode of thought and action. The
book sets out to answer the question of when, if ever, the search
for truth and the expression and practice of it ought to give way
before other considerations. Of course, as Morley reminds us at

the outset, everyone *says* that we should cling to truth even if the heavens fall. But "in practice all schools alike are forced to admit the necessity of a measure of accommodation in the very interests of truth itself." [20] Morley himself is no exception; for he was, like his master Mill, a humanist as well as a liberal, and he therefore was aware of what Lionel Trilling has described as the eternal dilemma of the humanist:

The aspects of society that humanism most exalts are justice and continuity. That is why humanism is always being presented with a contradiction. For when it speaks of justice it holds that the human condition is absolute; yet when it speaks of continuity it implies that society is not absolute but pragmatic and even anomalous. Its intelligence dictates the removal of all that is anomalous; yet its ideal of social continuity is validated by its perception that the effort to destroy anomaly out of hand will probably bring new and even worse anomalies, the nature of man being what it is. "Let justice be done though the heavens fall" is balanced by awareness of the likelihood that after the heavens have fallen justice will not ever be done again.[21]

Morley saw that a balance had to be struck between an ideal justice or truth, on the one hand, and the maintenance of the conditions of social union, on the other. But he thought that, in his own country and time, the boundary line had been grossly misplaced in the interests of maintaining the *status quo*.

Therefore, before dealing with the abstract question of "the boundary that divides wise suspense in forming opinions, wise reserve in expressing them, and wise tardiness in trying to realise them, from unavowed disingenuousness and self-illusion, from voluntary dissimulation, and from indolence and pusillanimity," Morley feels obliged to describe the spirit of his country at the time he writes. Its most notable and most disheartening trait is a profound and unreasoning distrust of all general principles, ideas, and ideals. His countrymen, preoccupied with the present, have not even a vision of the future. Among the great nations of the world, Morley groans (as Arnold had done earlier), only England lacks some national ideal toward which to strive; only England is publicly committed to none but petty and selfish ends.

For a variety of reasons, idea and aspiration in England are in bondage to fact; and undue reverence for things as they are limits the ability to conceive things as they might be. Morley, soon to

enter the realm of politics himself, sees a great danger in supposing that all problems yield their significance to purely political
tests. When it is forgotten that moral and religious ideas and
standards are often at least as relevant as political ones, thought is
debased; and the superstitious reverence for established facts
raises "the limitations which practical exigencies may happen to
set to the application of general principles, into the very place of
the principles themselves." [22] In too many areas of English life,
Morley charges, political considerations and social convenience
have taken priority over respect for truth.

Morley suggests several explanations for this state of affairs.
There is, as always in England, a terror of the French example of
premature application of systematic ideas to the social system.
Then there are the newspapers, which appeal to the popular mind
by cultivating prejudices and by displaying the worldly wisdom
that is above principles. Perhaps, too, the triumph of the historical
method (which was Morley's own) in making all truths relative
rather than absolute and in showing how the dogmas of one age
became the exploded prejudices of the next has made men wary
of committing themselves to positive and definite opinions and
ideals. But the most potent influences in impairing the Englishman's moral and intellectual alertness are the great increase in
material prosperity and the equally great decline in "sincerity of
spiritual interest." [23] The evil effect of wealth on moral seriousness
is, of course, a traditional commonplace; but the decline in spiritual sincerity itself is a phenomenon peculiar to what Morley (like
any number of his contemporaries) calls "an age of transition" in
which the old beliefs have lost their power but no new ones have
arisen to supplant them. In such an atmosphere, says Morley, "the
native hue of spiritual resolution is sicklied o'er with the pale cast
of distracted, wavering, confused thought." [24]

The "age of transition" and the intellectual and spiritual malaise
which accompany it will not disappear until men have acquired a
new faith. But new faiths are not acquired merely by wishing for
them, still less by timorously adhering to old faiths and to their
accompanying forms when these are no longer believed. Compromise with the old faiths and their forms merely serves to perpetuate them; and so Morley proceeds to answer the various arguments
promulgated to hinder the freedom of thought and expres-

sion and to prevent the realization of the new truths which such freedom from time to time discovers.

The first argument for the "utility of error" with which Morley deals is the one which says that we should speak to the wise according to their wisdom but to fools according to their folly; that is, that the so-called enlightened classes should pursue the truth unfettered by authority but that pious frauds should be carefully preserved for the unenlightened. Morley notes that many thinkers, such as Ernest Renan, who find no truth in a particular doctrine nevertheless think the doctrine should continue to be inculcated in those classes of persons whom it is supposed to keep from antisocial behavior, or who are supposed to gain an irreplaceable emotional consolation from their belief in the false doctrine.

That this argument—at least in its second, or psychological, form—could be forwarded by humane and sophisticated men in the Victorian period may be seen by glancing at Matthew Arnold's notorious essay of January, 1863, entitled "The Bishop and the Philosopher." It concerned the controversy, briefly described in Chapter 1, between John Colenso, bishop of Natal, and his ecclesiastical superiors over the right of a clergyman of the Church of England to publish a book questioning the historical accuracy of the Bible. Arnold issued a stinging rebuke to Colenso and thus ranged himself, whether he wished to or not, on the side of the poor bishop's persecutors. Nowhere in his essay does Arnold question the truthfulness or accuracy of Colenso's critique of the Pentateuch. What he questions is Colenso's assumption that a work dealing with truth in religious matters should be addressed (and, by being printed in English rather than Latin, it was so addressed) to the "uninstructed"; for "the highly-instructed few, and not the scantily-instructed many, will ever be the organ to the human race of knowledge and truth. Knowledge and truth, in the full sense of the words, are not attainable by the great mass of the human race at all." [25] If a liberal like Arnold was prone to such failures of realism—did he really suppose that the faith of the "uninstructed" in the literal truth of Scripture was still unimpaired?—and capable of such sophistries, we may readily imagine how quick were the friends of the established order to resort to the doctrine of "dual" truth.

Morley marvels at the way in which men of goodwill are inca-

pable of seeing the bad consequences of the "dual doctrine" system
(even assuming it accomplished what it claimed to accomplish).
If the "highly-instructed" are ready to surrender the field of debate to those who, by their own premises, are less instructed, are
they not thereby strengthening the power of the very persons who
have proved themselves incapable of using intellectual power correctly? If in religious matters—so we might apply Morley's arguments to Arnold's case—a liberal like Arnold is ready to surrender
the common people to the priesthood for religious purposes, does
he not see that he is also surrendering them to the priesthood for a
variety of other purposes—political, social, and cultural?

Why should a minority, holding what it takes to be true opinions, be willing to abandon the majority to what it takes to be
false ones? It can only be, answers Morley, that these men believe
no harm is done by being mistaken and that their belief rests on
the peculiar assumption "that error somehow in certain stages,
where there is enough of it, actually does good, like vaccina-
tion." [26] Thus, while everyone denies that error in the abstract can
be useful, a great many people act as if an error useless to them is
of the utmost utility to other people. Parents pay to have their
children educated in doctrines they themselves find incredible,
and husbands take care that their wives cling to beliefs they themselves have long abandoned.

The apologetics of error, Morley shows, is bewildering in its
variety and deviousness. But he gallantly attempts to answer some
of the most common pleas for the sanctity of acknowledged error.
Many will say that a multitude of good associations and habits
may be based upon a false opinion. But, if true notions are allowed to rest on false foundations, they are far more exposed to
destruction than if they were re-established on defensible
grounds. If one clings to the notion of hell-fire because he supposes good conduct to rest on the fear of horrible punishment,
how will he guarantee good conduct when the belief in hell-fire
has vanished? Should not the "instructed" rather bend themselves
to discovering the true foundations in the nature of things for such
good habits of thought and conduct as may exist? That would be
the truly conservative endeavor. As for Arnold's dismal conclusion
that the great mass of men is simply incapable of attaining truth,
Morley would contend that acquiescence in the processes that
have caused darkness is hardly the best way of re-establishing the

empire of light: "whatever impairs the brightness of such light as a man has, is not useful but hurtful. . . . Superstition, blind obedience to custom, and the other substitutes for a right and independent use of the mind, may accidentally and in some few respects impress good ideas upon persons who are too darkened to accept these ideas on their real merits. But then superstition itself is the main cause of this very darkness." [27]

But there is yet another line of defense for the friends of error. This one is that less harm would be done by retention of the false opinion than by its immediate destruction. But this argument, in Morley's view, simply begs the whole question, which is whether the practice of intellectual integrity is or is not preferable to the practice of intellectual deceit, and not merely whether or not one notion is false and another one true. The aim of those who believe in intellectual honesty must be to implant this ideal and its attendant state of mind in others; but the means must be the laborious correction of single wrong opinions. It may be a loss to destroy a false opinion without putting a true one in its place, but it would be a greater loss to postpone the search after intellectual honesty and the fairest mode of dealing with evidence merely in order to leave untouched a false opinion which is supposed to be of great usefulness. If it be objected that a vast, coherent, and harmonious system of thought and way of life may be destroyed at a stroke by the refutation of just one of its articles of belief, we may answer that a synthesis which rests even in part upon error must be either premature or simply false.

In concluding his argument against those who maintain the utility of error, Morley stresses, perhaps not altogether wisely, the consideration of progress: "whatever ease may be given to an individual or a generation by social or religious error, such error at any rate can conduce nothing to further advancement." [28] In other words, to discard a false faith is an act beneficial not merely to the individual but to the mighty cause of general progress toward a new faith and a new social order. Here, whatever credence we may give to the notion of progress, we must notice that Morley is shifting his ground of argument from the individual to the society as a whole. If he were dealing with a race of men who believed that their present actions and sufferings would be justified sufficiently if they received the thanks and admiration of posterity, Morley might be justified in dismissing arguments for the utility of error on the ground that error can never be helpful to progress. But, since he is addressing human beings who, for the most part, cannot see what the idea of progress has got to do with their own finite existence as mortal individuals, it seems unfortunate that he shifts his ground in this way, both here and in the remaining sections of *On Compromise.*

If, on the other hand, we share Morley's belief in progress, we must attend to his extension of the argument of Mill's *On Liberty* that we can never know what we lose by the suppression of opinion. Only the most uncritical optimist (and Morley has in mind the conservative Utilitarian Fitzjames Stephen) will maintain not only that whatever is, is good but that things could never at any point in history have been better than, in fact, they were. The pressure of Morley's language shows how much better he thinks the world might have been if a due regard for freedom and truthfulness had always been observed: "To me . . . the history of mankind is a huge *pis-aller,* just as our present society is; a prodigious wasteful experiment, from which a certain number of precious results have been extracted, but which is not now, nor ever has been at any other time, a final measure of all the possibilities of the time." [29]

Having disposed of the "dual doctrine" justification for compromise, Morley turns to the problem of the conflict between the practical or political spirit and the unfettered search for and expression of truth. He wishes to prove that it is worthwhile for the individual, however isolated he may feel, to seek truth and wisdom—even if the majority of his fellows seem unlikely ever to accept his views. We must remember, he says, that honor and integrity permit different degrees of compromise in different situations. We must be readiest to compromise when we are trying to realize an opinion and to convert theory into practice; here we may be opposed by a hostile and prejudiced majority, and simple expediency will demand a considerable deference to the status quo. When it is only a matter of expressing a heterodox opinion, however, "the reasons for respecting the wishes and sentiments of the majority are far less strong, though . . . such reasons certainly exist, and will weigh with all well-considering men." [30] But when we are in the process of making up our own minds about the relative merits of two courses of action or of two contending versions of truth, the fact that the majority of our contemporaries lean in one direction should in no way dispose us to believe it the right one.

England was, in Morley's view, the most "political" society that had ever existed. Every moral, religious, or philosophical issue was rapidly transformed by Englishmen into a political issue and seen only in its political aspect and relations. Politics, Morley is saying, is the art of the possible, of what can be achieved. As such, it is a highly valuable art. But we must be careful not to put the limitations which practical circumstances and requirements impose upon the application of general principles into the place of the principles themselves. Our realistic awareness of what is must not limit our capacity to imagine what may and should be.

We have seen how the *Fortnightly Review* was, in a sense, called into being as a response to Matthew Arnold's plea for a nonsectarian periodical disinterestedly devoted to seeing things as they are. *On Compromise* may be regarded as the continuation of Arnold's campaign for the de-emphasis of the political and practical spirit. Arnold had said, in "The Function of Criticism at the Present Time," that, whereas the French are often for suppressing the world of practice, the English are just as often for suppressing the world of ideas. He called for a genuine criticism, one which "obeys an instinct prompting it to try to know the best that is known and thought in the world, irrespectively of practice, politics, and everything of the kind. . . ." [31] Morley now, ten years after Arnold, urges (and in the pages of a review much concerned with practice and politics) that "In making up our minds as to what would be the wisest line of policy if it were practicable, we have nothing to do with the circumstance that it is not practicable. And in settling with ourselves whether propositions purporting to state matters of fact are true or not, we have to consider how far they are conformable to the evidence. We have nothing to do with the comfort and solace which they would be likely to bring to others or ourselves, if they were taken as true." [32]

The sense of political responsibility, admirable as it may be in itself, is too often at war with the virtue that it is Morley's main purpose to recommend: intellectual responsibility. Societies of the past, he points out, have rarely been simultaneously strong in both qualities. The more absolute the divorce between political and intellectual responsibility, between respect for practice and for disinterested thought, the more unfortunate the society. When the

political spirit unduly predominates over the intellectual, as it
does in England, people lose interest in the great and eternal
questions about the purpose and meaning of life; for these do not
seem obviously and immediately connected with social machinery.

In reaction against the mental and spiritual lassitude of his contemporaries, the agnostic Morley expresses a longing for the age
of belief when all were persuaded that having correct beliefs was
the indispensable precondition of salvation, though he does note
that later schools of thought, whether secular like the French *philosophes* or religious like the Oxford Movement, could also be
deadly serious about the true and the false. And Morley the democrat warns that "the House of Commons' view of human life," [33]
which counsels us to pay religious respect to the status quo, may
lead us, in modern times, into the tyranny of public opinion—
another term for Tocqueville's tyranny of the majority.

The question, however, remains of what the use of opinions is
that never do issue in practice. Morley's response is that no opinion really comes to naught because opinions furnish our minds
and thus help in forming our characters. It is of importance, as
Mill used to say, not only what men *do* but what they *are;* and
"what we think has a prodigiously close connection with what we
are." [34]

To add concreteness to his critique of the exclusively political
view of life, Morley tries to show (and here again he is following
in Arnold's footsteps) how liberalism itself has been partially depraved by carrying the political spirit out of its proper sphere.
Liberalism would be a more generous, a more attractive, and even
a more effective force than it is if it would refresh itself more
frequently at the fount of theoretic ideas which underlie and give
coherence to its practical programs.

Into no sphere has the political spirit obtruded itself more effectively or more improperly than into that of religion, where the
desire for emotional comfort rather than the love of ease is placed
ahead of truth. Morley knew this trait not only from observing his
foes in the theological camp but from observing even his friends.
For he had occasion in this very year to rebuke the late John
Stuart Mill for having, in his posthumously published "Utility of
Religion," so far dulled the edge of his logical scalpel as to allow

that in matters of religion, where the need for belief is so great, people may sustain themselves on hypotheses of which the best that can be said is that they are not certainly false.

The chapter "Religious Conformity" is in many ways the most interesting in *On Compromise*. Not only is it clearly the most eloquent and deeply felt, but it is also the one part of the book where we sense the whole man, and not just the logician. It is unique in dealing, as few works of the time did, with the day-to-day problems of the men and women for whom agnosticism had become a way of life as well as an abstract doctrine. We sense throughout the chapter what Morley states at its outset: "The main field of discussion touching Compromise in expression and avowal lies in the region of religious belief." [35]

Before launching into the discussion of whether or not and of when one should express heterodox religious opinions, Morley feels obliged to notice two recent changes in the religious mood and situation which affect his views. First of all, the contention between orthodox Christianity and its foes is now more polite and decorous than it once was; for the critics of religion are now more likely to explain it than directly to attack it. (This new mildness is, of course, partly due to the fact that Voltaire and his successors, by their harsher form of attack, succeeded in making established Christianity more humane; indeed, more "Christian" than it had ever been.) Second, modern free thought is not essentially skeptical but seeks to establish a new faith which incorporates the permanently valuable elements that may be salvaged from the old. Morley even goes so far as to say that the new faith (not necessarily Comtism) "will stand as closely related to Christianity as Christianity stood closely related to the old Judaic dispensation." [36] Both these facts should make it possible for free-thinkers to deal with established beliefs in a spirit that makes fair and disinterested controversy possible, and for the orthodox to dismiss their notion that heresy is the sign of moral depravity. But Morley does not seek to disguise the fact that conflict will inevitably ensue, or that "the future faith, like the faith of the past, brings not peace but a sword. It is a tale not of concord, but of households divided against themselves." [37] And it is precisely of such households that Morley now speaks.

Morley (in characteristic Victorian fashion) concedes without discussion that the relationship between child and parents is the single relationship which justifies a person in keeping his religious dissent to himself. A parent has a special claim on us, and "a man's self-respect ought scarcely to be injured if he finds himself shrinking from playing the apostle to his own father and mother." [38] Morley thus ranges himself, although with qualifications, with the parents and against the children in a debate that raged in many Victorian households. Among Victorian writers, there are several examples of the problem. Ruskin could never speak out fully and consistently on religion in his writings for fear of upsetting his intensely religious and Evangelical mother. Marian Evans (George Eliot) alienated her father for some time because her conscience would not allow her to attend church with him. Gerard Manley Hopkins decided upon his conversion to Catholicism in the knowledge that it would mean a partial break with his family.

Having committed himself to the position of "compromise" in this single instance, Morley carefully states the reasons why husbands and wives should feel no compunction about honestly avowing their religious opinions, however unorthodox, to each other. He insists that he does not seek to turn the household into a dialectical battlefield; but the freethinking husband or wife should know that there is no worthy reason why he should not speak freely when the moment arrives for speaking on religious subjects. To appear to assent to doctrines which one in truth rejects is to abnegate one's self-respect and to mislead others for no useful end.

Perhaps the best example in the discussion of religious conformity of Morley's willingness and ability to grope with the problems of free thought as a mode of life rather than a mere ideology is his analysis of the hypocrisy of unbelieving parents who conform to accepted religious practices in educating their children. Such parents belong in the large, growing class of people who "like to satisfy their intellectual vanity by scepticism, and at the same time to make their comfort safe by external conformity." [39] To have their children educated in the doctrines which they believe false is to betray either a total disbelief in the reality of truth and falsehood or a total unconcern for the welfare of future generations. As for the parent's plea that he is timid, not on his own behalf, but on behalf of his child Morley asserts: "To allow it to be done merely that children may grow up in the stereotyped mould, is simply to perpetuate in new generations the present thick-sighted and dead-heavy state of our spirits. It is to do one's best to keep society for an indefinite time sapped by hollow and void professions, instead of being nourished by sincerity and wholeheartedness." [40]

The final chapter of *On Compromise* concerns the application of beliefs to the practical conduct of life. Here, as Morley has implied through all the earlier chapters, more circumspection and flexibility are required than in the search for and expression of beliefs. Most men and women have to give all of their attention and energy simply to meeting the requirements of daily existence. To expect a community made up of men and women so occupied suddenly to accept ideas which have only just been discovered by the most advanced intellects and then to apply them as well is to show oneself incapable of all prudence and realism.

There is, however, a distinction between legitimate and illegitimate compromise. Compromise is legitimate when it means acquiescence in the fact that the majority of one's contemporaries are not yet prepared to accept the new idea in question or not prepared to bring their way of life into conformity with it. Compromise is illegitimate when it means the suppression or distortion of an idea in order to make it fit—or seem to fit—current prejudices and accepted opinions. It is far better to acknowledge failure (hopefully temporary) to effect changes in opinion and practice than to deceive oneself and others by pretending to a nonexistent success.

When we are dealing with the question of the applicability of new truths to the practice of life, illegitimate compromise is not merely a private failing but the betrayal of a social trust. If the discoverer of a new truth is too timid to express it, he is evading the social responsibility of advancing his community, of hastening the dissolution of worn-out beliefs and the acceptance of new ones. But, after chastising the timid, Morley goes on to show how little cause there really is for timidity. The heretic is rarely so isolated as he supposes, for a new idea rarely comes to one man without in some sense being "in the air," and the innovator is as natural a part of the environment as the conservative is. Furthermore, a person has something very like a moral obligation not to measure his speech and actions by the insidious criteria of immediate usefulness:

No man can ever know whether his neighbours are ready for change or not. He has all the following certainties, at least:—that he himself is ready for the change; that he believes it would be a good and beneficient one; that unless some one begins the work of preparation, assuredly there will be no consummation; and that if he declines to take a part in the matter, there can be no reason why every one else in turn should not decline in like manner, and so the work remain for ever unperformed. The compromiser who blinds himself to all these points, and acts just as if the truth were not in him, does for ideas with which he agrees, the very thing which the acute persecutor does for ideas which he dislikes—he extinguishes beginnings and kills the germs.[41]

Rationalizations of inaction are legion, but Morley does what he can to discredit the ones most frequently used. Many argue that they refrain from attacking such an institution as the Established Church, for example, because it performs many good and useful functions even though it is based on a false theology. In doing so, they forget that the inculcation of a false theology corrupts both morals and intelligence and that, if the established institution happens to be satisfying some exigencies of the present, it is failing to satisfy others and is preventing any preparation for the exigencies of the future. Other people, not quite willing to remain inactive, are yet too willing to settle for small reforms which perpetuate the evil principles that are the main drawback of the existing system or institution. Small reforms are not bad in themselves —in fact, Morley is full of counsels of patience for overhasty Jacobins—but they become pernicious when they divert the reformer's and the public's view from the larger aim which is the ultimate ideal.

Morley, as I mentioned at the beginning of this discussion, was a humanist as well as a liberal. He therefore saw social utility not only in the political and social improvement wrought by the expression and propagation of new ideas but in the moralizing and humanizing of the community which arise from the example set by individuals who are courageous enough to realize their own ideals of life. Like other Victorians—Arnold and Mill come to mind as notable examples—Morley saw morality as resulting not primarily from the adoption of correct ideas about society or about the universe but from emotional soundness. The aim of such sophisticated Victorian moralists was not to instill doctrines but to educate feelings and to refine sensibilities. Poetry was one means of such moral inspiration; the example of great men was another. Thus Morley asserts in *On Compromise* that even if the few men who have the courage of their convictions do nothing to advance the theory of conduct, "they have the art of stimulating men to a more enthusiastic willingness to rise in daily practice to the requirements of whatever theory they may accept." The love of virtue, Morley candidly confesses, depends not so much on a correct or up-to-date set of ideas as upon "affection, sympathy, association, aspiration." [42] If the conscientious heretic fails to make his heresy prevail, he nevertheless does good by encouraging conscientiousness and moral courage in his countrymen.

Almost the whole of the rest of the final chapter of *On Compromise,* as well as the appendix which follows it, is a résumé of the main arguments of Mill's *On Liberty.* Morley makes use of Mill's great defense of liberty to counter the (somewhat perverse) argument that, if the heretic is justified in being uncompromising in expressing *his* opinions, then the conservative is equally justified in being uncompromising in his resolve to preserve his cherished established institutions by destroying the heresies which challenge them. Mill's great argument, very briefly stated, is that reason and force are antithetical and that the essential precondition for the establishment of reason is liberty. Morley, perhaps too conscious of the onslaught which Fitzjames Stephen had recently made on Mill in his *Liberty, Equality, Fraternity* (1873), reiterates the master's major arguments in such detail that the reader is in danger, by the time he closes *On Compromise,* of forgetting its major theme. It is, however, a worthy theme and is worthily set forth; it should not be forgotten. Briefly stated, it is that moral courage is its own reward; that the moral action, though it often seems to go unobserved and unheeded, always is observed and always has its effect; but that, even if it went unobserved and had no effect, it should be performed simply because it is just. The emotional force behind Morley's attack on compromise can be sensed in his strong sentence upon religious conformity:

. . . how pitiful a thing seems the approval or disapproval of these creatures of the conventions of the hour, as one figures the merciless vastness of the universe of matter sweeping us headlong through viewless space; as one hears the wail of misery that is for ever ascending to the deaf gods; as one counts the little tale of the years that separate us from eternal silence. In the light of these things, a man should

surely dare to live his small span of life with little heed of the common speech upon him or his life, only caring that his days may be full
of reality, and his conversation of truth-speaking and wholeness.[43]

IV   Fortnightly *Literary Criticism*

Before we take a third sampling, as it were, of the direction of
Morley's liberalism as *Fortnightly* editor, we should examine that
aspect of his work as editor which shows what I have called the
humanistic aspect of his mind better than any of his political pronouncements, and more concretely than any of his ethical pronouncements, can. I speak of the literary contents of the *Fortnightly*, which, from the point of view of the present study, merit
special attention. Morley was always very proud of the list of
poets, novelists, and men of letters whose work graced his review;
and he was especially proud of those whom he had introduced to
the public, either by printing or reviewing their work.

Although George Henry Lewes was himself an intelligent and
sophisticated critic of literature, the general level of the *Fortnightly's* literary criticism during his editorship was low. An excerpt from Trollope's vulgar and philistine attack on Ruskin for
having turned from art criticism to criticism of society gives some
indication of the kind of thing which Lewes was willing to toler-
ate from his literary reviewers: "Mr. Ruskin had become a musi-
cian very potent, very powerful to charm as well as to teach. We
danced and were delighted that we could dance to such music.
But now he has become ashamed of his violin, and tells us that his
old skill was a thing of nought. He will leave talking to us of the
beauties of art and nature, of the stones of Venice, and the wild
flowers of Switzerland and will preach to us out of a high pulpit
on political economy and the degradation of men and the duties
of women!" [44] Here, surely, was an incongruity: an artist burdened
by a deep sense of social sympathy turns from art criticism to
social criticism and is chastised for doing so in a militantly liberal
and reformist magazine.

Morley saw that the literary criticism of the *Fortnightly* could
be improved, if it were made an integral part of the total enterprise of the review, by being connected with the magazine's social
and political aspirations. This decision, as subsequent events
proved, did not mean the imposition of the narrow, mindless, and
insensitive utilitarian notion of literature that was held by many

Victorian political writers;[45] but it did mean the constant recognition that literature is related to life and that good literary criticism must therefore be criticism of society, politics, and religion as well.

In 1873 Morley wrote in the *Fortnightly* a very favorable review of Walter Pater's essays on the Renaissance; and this review enables us to see Morley's view of the function of criticism; moreover, it illustrates his special function as a kind of promoter of young writers. Like Arnold, he calls sound, disinterested criticism the necessary precursor of great creative activity:

Criticism of the highest kind is the natural forerunner of such a movement as we are all hoping for; indeed criticism of the highest kind is the earliest form of the movement itself. The speculative distractions of the epoch are noisy and multitudinous, and the first effort of the serious spirit must be to disengage itself from the futile hubbub which is sedulously maintained by the bodies of rival partisans in philosophy and philosophical theology. This effort after detachment naturally takes the form of criticism of the past, the only way in which a man can take part in the discussion and propagation of ideas, while yet standing in some sort aloof from the agitation of the present.[46]

Although we can hardly doubt that Morley sympathized with the efforts of men like Pater and John Symonds to show the Renaissance as a far more attractive era than the one depicted by Ruskin or Browning, he was also committed to the idea that the promotion of young and iconoclastic writers was in itself a necessary and valuable activity. When Frederic Harrison asked him why his praise for Pater had been so unqualified—could one really suppose that Morley, a disciple of the great Utilitarians, approved Pater's doctrine of "art for art's sake"?—he replied: "I think it very desirable to call attention to any book like Pater's, which is likely to quicken public interest in the higher sorts of literature. And, moreover, a young and unknown writer like him ought to be formally introduced to the company by the hired master of the ceremonies, myself, or another to wit. So pray pardon my light dealings with his transgressions." [47]

Since we shall analyze in a later chapter the nature and direction of Morley's literary criticism, we may here restrict ourselves to assessing his performance as a "master of ceremonies" introducing and promoting literary talent. As we do so, it is hard to fault

either his courage or his taste. In a period when such writers as
Trollope, George Eliot, and Robert Browning were widely attacked for levity, irreverence, and even immorality, the *Fortnightly* was publishing and praising such writers as Meredith,
Swinburne, Morris, and D. G. Rossetti. Meredith's fictional studies
of radicalism, *Vittoria* and *Beauchamp's Career,* were serialized in
the review. Morley published many of Swinburne's poems (including his great elegies on Baudelaire and Gautier), and he also
used him often as a reviewer. In July, 1867, the review carried
Swinburne's important praise of William Morris' great volume of
pre-Raphaelite verse, *The Defence of Guenevere* as well as of the
narrative poem *The Life and Death of Jason.* In 1868 Morley
himself wrote a laudatory review of *The Earthly Paradise;* and he
published five of Morris' poems between that date and 1872. The
Fortnightly printed in March 1869 a group of sixteen of the sonnets in D. G. Rossetti's *House of Life* cycle, one of the major
achievements of Victorian poetry; and, when a storm of abuse and
vilification gathered about Rossetti's head and he was being sav-
agely and irresponsibly attacked in Robert Buchanan's notorious
Contemporary Review article "The Fleshly School of Poetry,"
Swinburne, reliable as ever in these matters, came forth to praise
Rossetti's work in the *Fortnightly.* Indeed, Swinburne himself had
earlier found in the pages of Morley's magazine not only a kind of
refuge from the hysterical attacks that had been mounted against
his *Poems and Ballads* but also an opportunity to continue his
poetic career.[48]

Morley's literary choices and policies were wise as well as courageous. In dealing with established and revered figures, the *Fortnightly* could show a detachment that we now suppose to be the
benefit of a twentieth-century perspective. Trollope was criticized
for his insufficient awareness of evil; Lewes raised doubts as to
Dickens' intellectual capacity; Tennyson was criticized for the inadequacy of his social philosophy. But a more certain proof of the
wisdom of Morley's literary policy as editor is simply the quantity
of good literature which appeared in the *Fortnightly* during his
reign. Rossetti's *House of Life* sonnets, according to two distinguished contemporary critics of Victorian poetry, achieved "a clar-
ity of imagery, a toughness and economy of diction which [gave]
a new sound to Victorian verse." [49] Pater's *Studies in the History
of the Renaissance,* a considerable part of which first appeared in

the *Fortnightly,* is now recognized to be the major work of a major writer and one which, in conjunction with the studies of John Addington Symonds, also first published in the *Fortnightly,* established the importance of the Renaissance for the late nineteenth and early twentieth centuries, and created a new enthusiasm as well as a new scholarship for that earlier era. Frederic Harrison published in the *Fortnightly* of November, 1867, a delightful satire of Arnold's doctrines of culture, disinterestedness, and (in Harrison's view) inaction. Arnold told Lady Rothschild that the piece made him laugh until he cried, but he decided that Harrison (as well as other critics of his Oxford lecture on "Culture and its Enemies") must be answered; and out of the controversy eventually grew the series of essays which by 1869 made up *Culture and Anarchy.* Arnold himself became a regular *Fortnightly* contributor in 1877 with an article on George Sand. This was followed in 1878 by "Equality," one of his most important political essays, and by the essays "Irish Catholicism and British Liberalism," and "'Porro Unum est Necessarium.'"

For a primarily political magazine edited by an astute political mind, the *Fortnightly* did extraordinarily well in literature. (Needless to add, its best poetry, fiction, and literary essays are now more read than its political manifestos.) Everett finds a political motive at work even in Morley's choice of literary contributors, but only in the broadest sense of encouraging fresh modes of thought, feeling, and expression as the surest guarantees of reassessing the old order and of groping toward the new. Any narrower political motive could not reasonably be imputed to Morley, for the medievalism of Morris or Rossetti may have been subversive of the existing spiritual order, but it can hardly be said to reflect Morley's ideas for renovating his society. It is, indeed, a commonplace of Victorian studies that Ruskin and the medievalizing Socialists who descended from him saw the liberalism of Mill and Morley as one of their chief enemies. In any case, there is no reason why Morley's idea of liberalism in its application to literature should have been any narrower than his application of it generally was. We should not be surprised that the man who printed Bagehot as well as Harrison, and who praised Burke as well as Voltaire, did not proscribe poets who failed to sing liberal principles.

V *Achievements*

For some indication of the direction of Morley's thoughts during the last years of his editorship of the *Fortnightly,* we may turn to two essays, one of 1878 entitled "Memorials of a Man of Letters" and another, written upon the occasion of his retirement from the editorship in 1882, called "Valedictory." In them, Morley tries to analyze the relationship that has existed between the review and liberalism, to sum up the fruits of his experience as an editor, and to assess the achievement of the *Fortnightly.* The occasion for the first article was the publication of some of the correspondence of Macvey Napier from the period 1829 to 1847, when he was editor of the *Edinburgh Review.* Any such volume, Morley says, must bring to the mind of one who is himself an editor the following questions: "What are the qualities of a good contributor? What makes a good Review? Is the best literature produced by the writer who does nothing else but write, or by the man who tempers literature by affairs? What are the different recommendations of the rival systems of anonymity and signature?" [50]

Morley compares the occupation of an editor to that of the manager of an opera house. The editor is "the impresario of men of letters, the *entrepreneur* of the spiritual power." [51] He too must balance and reconcile a great number of contending interests and factions; he too must humor his spoiled soprano—the writer who cannot bear the editorial alteration of a single syllable he has written. Few readers of organs such as the *Edinburgh* or *Fortnightly* can suspect how often their editors are concerned with such prosaic matters as poor paragraphing, slovenly manuscripts, disordered proofs.

In looking back to the great days of the *Edinburgh Review,* Morley concludes that a major change has overtaken the world of political journalism. The *Edinburgh Review* existed to express the coherent political creed of a distinct political school. No such creeds or schools exist any longer. The very spirit of liberalism has helped "to produce that sceptical and centrifugal state of mind, which now tends to nullify organized liberalism and paralyze the spirit of improvement." In an age when no substantial group of writers is united by a body of shared opinion, "the only motto that can be inscribed on the flag of a liberal Review is the general device of Progress, each writer interpreting it in his own sense. . . ." [52] The policy of affixing each writer's signature to what he prints would seem to be the natural outgrowth of this state of affairs.

In his "Valedictory" of 1882, Morley looked back over the fifteen years he had given to the *Fortnightly*. He had joined the review as a young man and was leaving it a middle-aged one. What had he accomplished? Had his performance lived up to his intention? Nothing, he confesses, is drearier than turning over thirty volumes of old reviews. Not only do most of their contents seem stale (as in the nature of things they must), but the experience calls to mind those contributors who were the chief support of the review and are now dead. Morley is particularly moved by his recollections of Lewes, J. E. Cairnes, Mill, Bagehot (who had written the first article in the first number), and W. K. Clifford. The *Fortnightly*, he reminds readers, owes a special debt to Mill as the man who encouraged him to conduct the periodical "on the principles of free discussion and personal responsibility." [53]

The essential success of the policy of signature would seem to be indicated, says Morley, by the number of periodicals that have adopted from expediency what the founders of the *Fortnightly* espoused from principle. Lewes had maintained, at the start, that a periodical could draw to itself a large number of distinguished writers of very different schools of thought only if it guaranteed each writer perfect freedom; and naturally such freedom could not be granted unless each writer took personal responsibility for what he wrote. But experience had shown that Lewes was only partly right, for it would be dishonest to pretend that the principle of signature did not carry with it serious drawbacks: it encouraged an idle curiosity about personalities; it tempted readers to think more of the man who wrote than of the value of his words; and it also narrowed the realm of the professional writer, for editors were now obliged to seek out specialists of known reputation and could no longer rely on the informed and intelligent general writer. Morley concludes that no general rule can be laid down as to whether or not men write best when they sign what they write. Some writers are made stiff and Olympian by anonymity; upon others, it has the opposite effect.

One of the most noteworthy changes that had come about in the world of letters since the *Fortnightly* was founded was, according to Morley, the "democratization" of speculation. Philo-

sophical, theological, and scientific questions which had formerly
been confined to books and treatises were now thrashed out in the
pages of popular periodicals in full view of a vast audience. In this
connection it is worth noticing that between 1867 and 1873, Morley raised the *Fortnightly's* circulation from 1,400 to 2,500. In
1873, he wrote: "With our present circulation, 2,500 in England
alone, we count, say, 30,000 readers; and they are readers of the
influential class." [54]

In his final estimate of the achievement of the *Fortnightly*, Morley frankly admits that it fell short of the ideal which its founders
had set. For one thing, though the editor welcomed many shades
of opinion, "the Review has unquestionably gathered round it
some of the associations of sect." [55] But the *Fortnightly's* critics
had never succeeded in accurately identifying the sect. At first
they labelled the review "Comtist"; then they implicitly admitted
that this was too narrow by calling it "Positivist." Even so they
remained wide of the mark, for how could Chamberlain's program, for example, so fully supported by the *Fortnightly*, be
subsumed under the Positivist label? Others unfriendly to the
Fortnightly had called it the organ of "Academic Liberalism,"
apparently forgetting its passionate commitment to political action.

Yet those who sensed a principle of unity underlying the apparent diversity of the *Fortnightly Review* were following a sound
instinct: "So far as the Review has been more specially identified
with one set of opinions than another, it has been due to the fact
that a certain dissent from received theologies has been found in
company with new ideas of social and political reform." This "suspicious combination" no longer arouses the anger it used to do, for
what were once the isolated heresies of the review—on trade
unions or national education—are now accepted elements of the
new climate of opinion. The *Fortnightly* had succeeded in bringing into prominence "principles and aims" which would not have
received a hearing twenty years earlier; and this achievement was
success enough for any periodical.[56]

Everett, in his study of the *Fortnightly*, has given the reasons
for Morley's success as editor. He was always on good relations
with his contributors; he knew what he wanted from each one and
how he could get it; and he conscientiously avoided favoritism.
He maintained a high standard of contributor—"I am always very

glad to have anything of mine in the *Fortnightly*," said Huxley, "as it is sure to be in good company." [57] He gave the review a cosmopolitan character by keeping it attentive to French, German, and American developments; by inviting contributions from foreign writers (Mazzini and Kropotkin were two); by including in it praise of such writers as Walt Whitman, Henrik Ibsen, Richard Wagner, and Emile Zola; and by campaigning to rehabilitate the French Enlightenment for English readers. Perhaps our last words on the achievements of the *Fortnightly Review* should be the last which Morley wrote in the review as its editor:

A certain number of people have been persuaded to share opinions that fifteen years ago were more unpopular than they are now. A certain resistance has been offered to the stubborn influence of prejudice and use and wont. The original scheme of the Review, even if there had been no other obstacle, prevented it from being the organ of a systematic and constructive policy. There is not, in fact, a body of systematic political thought at work in our own day. The Liberals of the Benthamite school surveyed society and institutions as a whole; they connected their advocacy of political and legal changes with carefully formed theories of human nature; they considered the great art of Government in connection with the character of man, his proper education, his potential capacities. Yet . . . it cannot be pretended that we are less in need of systematic politics than our fathers were sixty years since, or that general principles are now more generally settled even among members of the same party than they were then. The perplexities of to-day are as embarrassing as any in our history, and they may prove even more dangerous. . . . Yet ideas are hardly ripe for realisation. We shall need to see great schools before we can make sure of powerful parties. Meanwhile, whatever gives freedom and variety to thought, and earnestness to men's interest in the world, must contribute to a good end.[58]

CHAPTER 3

The French Enlightenment

The movement which went on in
France under the old *régime,* from
1700 to 1789, was far more really
akin than that of the Revolution itself to the movement of the Renascence; the France of Voltaire and
Rousseau told far more powerfully
upon the mind of Europe than the
France of the Revolution.
—Matthew Arnold,
Essays in Criticism

What we . . . were sometimes, by
a ridiculous exaggeration, called by
others, namely a "school," some of us
for a time really hoped and aspired
to be. The French *philosophes* of the
eighteenth century were the example
we sought to imitate, and we hoped
to accomplish no less results.
—John Stuart Mill, *Autobiography*

JOHN Morley's studies of the French Enlightenment cannot
be fully understood without grasping his motives for undertaking them. Victorians had the bad habit of confusing an interest
in France with an unqualified sympathy for all its ideas and institutions; as a result, they were highly suspicious of Englishmen
who devoted much of their time, energy, and prose to French
affairs. Morley did not escape from this suspicion, though in one
sense he certainly deserved to; for, unlike such genuine Franco-
philes as Arnold and Mill, he had remarkably little liking for the
country about whose great thinkers he wrote so fully and so well.[1]
We shall escape many of the errors of which Morley's Victorian

76

detractors were guilty if we attend to his essay of March, 1888, which carries the unfortunate title of "A Few French Models." He begins it by dismissing, with justifiable impatience, the parochial English view that the French Revolution was a blameworthy event because it retarded English reform by frightening Englishmen into confusing peaceful reform with violent revolution. He questions the causal analysis at work here and also remarks that "it is a curious implication that underlies all writing in this familiar vein, that France ought to have gone on with a bad government, in order to secure to England the advantages of a good one." [2]

Argument by analogy is always dangerous; and, when applied to politics, it is often pernicious. A certain school of conservative thought in England always sought analogues in the events of the French Revolution or in its intellectual antecedents for English reforms or reform movements which they disliked, and Morley was an ideal target for them. Not only did he think and act in ways which at once put hysterical conservatives in mind of the Reign of Terror; he had implicitly confessed his desire to reproduce the French Revolution in England by all the books he had written about the *philosophes* and the revolutionists. The chancellor of the exchequer at Dublin had labeled Morley "the Saint-Just of our Revolution." He had also been accused of finding "his models in the heroes of the French Revolution" and of looking for "his methods in the Reign of Terror." But would it not be just as rational to suppose that, because he had written a sympathetic appreciation of Joseph de Maistre, he sought his models among the heroes of the Catholic reaction and his methods in the supremacy of the Holy See over all temporal and secular authority? [3]

Morley says that he undertook his French studies not to discover spiritual icons or political models but to vindicate the eighteenth century and the thinkers of the French Enlightenment in particular from Carlyle's misrepresentations. Carlyle's essays on Diderot, Rousseau, and Voltaire were only the most forceful and articulate expression of the whole literary reaction against the French revolutionary group. But the influence of Buckle's history of civilization and, still more, of Comte's Positivism has, since the time Carlyle wrote, made it possible to see these thinkers through unbiased eyes. Morley readily admits that he and others who were in sympathy with the *philosophes* may have erred on the side of generous enthusiasm in their reassessments, but they did so because they were trying to redress an imbalance.

Nothing could be more foolish than to suppose that interest in and even sympathy with the *philosophes* are tantamount to an absolute allegiance to all their methods and doctrines. Morley could justly remind his readers of how often in his studies of the Enlightenment thinkers he had stressed the importance of studying doctrines which were untrue and yet had had great historical influence. In *Rousseau,* for example, he had written: "There has been no attempt to palliate either the shallowness or the practical mischievousness of the *Social Contract.* But there is another side to its influence. We should be false to our critical principle, if we do not recognise the historical effect of a speculation scientifically valueless." Morley also reminds his readers and critics that he has never looked to France as a model; he has, after all, always been a disciple of Mill, and the principles of Mill are far better illustrated by Abraham Lincoln in freeing the slaves than by the Frenchmen who fomented the French Revolution: "If we are to talk of ideals, of heroes, and models, I, for one, should hardly look to France at all." [4]

We must be careful not to accept these statements at face value. We may at once retort upon Morley that Mill himself did not seem to have noticed this absolute divorce between his political principles and those of the fomenters of the French Revolution, for he could write in his *Autobiography* of the Utilitarian Society: "What we were sometimes, by a ridiculous exaggeration, called by others, namely a 'school,' some of us for a time really hoped and aspired to be. The French *philosophes* of the eighteenth century were the example we sought to imitate, and we hoped to accomplish no less results." [5] Mill, to be sure, writes in the past tense; and Morley, like Mill, was to find fault with some of the precursors of the revolution, especially with Rousseau and his followers, for lacking certain eminently English qualities: a reverence for history; a suspicion of rationalistic utopianism; a respect (which Morley had learned from Burke) for the influence which particular circumstances have upon the application of general principles. But Morley knew as well as Mill that the spiritual foundations of Utilitarianism had been laid by the *philosophes,* and he wanted to examine those foundations as thoroughly as he could. His *apolo-*

gia for the French studies was certainly necessary, given English prejudices on the subject. But he was really more concerned to show the absurdity of political analogies than to prove that America rather than France is the proper model for a Utilitarian. The practical politician, he maintains, must see each problem as unique, for "there is no such thing as an essential reproduction of social and political combinations of circumstances." [6] Historical parallels and analogies are attractive to impatient people because they offer, as do racial stereotypes, a ready escape from thought and observation.

Having taken due note of Morley's *caveat*, we must observe that, if he had regarded his French studies as (to use his own words) "no more than an attempt to remind people of the place of French literature between Bayle and Rousseau in the progress of European emancipation," [7] it is hard to imagine him as writing them; for Morley's was not the disinterested scholarly mind. We need only compare the dry and abstract image cast by the words just quoted from his *Recollections* with the following expression of creative joy from a letter of 1871 to see that Morley was involved in something more than a scholarly adjustment of perspective: "a fortnight ago, I was seized, after the manner of poets, with a phrenetic and wholly invincible oestrus—to write a monograph—VOLTAIRE. Everything else has vanished from my mind. Night and day I am possessed with him, and I stick to my table like a slave. What a subject!!!" [8]

A genuine intellectual excitement was aroused in Morley by the vision of men possessed of great intellect and of the social passion for doing good who attempted, on a massive scale, to apply the precepts of reason to the vagaries of human society. He did not, of course, take these men as models all of whose ideas and actions he must emulate. But, whatever his disagreements with them, he must have recognized their effort as the prototype of Mill's and of his own.

Morley was no revolutionary, but neither was Voltaire. Morley was far more in sympathy with the movements of thought that had prepared the French Revolution than with the event itself. Nevertheless, whatever he might say about the false or premature application of ideas to practice in the French Revolution, he was certain that it remained, on balance, a great good, and that the *philosophes,* if they did indeed precipitate France into revolution, thereby saved her from a far worse fate—not despotism, but anarchy:

> What enabled the leaders of the nation to discern the horror and despair of this anarchic dissolution of the worn-out old, and what inspired them with hope and energy when they thought of the possible new, was the spiritual preparation that had been in swift progress since the third decade of the century. . . . The school of Voltaire, the school of Rousseau, and the schools of Quesnay and Montesquieu . . . all alike energetically familiarised the public mind with a firm belief in human reason, and the idea of the natural rights of man. They impregnated it with a growing enthusiasm for social justice.[9]

I Voltaire

Voltaire, the first of Morley's three books on the great men of letters of eighteenth-century France, appeared in 1872. Voltaire loomed in Morley's eyes as the first individual in modern history to exercise the kind of spiritual power that had previously belonged only to men standing within certain recognized institutions or systems, or to those institutions and systems themselves. In his essay on Condorcet, Morley wrote that "Voltaire filled a place before men's eyes in the eighteenth century as conspicuous and as authoritative as that of St. Bernard in the twelfth. The difference was that Voltaire's place was absolutely unofficial in its origin, and indebted to no system nor organisation for its maintenance."[10] Here was an individual who had transformed the mind of his country and to some extent the mind of the whole Western world; moreover, he had acted on a scale usually attributed to impersonal historical forces. An irony unnoticed by Morley is that one of Voltaire's contributions to historiography was to direct attention to the working of large impersonal forces, as opposed to outstanding individuals, in history; the heroic scale of his own life and the influence of his works became a powerful argument against his theory of history.

Voltairism, Morley believed, was a movement of the dimension and importance of Catholicism, the Renaissance, or Calvinism. Like those movements, it was not in itself a complete system of human nature but an attempt to develop sides of human nature which the prevailing system had either neglected or actively disparaged. It was, in fact, the Renaissance of the eighteenth century, both in its intellectual passion and its moral shortcomings.

The eighty volumes and more which Voltaire produced are "the monument, as they were in some sort the instrument, of a new renascence." [11]

Morley himself lived in an age of voluminous production by literary men, but the sheer volume of work from the Victorians must often be justified by the argument that there is a point at which quantity does change into quality. No such *apologia* is needed for Voltaire's plentifulness. He wrote on an immense variety of subjects, and always wrote, says Morley, originally. Morley is, of course, aware that Voltaire often acted as a great popularizer of philosophic and scientific ideas which he did not himself invent; his originality consisted in genuinely appropriating what he used and making it his own. To everything he touched, from history to biblical criticism to the ideas of Locke and the laws of Newton, he lent his extraordinary vitality; and the words *life, vitality,* and *alive* appear again and again in Morley's "Preliminary" chapter of *Voltaire.* What other writer has ever sustained through eighty volumes a wit whose magic no critic has yet analyzed and a style, in Matthew Arnold's words, "of unmatched incisiveness and animation," a "style compared to which the style of Lord Macaulay is tame, and the style of Isocrates is obscure."? [12]

Voltaire became a force in life as well as literature, Morley asserts, because he persistently carried himself and his ideas out of the study into the realm of action. Voltaire, perhaps the greatest man of letters who ever lived, nevertheless rated literature below action; and for this reason he has often been censured by contemptuous practitioners of belles-lettres. Yet, in actuality, he rated letters higher than his critics do, for he saw literature and ideas not as mere playthings but as legitimate instruments for criticizing and transforming the world.

In his struggles against infamy, religious or political, Voltaire did not temporize, as do the modern "compromisers" Morley attacked two years later. Though irreligious, he paid religion sufficient respect to treat it as the most important of subjects, something that could hardly be said of the pragmatic modern skeptic. But then Voltaire was no skeptic, either in temperament or in doctrine. The willing suspension of disbelief was a state which had no attractions for him, and he did not look upon the refusal to decide upon the truth or falsehood of any proposition, the good or evil of any institution, as a sign of intellectual sophistication.

Voltaire's impatience of mere skepticism, according to Morley, arose from the fact that he took ideas seriously, not as mere counters to be played with: "an irrational prejudice was not the object of a polite coldness, but a real evil to be combatted and overthrown at every hazard." [13] Forward as he was in helping the victims of injustice, he showed equal urgency in combating the prejudice and unreason that are the sources of injustice. Besides, eighteenth-century France provided him with many instances of the close union between a disrespect for the rational faculty and a disrespect for the human status of all men, regardless of their religious and political affiliation. In his mind, social cruelty was inseparable from intellectual repression; therefore, his own defense of reason was also a defense of his fellow human beings.

In view of his keen awareness of the inseparability of Voltaire's intellectual passion to know the truth from his social passion to apply it for good ends, it is surprising that Morley arrives at the conclusion that "Voltairism was primarily and directly altogether an intellectual movement . . . a reaction against the subordination of the intellectual to the moral side of men. . . ." [14] Surely someone whose reading of Voltaire has not even gone beyond *Candide* can see that Voltaire's primary purpose is not to criticize those philosophies and institutions that have an exclusively moral emphasis but to measure all philosophies and institutions by a simple standard: do they help to alleviate human suffering? This question, after all, is the one Voltaire asks in *Candide* of the church as well as of the philosophy of optimism (which had once been his own). His quarrel with the church itself does not arise primarily from his conviction of its falsehood but from his observation that devotees of the church are capable of treating nonbelievers with complete inhumanity and yet of enjoying the charms of good conscience. To test all doctrines by their conduciveness to human well-being rather than by their conformity to abstract standards of truth—and to dismiss, as Voltaire did, all "metaphysical" questions of a nonethical nature as futile—is hardly to exhibit an exclusively intellectual temper.

Morley is on surer ground when he establishes Voltaire as the destroyer, not only of the reigning system of his day, but of all systems and systematizers. In denying Christianity's claims to be a final and infallible system of belief, knowledge, and moral government, Voltaire was at war not only with erroneous belief but

with the tendency, not confined to the church, to arrive at a sup-
posedly final synthesis of all human knowledge and experience
when, in fact, a genuine analysis had hardly begun. He proved
that he had learned the lesson he taught others by refraining from
substituting a new system of society and belief for the old one.
Following a line of argument precisely opposite to that which had
been pursued by the Romantics and Carlyle—that Voltaire had
demonstrated the implausibility of the Christian religion but
had put nothing in its place—Morley praises Voltaire as "perhaps
the one great Frenchman who has known how to abide in patient
contentment with an all but purely critical reserve, leaving reconstruction, its form, its modes, its epoch, for the fulness of time and
maturity of effort to disclose." [15] Because he abstained from ill-
advised attempts at premature reconstruction—Morley has Comte
in mind—Voltaire became the butt not only of upholders of the
old system but of the believers in order at all costs who felt adrift
in the era of transition into which Voltaire had thrown nearly all
of Europe.

Peter Gay, the author of an excellent recent study of Voltaire's
politics, has said that a major fault of Morley's biography of Voltaire is its exaggeration of the influence which Voltaire's visit to
England had upon him. It is wrong to say, as Morley does, that
Voltaire left France a poet and returned a sage. In fact, Gay asserts and demonstrates, Voltaire had developed a social philosophy before leaving France.[16] If Morley did, in fact, exaggerate the
English influence upon Voltaire's mind and sympathies, he had
good reasons for doing so. When Morley wrote, England had for
some time considered the entire philosophy of the Enlightenment
as alien doctrines peculiar to the minds of renegade French pupils
of the Jesuits; to attempt to transfer this philosophy or any one of
its precepts to Protestant England was to go against nature and to
court disaster. Morley, without exactly intending that his countrymen should become converts to the philosophy of the Enlightenment, wanted to show them that many of the dominant ideas of
the mastermind of the whole movement were both English and
Protestant in origin. That he was, on the whole, successful is
proved by the fact that the English origin of many of the doctrines of the French Enlightenment is now a commonplace in the
history of ideas.

Morley's chapter on "English Influences" is mainly concerned

with Voltaire's *Lettres Philosophiques, ou Lettres sur les Anglais*
(published in England in 1732; in France in 1733), the book
which was the result of Voltaire's observation of England's people
and institutions between 1726 and 1729. Since he is writing not so
much a conventional Victorian biography as a biography of his
subject's mind, Morley touches only briefly on the events—such as
his two imprisonments in the Bastille—which made Voltaire flee
from France to England in 1726, and on the external incidents of
his three-year sojourn in England. In Morley's French studies, the
facts of a man's personal life are always incidental to the elucida-
tion of his ideas.

Morley takes the view that "Voltairism" originated in the flight
of its founder from Paris to London. For once, the outward
change in a man's life was a perfect reflection of an inward transformation. Before Voltaire's flight from his country, he had been
mainly preoccupied with imaginative literature; when he returned
from England, "he had tasted of the fruit of the tree of scientific
reason, and . . . he had become alive to the central truth of the
social destination of all art and all knowledge. In a word, he was
transformed from the penman into the captain and man-at-
arms." [17]

Morley could hardly have been blind to the striking way in
which the *Lettres Philosophiques* showed how the French Revolution had reversed the relative positions of France and England
on the road of social and intellectual progress. Voltaire, writing in
the early eighteenth century, celebrated England as the native
home of progress and enlightenment, in contrast to France, where
reaction and superstition ruled. Everywhere in his book, Voltaire
reported instances where England seemed to carry scientific and
philosophical light into the cobwebs of dark superstition that still
enveloped his own country. In England, John Locke, Isaac Newton, and smallpox inoculations had displaced Aristotle, René Des-
cartes, and witch-hunting. In politics, the same contrast was apparent. The English, Voltaire maintained, had fought for liberty
in their civil wars, whereas "the civil wars of France have been
longer, crueler, more productive of crimes than those of England;
but of all these civil wars not a single one has had a rational
liberty as its object" [18] (my translation).

Morley wrote in full awareness of how the French Revolution
and the subsequent English fear of all the principles which im-

pelled it had reversed the relative positions of England and France. France, however reactionary her governments might thereafter be (and Morley was almost never in sympathy with a French government), stood in the vanguard of Europe while England lingered cautiously in the rear. If Morley could show that the best principles of the Enlightenment thinkers—as distinct from those which led to the Terror—were rooted in Voltaire's experience of England, he could help to reopen the English mind to ideas it had wrongly supposed alien.

Among the first things which had impressed Voltaire in England was the superior position which men of letters held in English society. Patronage in the reign of Queen Anne (as Macaulay was to point out in his notorious essay on Samuel Johnson) was splendid—men of letters were respected, consulted, and supported. The alliance—or what seemed to be such—between mind and power must have been most attractive to a man who had already suffered considerable humiliation at the hands of arbitrary power in France. And Voltaire was filled with admiration for the way in which, in 1727, the death of Newton, whose name could hardly be mentioned in France, was the occasion for public mourning on a scale reserved in France for kings.

In discussing Voltaire's infatuation with Newton, Morley warns us against mistaking Voltaire's lightness of touch and tone for superficiality. Voltaire always did his homework on subjects he discussed. He set himself diligently to the study of Newtonian physics, and he received the Newtonian doctrines with something of the optimistic joy that characterized Pope's well-known lines "Nature, and Nature's Laws lay hid in Night./God said, *Let Newton be!* and All was Light." In Voltaire's own country, the Cartesian physics was still sacrosanct (as the Aristotelian physics had previously been). But it was not the substitution of, for example, the theory of attraction for the theory of vortices that was of primary importance for the development of Voltaire's mind; for Newton's methods and principles pushed his mind in the direction of empiricism and away from all metaphysics. This bent was confirmed by his reading of John Locke. Locke and Newton, instead of indulging, as their predecessors had done, in the invention of systems hatched by their own brains, laboriously observed phenomena. Both refrained from stating definitions of what they did not understand; instead, they set about examining what they

wished to understand. The main benefit which Voltaire derived
from Locke and Newton, according to Morley, was "a noble faith
. . . in the ability of the relative and practical understanding to
reach truth; a deep-rooted reverence for it, as a majestic power
bearing munificent and unnumbered gifts to mankind." [19]

Voltaire, then, had the great tradition of English empirical philosophy to thank for having saved him from the fate of so many of
his philosophically minded countrymen, with their fatal propen-
sity for system making. His study of Newton and Locke made him
"the very genius of good sense." Once again we may see how Morley, without in any way distorting facts, is trying, by an exercise in
the history of ideas, to disabuse his countrymen of the vulgar prejudice against Voltaire as a doctrinaire addicted to artificial systems.

It was not only in science and philosophy that Voltaire found
England advanced over his country. He was also profoundly impressed by the social differences between a country that had
emerged from feudalism and one which had not. Looking at the
English peasant, for example, he was impressed by the fact that
he, unlike his French counterpart, "doesn't have his feet bruised
by wooden shoes, . . . eats white bread, . . . is well dressed,
. . . is not afraid to increase the number of his cattle or to tile
his roof because his taxes will therefore be increased the following
year" [20] (my translation). He was amazed to see that, in England,
being a noble or priest did not exempt a man from paying certain
taxes; he looked approvingly on the (to him) novel practice of
arranging society in such ways as to encourage the sons of peers to
enter trade, thus giving to the merchant class a respectability it
had not found in France.

For England's political virtues, according to Morley, Voltaire's
eye was not so keen. True, he celebrated the freedom to think and
to express one's thoughts that existed in England; but he had no
sound grasp of the foundations of such spiritual freedom: "Liberty in spirituals was adorable to him, but for liberty in temporals
he never seems to have had more than a very distant and verbal
kind of respect. . . ." What Morley means in saying that Voltaire
failed to appreciate the positive side of political liberty is that
Voltaire was no democrat. Therefore, he was unable to see that
political liberty is "a gospel of duties" as well as a "doctrine of
rights": that it depends upon the degree to which the people of a

nation actively participate in the management of national affairs.[21] The England that Voltaire observed was, of course, no democracy, but it had moved in the direction of representative institutions which encouraged a great many men from all stations of life to participate actively in the workings of government. What Voltaire failed to see was the educative value of democratic institutions which obliged men to concern themselves with issues larger than their personal welfare and advancement. Fond as he was of liberty, much as he did to secure it for others, Voltaire was too content to rest satisfied with the shortsighted expedient of a benevolent despot as the readiest means of obtaining it. (It is noteworthy that Morley, devotee of the "historical" method though he was, feels no qualms about judging Voltaire's political tastes by the democratic ideals of a much later age.)

Voltaire's other oversight in assessing the England of his day was, according to Morley, his inadequate awareness of the role of Protestantism in fostering the spiritual liberty he so admired. Far as Morley wandered from the Evangelical Protestantism of his youth, he always believed Protestantism conducive to political virtue, at least when compared with its chief rival, Catholicism. Voltaire, he complains, was unable to see that Protestantism had been responsible, in England and other countires, for weakening both the idea of and the respect for authority. Voltaire admired English liberty without seeing that it could not have arisen if the English had not been leavened by Protestantism. Admittedly, many Protestants, as well as many branches of Protestantism, have been guilty of persecution and of the denial of intellectual independence; but this fact does not alter the other fact that "Protestantism was indirectly the means of creating and dispersing an atmosphere of rationalism, in which there speedily sprang up philosophical, theological, and political influences, all of them entirely antagonistic to the old order of thought and institution." [22]

Morley's analysis of Voltaire's *Lettres Philosophiques* reveals much not just about his preoccupations at the time of composing the book in 1871 but about his fundamental outlook on life. The *Lettres Philosophiques* is composed of twenty-four chapters devoted to English men, customs, religious sects, philosophies, and a single chapter, the last in the book, devoted to a furious attack on Pascal's *Pensées*. Why should Voltaire, with his rather strict notions of artistic unity, have attached a critique of Pascal to a book

devoted to England and the English? Morley does not directly
address himself to this question, but he is surely aware of it. After
three years in England, Voltaire was filled with boundless hopes
of the good which men might make for themselves in this world if
they followed the precepts of reason and simple humanity. But
Pascal's doctrine of original sin denied that man could ever escape
from his fallen state in this world; to him, all man's hurryings to
and fro were mere searches for anodynes which enabled him to
ignore the truth of his situation. Man's situation, in Pascal's view,
was that of a creature who was, in Cardinal Newman's description, "doubled up in a cage in which he can neither lie, stand, sit,
nor kneel." [23] Progress, whether intellectual or social, could do
nothing more than make man a bit less uncomfortable in this
rather hopeless situation.

Voltaire, although his attack on Pascal is telling in many ways,
shows himself spiritually deaf to the very questions Pascal is pos-
ing about the possibility of an inherently sinful being finding happiness by ignoring his spiritual predicament. For Voltaire saw the
evils about him not as sins but as crimes which could be prevented once their causes were known. He was quite indifferent to
questions of man's metaphysical status, of his exact location in
between the extremes of pure being and mere nothingness, God
and the worm; for such questions could never be answered. And if
every metaphysician should answer in the negative to the question of the possibility of moral progress, empirical evidence (like
that which he had collected in England) could prove otherwise.
Whatever we may think of the adequacy of Voltaire's response to
the charge of ignoring "ultimate" questions, it is important to note
that Morley accepts it: "This sage strain," he says about Voltaire's
rebuke to those who despair because they have not found the final
secret of human nature, "was the restoration to men of their self-
respect, the revival of that intelligence which Pascal had so humil-
iated and thrust under foot." [24]

Voltaire was the one genuinely literary figure to whom Morley
devoted an entire book. It is therefore not surprising that he reveals, in his discussion of Voltaire's more purely literary output—
his tragedies and his narrative poetry—much about his own conception of literature. What is surprising is that the chapter called
"Literature" in Morley's study of Voltaire hardly mentions the

philosophical tales which are most read and by which Voltaire is best-known today: *Zadig, Candide, Micromégas.*

At the outset, Morley defines his critical role as the relatively modest one of measuring how well a man uses his gifts and his opportunities rather than of pronouncing him a failure or a success in absolute terms. What he will try to do in his analysis of Voltaire's literary achievement—or of any writer's for that matter —is to depict the writer's character as the result of a "complex interplay" between "the first innate conditions of temperament" and "the fixed limitations of opportunity." [25]

If ever a man was called by the inmost law of his nature to literature, that man was, Morley asserts, Voltaire. He was called to literature as the unsurpassed art of "showing the ideas of all subjects in the double light of the practical and the spiritual reason." Voltaire's literary practice affords Morley the opportunity for defining his own conception of literature as a moral agent which acts upon society by communicating to its members "the two precious qualities of breadth of interest and balance of judgment; multiplicity of sympathies and steadiness of sight." [26] Here, as elsewhere in the book, Morley praises Voltaire for complementing his intellectual impulse with the social impulse to impart his knowledge. He performed his social task in two ways: by popularizing scientific and philosophical knowledge in his essays, dialogues, and dictionaries; and by transmuting this knowledge into emotional equivalents in his plays and tales.

Truly to understand the nature of Voltaire's literary commitment, Morley argues, one must remember that the role of a man of letters in the mid-eighteenth century in France was not what it is in the Victorian period in England. In modern times, the profession of letters is as polite and safe as that of the clergyman, lawyer, or physician; for its members accept the reigning opinions and prejudices quite as readily as do their counterparts in the church, the law, or medicine: "To be a man of letters in France in the middle of the eighteenth century was to be the official enemy of the current prejudices and their sophistical defenders in the church and the parliament." Parents in the France of that day heard of their son's decision to enter the world of letters with the same horror that overtakes a Victorian parent when informed of his son's conversion to Positivism.

But, if Voltaire's commitment to letters was tantamount to a
declaration of war against his society, it did not mean that he was
going to be a mere pamphleteering playwright. Morley's insistence that the best of Voltaire's plays—*Mérope, Sémiramis,
Tancrède*—are very far from being propaganda, or "tendency"
plays, reveals his own feeling that didactic drama is by definition
of a low order. A fair examination of Voltaire's plays, Morley
maintains, shows him to be innocent of "the offence of art with a
moral purpose." Morley's irony at this point suggests an uneasiness with his defense of Voltaire's literary purity—and rightly so;
for Morley does not really mean to go further than to say that,
although Voltaire often chose subjects (especially, for example,
religious ones) upon which he hoped to correct prevailing modes
of thought, he was too respectful of traditions of propriety and
congruity in dramatic art to turn his dramatic actors into contentious ideologues. He therefore wisely retreats to this conclusion:
"With Voltaire tragedy is, as all art ought to be, a manner of disinterested presentation." [27]

It has often been charged that Voltaire's concern with Classical
rules of fitness and propriety in drama was excessive and that in
literature he was a spokesman for the kind of conservatism that he
opposed in all other areas of life. But Morley credits Voltaire with
several happy innovations in the tradition of the French classical
drama. Voltaire, he points out, made the subjects of tragedy more
"masculine"; that is, less exclusively concerned with the love relation. In his treatment of Roman subjects in *Brutus* and *La Mort
de César*, he introduced politics to French drama; for his predecessors had used similar historical subjects primarily to elucidate
some commanding human passion. By such plays, Voltaire added
a dimension not just to French drama but to French life; for, during the revolution, France was to witness many attempts to emulate the ways of ancient Rome. Finally, Voltaire enlarged French
drama in the simple geographical sense by introducing nearly
every corner of the universe upon his stage. Here again Morley
searches for the social significance of a change in artistic conventions:

This revolutionary enlargement of subject was significant of a general and very important enlargement of interest which marked the
time, and led presently to those contrasts between the condition of

France and the imaginary felicity and nobleness of wilder countries, which did so much to breed an irresistible longing for change. Voltaire's high-minded Scythians, generous Peruvians, and the rest, prepared the way along with other influences for that curious cosmopolitanism, that striking eagerness to believe in the equal virtuousness and devotion inherent in human nature, independently of the religious or social form accidentally imposed upon them, which found its ultimate outcome, first in an ardent passion for social equality, and a depreciation of the special sanctity of the current religion, and next in the ill-fated emancipating and proselytizing aims of the Revolution, and in orators of the human race.[28]

This speculation may seem a bit fanciful, especially when we recall that Voltaire's Chinese and Moors are by no means uniformly virtuous; but it does show how Morley works as a critic. Another writer might have found in the fact of his geographical enlargement of French drama an indication of the geographical restlessness that was so characteristic of Voltaire's life; still another might have argued that Voltaire's aim in carrying his readers and audiences to every corner of the earth was to disprove, in a laboriously empirical way, the belief that this is the best of all possible worlds, one in which partial evil is canceled out by universal good. But Morley chooses to move out from the work and its author to the world in which they acted.

If Morley shares with the best Victorian critics of literature and art the strength of a sensibility which integrates literature with society, he also shares their common weakness: prudery. Disturbed by Voltaire's licentiousness and sensuality, he reminds his English audience (though a Victorian audience hardly needed reminding) that "the unclean Swift," the closest thing to a counterpart of Voltaire that ever existed, was far worse; Swift was, in fact, "truculent and often gross," [29] which Voltaire never was. Nevertheless, the fact remains that in "La Pucelle," the poem about Joan of Arc, as well as elsewhere, Voltaire seemed to give his approval to that liberty in the relation of the sexes which was accepted and practiced by so many of the leaders of the progressive movement of the time. All other movements known to history, Morley points out, and not for the first time in the book, had been characterized by the principles of asceticism; here was a complete reversal. Perhaps, Morley conjectures, the leaders of the Enlightenment felt obliged to espouse the opposite extreme to the

sexual continence practiced, or at least preached, by their main
adversaries. He then delivers Voltaire a lecture on the sanctity of
family life (though Voltaire's writings contain many celebrations
of this bourgeois desideratum); and he invokes, with an astonishing complacency, the supposed moral superiority of his own civilization. He does not stop to consider what, if any, relationship exists between the "libertinism" of such men as Voltaire and Diderot
and their tolerance toward their foes, and, on the other hand,
between the asceticism of the Cromwells, Robespierres, and
Rousseaus and their bloodthirstiness toward *their* foes.[30]

In 1750, after years of coaxing, Frederick the Great succeeded
in persuading Voltaire to take up residence in his court at Pots-
dam. The move, according to Morley, was an error for both men.
"If the visit to London did everything for Voltaire, the visit to
Berlin did nothing." [31] Prussia was as far behind France in art and
science (saving military science) as France was behind England;
therefore, Prussia had nothing to teach Voltaire. Neither did Prussia's king have anything to learn from Voltaire, for he was a convinced Voltairian long before the great philosopher joined his
court. However, there was an intellectual and spiritual relationship between the two men far more worth recounting than their
personal one, and this Morley attempts to do. Frederick and Voltaire were the leaders of the two great movements then at work in
transforming the old European order: Voltaire was overturning
the spiritual hierarchy of Europe, while Frederick was disman-
tling the political order. The main tangible target of Voltaire was
the Roman Catholic Church; that of Frederick, the German Empire.

For Morley, who throughout his life showed a strange tendency
to suspend ordinary standards of moral jugment when dealing
with Prussian power, the military exploits of Frederick in the
Seven Years' War (1756–63) were far more than just another
struggle to maintain a dynasty or to extend the power of a royal
house. "It was the entry of Frederick the Great upon the scene
which instantly raised international relations into the region of
real matter . . . into a vital competition between old forces and
principles and new." [32] Here at last was a war to settle not mere
questions of the triumph of one dynasty or another but of what
form future civilization would take; at last men were to die not for
vested interests but for principles.

Mindful, perhaps, that in the course of his lengthy pragmatic defense of Frederick's aggressive policies, he has left Voltaire out of view, Morley insists that these policies were the logical and necessary complement to Voltaire's war of ideas. In fact, one of the best pragmatic defenses of the Voltairian philosophy itself is that it produced—usually when working in conjunction with Protestant traditions—so many "active, wise, and truly positive statesmen" in Europe between 1760 and 1780. "The application of reason to the amelioration of the social condition was the device of the great rulers of this time, and the father and inspirer of this device was that Voltaire, who is habitually presented to us a mere mocker." [33]

Seemingly, Morley, in his eagerness to demonstrate the value of Voltaire's precepts and spirit in the realm of action, has involved himself in a contradiction. At other points in his study of Voltaire, as we have already seen, he rightly chastises his subject for overlooking the educative value of representative institutions and for acquiescing too readily in enlightened despotism; but, in order to rebuff those critics who accuse Voltaire of exerting an exclusively negative and destructive influence, Morley himself falls to the temptation of vindicating the "positiveness" of Voltairism by showing that it often moved despotic rulers to follow policies of enlightenment and religious tolerance. He has too quickly forgotten that, by his own testimony, one of the most praiseworthy characteristics of Voltaire was his patient ability to abide a period of transition between old and new beliefs. This is not, of course, to say that Morley recommends enlightened despotism as an acceptable form of government; but he does relax his moral standards in order to vindicate the "practicality" of the principles of the Enlightenment.

At some time early in the 1830's, John Stuart Mill decided against writing a history of the French Revolution, a subject he had long studied, because he was convinced that the time had not yet come when the subject of Christianity could be openly discussed in England. He therefore turned his books and materials over to Carlyle, who knew no such hesitation. But then Carlyle did not share the dangerous religious views of the *philosophes*, and he constantly charged them, not with having argued falsely, but with having been merely destructive in their arguments: had they not, after all, deprived Carlyle himself of his inherited Christianity without supplying him with a new faith? Morley, who was moved by Carlyle's misrepresentations of both the *philosophes* and the revolution itself to revalue the eighteenth century, set out to complete the task that Mill had left undone. He would be the first English writer to present the religious views of the *philosophes* in a sympathetic light; and his chapter on "Religion" in the study of Voltaire is the first major step in this direction.

This crucial chapter is broken into three sections. In the first, Morley analyzes the causes of Voltaire's hatred for the Christianity of his time and country. In the second, he examines Voltaire's method of attack upon his chosen enemy. In the third and last section, he asks for Voltaire's answers to those ultimate questions with which religion has always had to deal. There were, according to Morley, two main causes for Voltaire's enmity to Roman Catholicism: one intellectual, one moral. In the first instance, he was disgusted by a system of belief resting so largely upon the irrational and unnatural, miracles and mysteries. In the second instance, and the more important one, he was horrified by the cruelty, intolerance, and mean jealousy of the Catholic Church. The movement which was to go by his name was not, then, Morley insists, primarily an "outbreak of reckless speculative intelligence, but a righteous social protest against a system socially pestilent." [34]

But although Voltaire's moral horror was greater than his intellectual disgust, he knew that he would have to undermine a fanatical set of beliefs before he (or his successors) could do away with the fanatical practices that followed from them. It was all very well to say that religious tolerance was often a mask for religious indifference; but, if indifference was the price that had to be paid to create a respect for the human status of all people, regardless of their beliefs, then it was the duty of philosophy to create that indifference by throwing the light of reason upon the mystical foundations of revealed religion.

Protestant countries, Morley hastens to interject, were not faced with such hard choices between irreconcilable antagonists. In England, for example, Protestantism intervened between Catholicism and scientific modes of thought to prevent a violent breach with the past; and the cause of toleration could be defended—as it never was in France or Italy—by men who were also staunch

defenders of Christianity. The opposition of extremes is, according to Morley, inevitable in countries where Protestantism has not
interposed itself as a mediator. For Morley Protestantism is, like
Voltairism, a dissolvent of the theological spirit; but it is a less
acrid dissolvent.

In fact, an English audience may be unable to picture to itself
the abomination which Voltaire attacked under the label of Christianity: "It cannot be too often repeated that the Christianity
which Voltaire assailed was not that of the sermon on the
mount. . . ." Voltaire's principles and practice alike were far
closer to those of the speaker of that sermon than were the principles and practice of the Christianity he opposed. For Christians
like the Quakers—who attempted to model their lives upon the
precepts of the sermon, without sophisticating them into theology
—Voltaire often expressed his admiration. He may not have
shared the Quakers' convictions, but he always set conduct above
convictions and was content to keep his hands off convictions that
he believed false so long as they did not lead to evil conduct. The
one target of his attack was "that amalgam of metaphysical sub-
tleties, degrading legends, false miracles, and narrow depraving
conceptions of divine government, which made the starting point
and vantage ground of those ecclesiastical oppressors, whom he
habitually and justly designated the enemies of the human
race." [35] The courage which Voltaire displayed in going to the aid
of victims, as well as of their families, of Catholic atrocities in
France was for Morley visible proof of the guiding motive of his
onslaught upon religion.

But the admirableness of Voltaire's motives for attacking the
Christianity of his day does not, in Morley's view, excuse the
methods he used. These methods were chiefly literary and dialectical, and they were woefully defective when measured by the
canons of scientific and philosophical criticism. To forgive Voltaire his means because we sympathize in his ends "is deliberately
to throw away the advantage of our distance from the contest,
and to sell for a momentary self-indulgence in the spirit of party
the birthright of a free and equitable historic vision." [36]

Having made this statement Morley admits, however, that Voltaire was to some degree the victim of his circumstances. The defenders of religion had themselves set the terms of the argument
by fastening their apologetics to the flimsiest superstructures of

their system rather than to its more substantial foundations. Voltaire, even if he had wished or been able to go beyond the immediate points of a particular controversy—whether about miracles or about chastity—to the general principles upon which it really depended, would have been prevented by the knowledge that doing so would have caused him to miss his target and to lose his audience. "He was making war on an institution, and it was not his concern to fight on ground which his adversary had never thought, and was too blind and demoralized to be able to think, of taking up." [37] Voltaire chose to answer fools according to their folly. Sophisticated modern students of religion may chide him for doing so, but they forget that only the defeat of the religionists on lower ground by Voltaire forced them to the defense of the higher ground. The defense of Christianity on the basis of its appeal to the human heart rather than upon its historical verifiability or miraculous character has only been heard since Voltaire did his work; it was not in evidence before that time.

Voltaire borrowed many of his methods of attack, says Morley, from the English Deists, using these methods with less gravity but more skill. He would bring into prominence those points in scripture and doctrine most contradictory to ordinary human experience—and he insisted upon evaluating scripture and doctrine by experience and not authority. Is it conceivable, he would ask, that God would choose to reveal himself but in one remote place to a handful of people? Does the sun shine in just one place? Is there anything in our experience which suggests the equivalence between the idea of three and the idea of one? If he did not appeal to experience to discredit the stories of scripture, he could appeal to history or to what a later age would call "comparative religion." He would show how many of the doctrines, characters, and incidents of Jewish and Christian history had their counterparts in one or another of the pagan religions, or in the books of Oriental philosophers, or in fables.

Voltaire, according to Morley, was too concerned with the immediate world of practice to see the philosophical inadequacy of his ridicule of the church and its creed. He might win the applause of readers disgusted with the proliferation of miracle mongering and pious frauds by collecting innumerable instances of the ludicrous, the inconsistent, and the immoral in scripture and doctrine; but, by doing so, he left untouched the most fundamental and comprehensive general ideas of the Christian religion. He concentrated his attack on the superstructure and left the foundations intact; he criticized endlessly the evidence for particular miracles but devoted very little attention to the general idea of the miraculous.[38]

Morley's main criticism of Voltaire's method of attacking religion, then, is that it failed to rise above concrete details to the abstract general questions which were the heart of the matter. The criticism is a valid one from the point of view of a philosopher, but we must remember that Voltaire was not primarily a philosopher but a literary man. To translate and thereby reduce the abstract doctrines of transubstantiation or baptism into their constituent concrete elements is, of course, to be both unphilosophical and irreligious; it is to substitute, as Voltaire habitually did, the concrete for the abstract and the letter for the spirit. But this, Morley seems to forget, is the way that literature works. In literature, it is assumed that abstractions are not true until, as Keats liked to say, they are proved on the pulses; and to be thus "proved" they must be given concrete form. Literature is neither religion nor philosophy; for in literature, as T. S. Eliot once said, the spirit killeth, and the letter giveth life.

The final section of Morley's discussion of Voltaire's treatment of religion deals with Voltaire's answers to what Morley takes to be the great ultimate questions raised by religion: what is the nature of God (assuming that He exists), and what are the prospects of a future life beyond the grave? Dealing with Voltaire's answers from the absolute point of view of man's permanent needs, Morley finds them sadly wanting; dealing with them from the relativistic point of view of the historian, Morley finds them satisfactory for the period in which they were expressed.

Morley says that Deism itself is vague in its definitions of God and His attributes, is insufferably optimistic, and is therefore generally the creed of a wealthy and complacent minority of individualists. To the ordinary person, Deism holds out none of the joy and consolation which he has been accustomed to receive from less rational religions. Voltaire, to be sure, moved away from the optimism that seems to be inherent in Deism by the time he came to write *Candide*. In this great work, Voltaire expressed anger at a great many things but most of all at himself for once having espoused the philosophy of optimism. Seeing now that the denial of evil was itself the worst of evils, he rejected the Deistic conception of a rational providence, but he did not reject Deism. Henceforth, however, his Deism was mystical rather than rational, as much a *faith* as the many faiths he decried. The final issue of *Candide*, therefore, was doubt—a doubt which was to be soothed —a monkish solution indeed!—by work. So far as Morley is concerned, therefore, Voltaire may have freed himself from Deistic optimism, but he did nothing to furnish Deism with positive answers to the great leading questions that religion persists in asking.

Thus, Morley confesses, the old charge that Voltaire's religious creed is one of negation is true: "But still, be it always understood, negation of darkness. And this inevitably leads in the direction of the day. It was an indispensable step in the process of transition." Voltaire, Morley insists, was a transitional figure who proposed a kind of *via media* between those like Rousseau, who affirmed the practice of Christianity when they no longer believed its dogmas, and the atheistic school of Diderot, who were annoyed by Voltaire's reactionary lingering among the believers. Negative Voltaire was, but his negativism enabled great numbers of men to glimpse a ray of light breaking into the prison where they had long been; and men "do not decline a reinvigorating article of faith because it is not a system, nor do they measure a deliverer by syllogism." Voltaire, as Morley seems never to tire of repeating, did not come armed with a new system and did not pretend that he had one. It was his faith that an advanced society could survive an age of transition and analysis, "if the activity of human intelligence were only sufficiently stimulated and the conditions of social union were once so adjusted as to give it fair play." [39] This faith in the resilience and creative power of human intelligence was what made Voltaire, as distinguished from Rousseau, whose first concern was emotional complacency, a precursor of the rational reform of religion and society.

In Morley's time, there was no necessary connection between the passion for reform of religion and society and the passion for history. From Burke to Coleridge to the Oxford Movement, in fact, a strong tradition had grown up that history supported the conservative belief in the slow growth of societies and institutions and that rationalistic reformers were either ignorant or disrespectful of history. In the eighteenth century, Morley knew, just the opposite had been true: "the best secular histories which remain from this period, one of them the most striking monument in historical literature, were written by the most marked assailants of reigning superstition." [40] Voltaire had been not just a great historian but a great innovator in historiography—in fact, the father of modern historical study. His two main principles for the study of history were that laws, arts, and manners are history's chief concern. Circumstantial details which led to nothing—which made no contribution to intellectual, moral, or material progress—are of little concern to the historian, who must keep his eyes focused upon large, general movements and not be diverted by *minutiae*. The true historian is not a retailer of innumerable unconnected facts; he is one who searches for the general laws behind those facts.

It was Voltaire who reversed history's emphasis upon great single personalities. According to his concept of history, the heroic names of history were but convenient labels for critical turning points in the movements of whole peoples. He looked past the famous and infamous men of each epoch to the large impersonal currents which brought them to the surface—the nebulous forces which in Morley's period were called "spirit of the age," or "Zeitgeist" or "climate of opinion." Unlike most of his predecessors, and even some succeeding historians like Carlyle, Voltaire attributed the movement of history, not to the actions of great individuals, but to the movement of the human spirit in its various guises and moods.

The particular consequence for historical study of Voltaire's transformation of its general principles were several. If a nation's history is equated with its progress toward intellectual enlightenment, material prosperity, and moral elevation, then certain onceprominent features of historical works fade into the background. Especially diplomacy and war—once the staples of so much historical study, and always the causes of so much evil—receive less honor than formerly from the historian. Morley, himself inclined to pacifism, naturally exults in Voltaire's simultaneous degradation of and protest against war. (Ironically, it was to be Morley's own failure to recognize that, in the twentieth century, war is the ultimate reality that brought about the end of his political career.)

The work in which Voltaire set forth the principles of the "new" history was the *Essai sur les Moeurs et l'Esprit des Nations, et sur les principaux faits de l'Histoire depuis Charlemagne jusqu'à Louis XIII.* Morley is critical of the way in which Voltaire reacts against Jacques Bossuet's narrowly Catholic interpretation of the course of universal history by denying even a historical value to either Judaism or Catholicism; and he chides Voltaire for lacking the disinterestedness needed to recognize that ecclesiastical power sometimes developed at the expense of a far more immoral secular power. Nevertheless, Morley thinks the work provided one of the foundations of modern history because it showed the importance and necessity of "comprehending in a single idea and surveying in a single work the various activities, the rise and fall of power, the transference from one to another of political predominance, the contributions to the art of living, among the societies which were once united in a single empire." [41] In the *Essai,* Morley sees the germ of the scientific idea of history which has since grown up: societies are viewed as related parts of a collective, familial unity; but the relations are not yet articulated, nor the laws discovered according to which qualities are transmitted from one society to another. Voltaire, whose influence upon Europe is so often seen as a disintegrating and dissolving influence, led future historians to study the history of modern Europe as an organic whole.

In the last chapter of *Voltaire,* we see Morley already looking ahead to his study of Rousseau; for, he institutes a remarkable comparison between the two men and their social influences which is one of the high points of this book. He begins by reminding us of a point that has often been made in the course of the book: namely, Voltaire's indifference to political action and his willingness to acquiesce in the temporal order while he gnawed away at the spiritual order. This political indifference was, in Morley's view, a major strategic error on Voltaire's part; for "it was impossible to revolutionize the spiritual basis of belief without touching the social forms, which were inseparably connected with the old basis by the strong bonds of time and a thousand fibres of ancient association and common interest." Rousseau took quite another path, and in doing so became the founder of the rival revolutionary school. The followers of Voltaire, concerned above all with the sacred rights of reason and with the promise of what reason could achieve, appealed to the intelligence of men; the followers of Rousseau, seeking an immediate remedy for human

suffering, appealed to the sentiment of men. "The Voltairean principles of the strictest political moderation and of literary common
sense, negative, merely emancipatory, found their political outcome . . . in the Constituent Assembly, . . . while the spirit of
Rousseau, ardent, generous, passionate for the relief of the suffering, . . . came to life and power in the Convention and the sections of the Commune of Paris which overawed the Convention." [42]

The inability of these two revolutionary schools to find common
meeting ground in social principles was to receive painful expression in the catastrophe which finally overtook the French Revolution. Voltaire's political theory, so far as he had one, was that the
political order would—and should—continue to exist until rational criticism had done its work of transforming thought and
sensibility, which in their purified form would then create a humane and enlightened political order. Rousseau, on the other
hand, directed all the force of his revolutionary passion against
the existing temporal order, and he was as indifferent to freedom
of thought as were the princes who persecuted him. Whereas Voltaire was blind to the fact that the assault upon the power of the
church, to be effective, had to be part of a comprehensive philosophy of social regeneration, Rousseau failed to see that no society
can be regenerated without the aid of moral and spiritual forces
such as are incompatible with ecclesiastical domination.

But Morley does not allow himself to be overcome by the
charms of symmetry. Rousseau's blindness was greater than Voltaire's; for Voltaire at least had his priorities in order, and he saw
that the weakening of theological ideas and church power was the
indispensable prerequisite for the diffusion of truly social ideas.
Voltaire was, moreover, an extraordinarily humane and courageous man; and Morley cannot but respond to his expression,
however unscientific, of a hope for the future that matched Morley's own: "Everything that I see appears the throwing broadcast
of the seed of a revolution, which must inevitably come one day,
but which I shall not have the pleasure of witnessing. The French
always come late to things, but they do come at last. Light ex-
tends so from neighbour to neighbour, that there will be a splendid outburst on the first occasion, and then there will be a rare
commotion. The young are very happy; they will see fine
things." [43]

II   Rousseau

Morley's study of Rousseau, published in 1873, is a more conventional biography than *Voltaire;* for Morley is obliged to give far more personal history in it than was necessary with Voltaire. Voltaire stood for the claims of intelligence and so a biography of his mind seemed the appropriate treatment; Rousseau stood for a revolution in sensibility and emotion, and so his position was inextricably bound up with his personality. His personality, moreover, had struck many of his readers as highly repulsive; and Morley took it upon himself to show that Rousseau's personality had more than one side and that the repulsive side should not be allowed to discredit his work, much as it appeared to support old adages about the disparity between profession and practice. Finally, no English biography of Rousseau existed, and Morley could not assume, as he could with Voltaire, that his readers had a reasonably full and accurate idea of the facts of his subject's life.

Among the three great speculative revolutionists—Voltaire, Rousseau, and Diderot—Rousseau was, according to Morley, the most directly revolutionary. He was the first to turn his sights directly upon those social conditions which the revolution sought to modify: he was the first great voice of the common people, the first who articulated to the world their plight and their aspirations. He was the bringer of enthusiasm, depth, and fervor—as opposed to correct and lucid thought—to the revolutionary movement. He was the most perfect embodiment of the revolutionary passion to simplify:

The impulse to shake off intricacies is the mark of revolutionary generations, and it was the starting-point of all Rousseau's mental habits, and of the work in which they expressed themselves. . . . Simplification of religion by clearing away the overgrowth of errors, simplification of social relations by equality, of literature and art by constant return to nature, of manners by industrious homeliness and thrift,— this is the revolutionary process and ideal, and this is the secret of Rousseau's hold over a generation that was lost amid the broken maze of fallen systems.[44]

But Rousseau was more than a revolutionist. In the aspect of his thought which touched on religion, he was profoundly reactionary in spirit. If, therefore, his political thought stirred Robespierre and Paine to action, his religious influence was felt by men like Chateaubriand and other French leaders of the Romantic reaction. Morley sets himself the task of showing how and why the same man gave "direction to the first episodes of revolution, and force to the first episode of reaction." [45]

In Morley's account, which relies heavily on the *Confessions,* of the early part of Rousseau's life—the years prior to 1749, when he composed his first discourse—our attention is repeatedly directed to two themes. One is that Rousseau's character and the circumstances of his youth decisively set him apart from the other leaders of the revolutionary movement, the *philosophes;* the other is that Rousseau was a strange combination of opposites and that disgust with certain of his traits and actions should not blind us to the more admirable sides of his many-sided nature.

Rousseau came late not only to writing but to reading. As a result, says Morley, he may be said, by contrast with such men as Voltaire and Diderot, to have been formed by life rather than by literature. In fact, "scarcely any great writer since the revival of letters has been so little literary as Rousseau. . . ." [46] Morley does not mean that Rousseau had an unusually wide and varied experience but that he always lived in the belief that his own impressions were the best source of knowledge. They were not, at least at first, the source of literature, for he surrendered himself to his feelings and impressions without any thought of writing them down.

But his experience as well as his attitude was different from that of contemporaries like Voltaire, Hume, and Diderot. While these men, the leaders of the eighteenth-century intellectual movement, were developing their minds and sharpening their rhetorical weapons in the study and practice of literature, "Rousseau, the leader of the reaction against that movement, was wandering a beggar and an outcast, craving the rude fare of the peasant's hut, knocking at roadside inns, and passing nights in caves and holes in the fields, or in the great desolate streets of towns." [47] Rousseau, when he came to write about poverty, could claim, as the older philosophers could not, to be writing from experience.

Morley does not, it should be added, consider that Rousseau had the advantage over his prominent contemporaries in being so exclusively reliant upon his own impressions and experiences. The way in which he habitually allowed feeling to predominate over reflection brought with it many drawbacks, as well as a few advantages, for himself and also for future generations of men. Among the former was his almost entire inability to learn— whether Latin, dancing, fencing, or chess; and this weakness is attested to not only by many of his would-be instructors but by Rousseau himself: "One would say that my heart and my intelligence do not belong to the same individual. . . . I feel all, and see nothing; I am carried away, but I am stupid. . . ." [48] Morley does not mean to discredit Rousseau's ideas by locating their source in sensation rather than in thought, but he does think the biographer's duty is to show just how a man, who presumes to teach other men, came by his own ideas.

The other impulse of Rousseau's formative years which was to set him apart from the *philosophes* was his fondness for religion and for nature—or, rather, for the religion of nature. Voltaire, before his disillusionment with optimism, may have looked upon the natural world as the handiwork of God; but it is hard to imagine his following Rousseau about the countryside each morning and joining in worship of the scenery, a worship Rousseau described as "a sincere elevation of heart to the author of the tender nature whose beauties lay spread out before my eyes." [49] While Voltaire and the Encyclopedists were laboriously adding to the sum of human knowledge, Rousseau walked about with his head in the clouds maundering about the beneficent author of nature.

The other main concern of the early biographical chapters of Rousseau is the dark side of Rousseau's personality and the proper response to it. Morley, as we have seen and shall see elsewhere, shared the conventional Victorian uneasiness with all overt discussion of sex. Naturally, therefore, he is unnerved by Rousseau's candid account of his sexual experiences. Writing of Rousseau's description of the birth of sensuality in his boyhood, Morley fulminates: "It is here that the flesh spreads gross clouds over the firmament of the spirit. Thinking of it, we flee from talk about the high matters of will and conscience, of purity of heart and the diviner mind, and hurry to the physician." [50] Morley is even ready to cite all of Rousseau's youthful dealings with sex or women, none of them "wholesome or manly," as an argument (not that Morley does not have plenty of his own) against the theory of the natural goodness of man.

We might expect that, after he has dealt so harshly with Rousseau's sexual weaknesses and with his freedom in advertising them, Morley would be scathing in his criticism of Rousseau's refusal to accept responsibility for the results of his sexual indulgence: the five children he had by Theresa Le Vasseur. But this is not so; apparently it was easier for Morley to forgive cruelty than sexual candor. He begins his discussion of this sorry episode in Rousseau's life by chiding those writers who have expressed shock that Rousseau would have formed an alliance with an ignorant kitchen maid like Theresa. Rousseau, Morley wisely points out, "would not have been what he was, nor have played the part that he did play in the eighteenth century, if he had felt anything derogatory or unseemly in a kitchen wench." [51] He never, after all, set any store by literary culture, social position, and accomplishments.

Neither Rousseau nor Theresa had any money; and, when their first child arrived, Rousseau, whose writings on education were to stress the supreme importance of parental influence, deposited it in the box of the asylum for foundlings. The experience was not, apparently, sufficiently traumatic to make Rousseau practice what the Victorians called "moral restraint" or to resort to artificial interference with pristine nature; he went on, with Theresa's help, to produce four more children, each of whom was sent the way of the first. Morley has no wish to extenuate Rousseau's crime, but he does surround his condemnation with certain reminders. The first is that Rousseau abandoned the children from wholly material motives; he could not afford to support them and did not want to be disturbed by their presence. The second is that Rousseau lived in a lax time when the family structure had been weakened, and his crime differed from many others of the time only in that he did not erect a social theory to transform his vice into a virtue—in fact, he suffered bitter remorse for it. Finally, it must be recalled that "the atrocity of the offence owes half the blackness with which it has always been invested by wholesome opinion, to the fact that the offender was by and by the author of the most powerful book by which parental duty has been commended in its full loveliness and nobility." [52]

But, since there are so many events of this kind in Rousseau's life, Morley is obliged to define his method of dealing with them. How, for example, is one to relate Rousseau's profoundly immoral desertion of his children to his role as the founder of a great reli-

gious reaction? Not, Morley replies, as the practice which negates
the profession by belying it. There are innumerable cases in religion and philosophy which require us to do as the sage says and
not as he does. We must recognize the mystery and complexity of
the human spirit—all men are fallible; and we must be able to
take from each man that which is fruitful in him and leave the rest
behind. After all, Socrates was the husband of Xanthippe; David
murdered Uriah; Peter denied his master. "Our vision is our blindness, if we can never bring ourselves to see the possibilities of
deep mystic aspiration behind the vile outer life of a man, or to
believe that this coarse Rousseau, scantily supping with his coarse
mate, might yet have many glimpses of the great wide horizons
that are haunted by figures rather divine than human." [53]

Rousseau was launched upon his relatively brief (twelve-year)
literary career by the announcement by the academy of Dijon in
1749 of an essay competition on the question, *Has the restoration
of the sciences contributed to purify or to corrupt manners?* and
by the inspiration which entered his soul when he read the announcement:

If ever anything resembled a sudden inspiration, it was the movement
which began in me as I read this. All at once I felt myself dazzled by
a thousand sparkling lights; crowds of vivid ideas thronged into my
mind with a force and confusion that threw me into unspeakable agitation; I felt my head whirling in a giddiness like that of intoxication.
A violent palpitation oppressed me; unable to walk for difficulty of
breathing, I sank under one of the trees of the avenue, and passed half
an hour there in such a condition of excitement, that when I arose I
saw that the front of my waistcoat was all wet with my tears, though
I was wholly unconscious of shedding them. Ah, if I should ever have
written the quarter of what I saw and felt under that tree, with what
clearness should I have brought out all the contradictions of our social
system; with what simplicity I should have demonstrated that man is
good naturally, and that by institutions only is he made bad.[54]

Rousseau recovered sufficiently from his transport and retained
enough of his vision to enter the essay competition and to win the
prize. He had thus begun a literary career that was to be perfectly
unified, according to Morley, by its devotion to the principles dictated to him by this vision.

Before summarizing the argument of Rousseau's first discourse, on the sciences and the arts, Morley makes it unmistakably clear where he stands in respect to it and to the remaining expressions of Rousseau's social philosophy. Rousseau's fit of enthusiasm, says Morley, deprived him of all opportunity to discover a *modus vivendi* whereby he could secure his happiness in the midst of a society and a generation to which he was profoundly antipathetic. "In this way the first Discourse was the letting in of much evil upon him, as that and the next and the Social Contract were the letting in of much evil upon all Europe." [55]

In this discourse and in its successor (on the origins of inequality), Rousseau established the primitivist position that in later ages was wrongly supposed to have been shared by Voltaire and the *philosophes*. Rousseau argued that, whereas the manners of men living in a natural state perfectly reflected their conduct, the modern influence of the arts and sciences had brought about an unfortunate and deceptive uniformity of manners which prevented us from ever knowing what kind of person we were dealing with and so bred suspicion, treachery, and hypocrisy. A study of the decline of such great states as Egypt, Greece, Rome, or China shows that the development of the arts and sciences brings about a fatal enervation. Though there is one kind of ignorance that springs from a bad heart and is brutal, there is another kind which is admirable because it limits our curiosity to what we need, are able, and are intended by God to know. Why did God hide so many secrets of Nature from us if he wished us to know them? Is it not pride that is at the bottom of scientific curiosity, and do not low motives of greed and curiosity impel men to pursue certain sciences? Even if it could be shown that the study of sciences leads to truths, are they truths which make anyone better off or which improve government or commerce? And could not those who pursue the sciences be diverted to more useful functions? Bad as science and art are in themselves, they are worse in their influence upon those who are not themselves scientists or artists.

Morley, aware that in his own age those who defend the thesis that man has been progressive and that the arts and sciences have been the grounds of his progress are in nearly full possession of the field, does not bother to refute Rousseau's contentions in detail; he satisfies himself with a refutation of the main assumptions of the discourse. First of all, he points out, the discourse is absurdly one-sided in admitting none of the benefits and conveniences which the pursuit of knowledge has brought to the human race. Moreover, Rousseau entirely ignores the possibility—nay certainty—of multiple causation in the downfall of once mighty nations, imputing all blame to intellectual progress. Most importantly, he bases his argument on the entirely unsubstantiated "assumption of there having once been in the early history of each society a stage of mild, credulous, and innocent virtue, from which appetite for the fruit of the forbidden tree caused an inevitable degeneration." On the contrary, Morley maintains, both available evidence and scientific analogy make it much more likely that mankind has progressed than that it has declined from some Golden Age or Garden of Eden. As for Rousseau's attribution of the ills of civilization to the arts and sciences, Morley allows Voltaire's excellent reply to do service for one of his own: "What really makes, and always will make, this world into a valley of tears, is the insatiable cupidity and indomitable insolence of men, from Kouli Khan, who did not know how to read, down to the custom-house clerk, who knows nothing but how to cast up figures." [56]

But there is, in Morley's view, a positive side to Rousseau's discourse, however well concealed it may be among his extreme statements. This side is, simply expressed, that, if one is put to a choice, virtue without science is better than science without virtue. Rousseau, in his crude way, was trying to remind those of his contemporaries who considered knowledge the sure way to individual sanctity and social well-being that cultivation was no guarantee of morality or of public spiritedness; that a society with a low degree of knowledge might yet be ordered and contented; and that, in Morley's words, "the well-being of a country depends more on the standard of social duty and the willingness of citizens to conform to it, than on the standard of intellectual culture and the extent of its diffusion." [57]

Rousseau's aspersions on the utility of knowledge demanded a firm response from a practiced Utilitarian like Morley, and he was ready to give it. At first, he seems ready to accept the terms of the argument that Rousseau has laid down; for he argues, empirically, that the greatest material benefits have always been derived from knowledge in just those periods when intellectual activity was freest. That is, he answers Rousseau by asserting that it is precisely when the intelligence works most disinterestedly and independently that it subserves social interests. But this is only a part of his reply. His concluding remarks on Rousseau's first discourse show that he has only temporarily adopted Rousseau's narrow standard of utility so as to meet him on common ground. Finally, he must point out that Rousseau went to the opposite extreme from the "knowledge" school in asserting the place of simple virtue in social arrangements because he had no conception of "the central truth, namely that the full and ever festal life is found in active freedom of curiosity and search taking significance, motive, force, from a warm inner pulse of human love and sympathy." [58]

In 1753, the academy of Dijon once again spurred Rousseau into activity by offering a prize for the best response to the question: *What is the origin of inequality among men, and is it authorized by the natural law?* Morley, before summarizing the argument of the discourse on the origin of inequality, feels obliged to chide Rousseau for a speculative weakness that he shared with most of his contemporaries. Morley is not often humorous, and so he must be rewarded with full quotation when he is: "One who had watched bees or beetles for years could not give us a more full or confident account of their doings, their hourly goings in and out, than it was the fashion in the eighteenth century to give of the walk and conversation of the primeval ancestor. The conditions of primitive man were discussed by very incompetent ladies and gentlemen at convivial supper parties, and settled with complete assurance." [59] Rousseau filled more than half the pages of his *Discourse on the Origin of Inequality* (1754) with description of these primitive conditions.

Rousseau commences his argument with a distinction between the physical inequalities which exist naturally, and the moral or political inequalities, such as differences of privilege or wealth, which are created by society. In the natural state, physical inequalities were of small or no importance because each man lived in isolation. As a result of the accretion of changes over the course of centuries, however, there was increased communication among men, a small development of the rational faculties, and a growth of the sense of mutual obligation. Although the pristine state of nature, when perfect uniformity among men existed, was good and pure, the later (or second) state was the truly perfect one. But it too was undermined as a result of a series of changes which accentuated the natural or physical inequalities and led to the institution of property. The results of these changes were thus summed up by Rousseau:

The first man who, having enclosed a piece of ground, could think of saying, *This is mine,* and found people simple enough to believe him, was the real founder of civil society. How many crimes, wars, murders, miseries, and horrors would not have been spared to the human race by one who, plucking up the stakes, or filling in the trench, should have called out to his fellows: Beware of listening to this impostor; you are undone if you forget that the earth belongs to no one, and that its fruits are for all.[60]

Social constitutions, in Rousseau's view, came into existence to protect property and to perpetuate the inequality between rich and poor.

Once again, Morley finds much that is objectionable in Rousseau's argument. To start with, his exposition is faulty because he does not define the kind of inequality he is discussing; the reader does not know when he refers to inequality of wealth, when to political inequality—and, oddly enough, he shrinks from suggesting concrete ways of modifying either of the institutions which he finds responsible for all social evils. But what Morley mainly objects to in the second discourse is Rousseau's method. Simply put, it is the grossly unscientific method of "guess" about the early state of the world. Rousseau's guess is that all movement away from this early state has been corruption; Morley's view—though some might call it merely *his* guess—is that there is far more evidence to support the assumption that this movement has been progressive and upward. Rousseau, he asserts, can produce no evidence to show that there ever was some single, uniform state of nature, any more than there now exists some normal or standard social state. Since Rousseau knew full well that no such thing as a standard or "general" tree or triangle existed, he should have deduced that no such thing as "a state of nature in the general and abstract, fixed, typical, and single" ever existed.

Rousseau's fantasy of some absolute divide between the natural and the social state also led him to misconceive the latter. In arguing that civil society was brought into existence in order to preserve property and foster inequality, he implied that man was a logical, rational animal rather than a social one. But Morley finds more wisdom in Aristotle's belief that sociability was an inherent quality of human nature rather than the result of syllogistic reasoning on the part of property-owning barbarians. Yet, sane as Morley's criticism of Rousseau's procedure seems, he appears himself to have fallen into the trap of "instinctual" explanations for human behavior. He implies that man is instinctively sociable, but he goes on to rebut Rousseau's assumption that the "advance" into a social state has everywhere been part of a single uniform process by pointing out differing rates of movement toward civilization and by attributing the differences to race: "There is no sign that Rousseau, any more than many other inquirers, ever reflected whether the capacity for advance into the state of civil society in any highly developed form is universal throughout the species, or whether there are not races eternally incapable of advance beyond the savage state." [61] If the myth of the goodness of the state of nature was an eighteenth-century superstition, then the myth of racial superiority was a nineteenth-century (as it is a twentieth-century) superstition; and Morley did not entirely escape from it or from simplistic European ideas of cultural superiority.

But Morley knows that most great social critics create some myth of the past or of the future against which they can measure their own society; and he reminds us that the positive element of this discourse—which could not have been as greatly influential as it was unless it contained something which seemed truthful and urgent to men of the time—was not its description of the state of nature but its attack on existing society. Whatever else he may have missed, Rousseau saw the spectacle of masses of men passing their lives in the most abject misery, without light and without hope, as one which could be borne only in the conviction that it was temporary and remediable. But, whereas Morley looked upon the spectacle as the by-product of an upward, forward-moving process, Rousseau saw it as a decline from a happier state.

Morley does not find Rousseau's theory of equality objectionable if properly understood. Many preachers of equality, writes Morley, tend to confuse equality of opportunity, which is admirable, with equality of result, which is impossible. Rousseau, he reminds his reader, did not say that all men are born equal; on the contrary, he admitted many natural inequalities. What he did say was that the artificial differences generated by the social state do not coincide with the original, natural inequalities, and that the

tendency of society, as we know it, is to deepen and perpetuate
the artificial inequalities of wealth, property, and privilege. If, at
the time Morley writes, society is no longer so guilty as it once
was of widening the artificial gulf between rich and poor, Rousseau is one of those to be thanked for the improvement.

Yet Morley's final word about the discourses is a negative one.
In his book on Voltaire, he had contrasted the two men by pointing out Rousseau's almost complete indifference to history. Now
he goes even further and charges that the two discourses were the
beginning of an unfortunate reaction against the historic mode of
inquiry that had been initiated by Montesquieu. He holds Rousseau responsible for diverting the minds of innumerable social
thinkers "away from patient collection of wide multitudes of facts
relating to the conditions of society, towards the promulgation of
arbitrary systems of absolute social dogmas." [62] And one of the
social dogmas for the promulgation of which Rousseau must be
held partly responsible, says Morley with a wary eye on the future, is dogmatic communism.

After discussion of the discourses, Morley returns to the story of
Rousseau's personal life during his years in uncongenial Paris and
then in his rural refuge at the Hermitage given him by Madame
d'Épinay. In analyzing this section of the book, we would do well
to keep before our minds Morley's view of his own work. He referred to his books on such great men of letters as Rousseau, Voltaire, and Diderot as "historical" studies." In the Preface to his
historical study of Burke, he distinguished this form from biography because, whereas in biography the writer's aim is to abstract
his subject from his historical surroundings, the writer of the historical study "aims not at a reproduction of the central figure of
his meditations, but at a criticism of his hero's relations and contributions to the main transactions of his time." [63] In *Rousseau,* for
reasons already noted, Morley is often obliged to supply a great
deal of personal detail; but, if we read carefully, we can see how
he always keeps in view the need to see Rousseau's life in relation
to his ideas and those ideas in relation to the age.

Rousseau, Morley shows, was always miserable in Parisian society and in the company of the *philosophes* because his two chief
qualities, reverence and sensuousness, set him apart. He had imbibed far too much of the Calvinism and Republican earnestness
of his native Geneva ever to feel at home among people who took

nothing on faith, who were forever analyzing, questioning, doubting; whereas he looked forward to a time when men might again live in devotion to unquestioned beliefs, the followers of Voltaire, Diderot, and D'Holbach reveled in an atmosphere where everything was an open question quite as if it were the normal state of things.

If his innate reverence (and consequent passion for the objects of reverence) set Rousseau apart from Parisian society in one way, his sensuousness did so in another. First of all, it made him religious; and then, as Morley puts it, "the sensuous temperament in its full strength is essentially solitary. The play of social intercourse . . . [is] fatal to free and uninterrupted abandonment to the flow of soft internal emotions." [64] Consequently, the more Rousseau frequented Parisian society, the more irritated with it he became, the more desirous of fleeing to Geneva or to the country.

Morley is of two minds about Rousseau's sensuousness and the resultant love of isolation from society. On the one hand, he rather admires Rousseau's asocial qualities. They showed that he was truly indifferent to social approval, the charms of flattery and the temptations of sinecures; here, if anywhere in Rousseau's life, preaching and practice were in perfect harmony: "It is a permanent source of comfort to all who thirst after reality in teachers, . . . to find that the prophet of social equality was not a fine gentleman, nor the teacher of democracy a hanger-on to the silly skirts of fashion." [65] Men like Voltaire and Diderot, fully committed to the social idea, had no comprehension of solitude and none of the special strengths and graces which it can impart. On the other hand, Morley must admit that his taste for solitude laid Rousseau open to the charge that he "loved man most when he saw men least."

The charge, Morley says, is justified and does point out the lack of actuality and concreteness in Rousseau's sympathy with mankind. Yet we would be both bigoted and wasteful if we therefore dismissed Rousseau's love of mankind as artificial; the ideal has its own reality, and its own power to stir men, as it stirred Rousseau, to a devotion both genuine and effective. Finally, Rousseau's solitary character was an outgrowth of his sense of the freedom and of the wholeness of the individual, a sense which ran through much of his teachings and which a Catholic country like France greatly needed; but the French Revolution—this is one of Morley's main contentions—absorbed only those of his teachings which affirmed the idea of collective organization and passed over those which celebrated the free life of the individual.

The action of Rousseau's life which, according to Morley, made definite and permanent the schism between himself and Voltaire and the *philosophes* was his publication of his *Letter to D'Alembert* condemning the immorality of the stage and opposing the establishment of theater in his beloved Geneva. The letter was not in itself of great importance, says Morley, since it was but a supplement to the first discourse condemning the arts and sciences. In the letter, as in the more ambitious work, Rousseau is joining in the reactionary protest against the pernicious influence of philosophers, poets, and men of letters. He argues that the stage can never by itself produce morality but that it often produces immorality, to say nothing of the wasteful and luxurious tastes it encourages in its devotees.

We shall deal with Morley's defense of the moral influence of drama in the next chapter, but we must follow here his attempt to connect the letter with the wider issues that separated Rousseau from the *philosophes*. We have already seen how, at the end of *Voltaire,* Morley contrasted the political ideas and impulses of Voltaire and Rousseau. In the concluding section of the first volume of *Rousseau,* he returns to the comparison to find in it the seeds of the schism between the rationalist and the emotional schools of eighteenth-century French thought. None of their contemporaries, Morley asserts, could see so clearly that which is now apparent—that Rousseau and Voltaire represented antithetical rather than complementary powers: "Voltaire's mental constitution made him eagerly objective, a seeker of true things, quivering for action, admirably sympathetic with all life and movement, a spirit restlessly traversing the whole world. Rousseau, far different from this, saw in himself a reflected microcosm of the outer world, and was content to take that instead of the outer world, and as its truest version." [66] The contrast between the objective and the subjective temperament was increased by the contrast between satire and sarcasm on Voltaire's side and reverence on Rousseau's, between the religious indifference of the former and the fervid religious spirit of the latter.

On most of the great questions which divided Voltaire and

Rousseau, Morley is on the side of the Voltaire. He shares Voltaire's sympathy for "civilization," in opposition to Rousseau's primitivism; he admires Voltaire's courage and integrity in breaking with the philosophical optimists (and thus his own past); and he reproves Rousseau for siding with those who deny the existence of evil and for complacently deriding the Voltaire of *Candide* and of the poem on the Lisbon earthquake as a man ungrateful for the wealth and happiness with which God had blessed him. "It is hard," says Morley, himself for once shocked by Rousseau's inanities, "to imagine a more execrable emotion than the complacent religiosity of the prosperous. Voltaire is more admirable in nothing than in the ardent humanity and farspreading lively sympathy with which he interested himself in all the world's fortunes, and felt the catastrophe of Lisbon as profoundly as if the Geneva at his gates had been destroyed." [67] Having called upon the last resources of his sentimental theism to offer a "justification" of the Lisbon earthquake as the vindication of nature against artifice, Rousseau was certain that Voltaire had maliciously directed *Candide* (which, however, he did not bother to read) against himself.

Despite the external symmetry of Morley's persistent comparisons between Rousseau and Voltaire, it is apparent that he thinks of Voltaire as a touchstone for detecting the most radically unsound elements in Rousseau. The method of comparison helps him to re-enforce the point that he is more respectful of Rousseau's influence than of his ultimate value as a thinker or writer; and it serves to remind us that Morley, far from being a neutral student of those ideological quarrels which were brought to a head by the publication of the *Letter to D'Alembert* in 1758, was carefully sifting the articles of his own social creed. "After 1760," he concludes, "the great stream divided into two; the rationalist and the emotional schools became visibly antipathetic, and the voice of the epoch was no longer single or undistracted." [68] In the years immediately following the "schism" came Rousseau's best-known works: the didactic novel *La Nouvelle Héloïse* in 1761; *Le Contrat Social* in 1762; and *Émile*, a novel on education, in the same year.

Morley chooses to treat *La Nouvelle Héloïse* not primarily as a novel but as—what it undoubtedly is—a fictional continuation of the argument of the two discourses. Though Morley pauses to comment on the inadequate characterization, the slightness of plot, and the simplistic presentation of motives, he is mainly concerned to show how *Julie* (to call the novel by its shorter name), like the discourses, was an attack upon the present ordering of society and upon the ways in which society corrupted human nature. The aim of the book, according to Morley, was "to rehabilitate human nature in as much of the supposed freshness of primitive times, as the hardened crust of civil institutions and social use might allow." [69]

Morley's judgment of the novel in relation to its aim of reordering existing society is that it had a salutary effect upon sensibility but a negative one upon intellect. The dual effect, he argues, can be seen by examination of the character of Julie. In allowing herself to be seduced by her tutor, she simultaneously violates her purity and betrays her class. At once overcome with remorse, and anxious to do her duty by her father (whose reverence for class lines stood in the way of her marrying the tutor), Julie agrees to marry a foreign baron named Wolmar. She then returns, not reluctantly, but with a vengeance, to the path of honor and duty, preaching to others a sanctity she had had to learn from experience. Her own moral awareness had arisen not from doctrine but from her powerful sense of sympathy for others, starting with her father.

In Morley's view, the influence which Julie's emotional fervor had over innumerable female readers was a good, but one which brought evil consequences in its train: "The women who wept over her romance read in it the lesson of duty, not of whimpering introspection. The danger lay in the mischievous intellectual direction which Rousseau imparted to this effusion." [70] In other words, the kinds of emotions which Julie liberated in her readers revised sensibility in an admirable and "progressive" way; but the furniture of Julie's mind was irredeemably reactionary. She preaches not only to her husband who, though kind and virtuous, is an atheist but also to Saint Preux about the efficacy of prayer and the depravity of man, much in the manner of Pascal or Fénelon. Julie symbolized at one and the same time emotional progress and intellectual reaction; and her popularity as a literary heroine aided Rousseau in his effort to replace reason with emotion as the sovereign power in man.

The other aspects of the novel which Morley finds important are its idyllic descriptions of rural middle-class life as "frugal, decorous, wholesome, tranquilly austere." [71] Within this atmosphere Rousseau depicted the sanctity of marriage and its dependence upon both religion and equality. Democratic sentiments, in fact, abound in these sections of the book and others, and help explain why the book had the effect of stirring up the spirit of insurrection among many of its readers, even in spite of itself. Rousseau helped to undermine the existing social order not by directly denouncing it and demanding its overthrow but by presenting, in the domestic scenes of the second half of *La Nouvelle Héloïse,* pictures of an ideal social state in which no miseries exist but those which are inseparable from the human condition.

Morley's final estimate of the book shows his admirable flexibility and detachment as a critic and historian of ideas. Although he deplores many of the economic and political doctrines embodied in the book, he is sure that it imparted to many men and women the desire for simpler lives and a more harmonious social order, and in this way did good. Speaking with the voice that Mill had used in his great essays on Bentham and Coleridge, Morley says that we cannot reasonably expect one teacher of mankind to fulfill more than one vast task. "We owe a place in the temple that commemorates human emancipation, to every man who has kindled in his generation a brighter flame of moral enthusiasm, and a more eager care for the realization of good and virtuous ideals." [72]

The *Social Contract,* Rousseau's most influential single work, represented both a departure from some of the opinions of his earlier works and a continuation of their worst vices. Morley points out that, in the *Social Contract* as in his earlier works, Rousseau set himself against the belief in progress and perfectibility which dominated the best minds of the century. But he no longer celebrated the natural state as the consummation of man's highest wishes, and he greatly altered his notions of equality and of where it is to be found. He now argued that the civil state conferred upon man advantages far outweighing those he enjoyed in the natural state; and that equality, far from being the peculiar happiness of a state of nature, is attainable only through society and its laws.

But, if Morley regards these changes in opinion as improvements, he finds no improvement whatever in Rousseau's method of inquiry. In the *Social Contract* as in the discourses. Rousseau repudiated the historic method which, in Morley's words, "traces

the present along a line of ascertained circumstances, and seeks an
improved future in an unbroken continuation of that line." [73] Instead, he persisted in deducing all his maxims from a purely imaginary set of conditions. Rousseau was impatient (as well as ignorant) of history because it was rife with disorder and illogic; his
very mental comfort, according to Morley, required him to set up
models of perfect order both in the state of nature and in the
movement into the social state.

The other defect of Rousseau's method which appeared only
too clearly in the *Social Contract* was its dogmatism. Morley
forcefully states the reason the *Social Contract* was to become the
gospel of the Jacobins:

The Social Contract is worked out precisely in that fashion which, if
it touches men at all, makes them into fanatics. Long trains of reasoning, careful allegation of proofs, patient admission on every hand of
qualifying propositions and multitudinous limitations, are essential to
science, and produce treatises that guide the wise statesman in normal
times. But it is dogma that gives fervour to a sect. There are always
large classes of minds to whom anything in the shape of a vigorously
compact system is irresistibly fascinating, and to whom the qualification of a proposition, or the limitation of a theoretic principle is dis-
tressing or intolerable.[74]

Rousseau aggravated the harm done by a dogmatic method by
employing the favorite language of traditional dogmatists: abstract terms and logical definitions untainted by the disorder of
mere experience. Throughout the *Social Contract,* Morley
charges, Rousseau manipulates abstractions and makes logical de-
ductions from verbal definitions; meanwhile he leaves entirely out
of view the visible objects of the world to which the words are
supposed to refer. Among the black marks which Morley gives the
work, as we have already seen, is the fact that it became the practical handbook of the Jacobins during the early months of 1794.
He does so not because he wishes to make Rousseau responsible
for them—"The author of a theory is not answerable for the applications which may be read into it by the passions of men and the
exigencies of a violent crisis." [75]—but in order to prove that Rousseau built his theory with too little consideration of the actualities
of human nature and human society; consequently, he had too
little awareness of the uses to which the theory might be put.

Given Morley's thoroughgoing rejection of Rousseau's method, we need not be surprised at his low estimate of the central doctrines set forth in the *Social Contract*. In Rousseau's major premise—that the origin of society rests in a social compact according to which each person places his person and power under the direction of a general will that is the sum of all individual wills—Morley sees both error and a fruitful source of mischief. According to Morley, the great error of Rousseau (as of all thinkers who imagined some kind of social contract) was that he allowed society to rest on conventions which the human will had made and which—it naturally followed—the human will could unmake when it wished. Rousseau assumed, or at least implied, that human nature was passive and infinitely malleable; and he took no account whatever of the infinitely varied influences of time and place upon human action. Morley thus tries to rebut Rousseau with arguments that sound surprisingly like the stock-in-trade of the conservative social philosopher: there is an unalterable human nature which should define the limits beyond which the legislator's experiments must not venture and which negates "Rousseau's conception of the lawgiver as one who should change human nature, and take away from man the forces that are naturally his own, to replace them by others comparatively foreign to him." [76]

Morley considers Rousseau's entire concept of a social contract which lapses the moment that a government, which is the minister of the sovereign people, usurps the sovereignty, to be an invitation to anarchy. For example: in 1788, when George III suffered his first attack of madness, the Parliament usurped regal authority by meeting, deliberating, and passing a Regency bill, without his consent. The Whigs furiously denounced these proceedings as fraudulent; but, if they had been like many of their French counterparts of that day, they would have declared the social compact violated and all British citizens entitled to resume their liberty and natural rights. The alternative to this anarchic doctrine, Morley insists, is not slavish submission either to a parliament or to a monarch but "the right and duty of throwing off any government which inflicts more disadvantages than it confers advantages." Morley, in his English way, is sure that, by shifting the ground of argument from rights to "advantages" or interests, he has found a more substantial and objective basis of social cohesion. But whatever force his argument has seems to derive more from experience than from logic: "Rousseau's whole theory tends inevitably to substitute a long series of struggles after phrases and shadows in the new era, for the equally futile and equally bloody wars of dynastic succession which have been the great curse of the old. Men die for a phrase as they used to die for a family." [77] They may do it in France, but in England men talk of expediency and not rights; one can compromise about interests but not about dogmas.

The second most important proposition of the *Social Contract* finds more favor in Morley's eyes: that the body constituted by the social compact is the sovereign, that each citizen is a member of the sovereign yet also a member of the state and subject to the sovereign. The citizen thus has, in a sense, two identities. His individual self obeys, not a body wholly external to himself, but one of which he himself constitutes a part, or his collective self. This doctrine, Morley asserts, played a useful historical role because it broke up the feudal idea of political authority as a property of landownership or noble birth and lodged it with the simple fact of participation as a citizen in the social union. The doctrine of the sovereignty of the people—though Morley never quite commits himself to saying it is true—embodies for him whatever positive content the *Social Contract* has; for it instilled in innumerable peoples the undoubted truth "that a nation with a civilised polity does not consist of an order or a caste, but of the great body of its members, the army of toilers who make the most painful of the sacrifices that are needed for the continuous nutrition of the social organization." [78] Morley also finds in this doctrine and in the kindred idea of association among equals the germ of the various modern schemes, including socialism, of collective action for the common social good.

In view of Morley's critique of the *Social Contract*, it is hard to understand how his contemporaries could have thought of him as a doctrinaire who found his principles in Rousseau and his methods in the Reign of Terror. In combating Rousseau's conception of a social contract, Morley sets himself squarely on the side of the Utilitarians and Burke (who in Elie Halévy's great study of the Utilitarians is counted a precursor). For Morley, the obedience of subject to sovereign depends not upon contract but upon force; and all maxims of society and government are tested not by their conformity to some abstract standard of right but simply by their expediency. Morley uses the favorite terms of Burke and Coleridge—though also of Mill—when he condemns Rousseau for viewing society as a machine and without any awareness of the forces which impart movement to it and make of it a "living organism." Nothing, in short, could be more "English" than Morley's critique of Rousseau's social and political methods and doctrines. He departs from the common English attitude toward the *Social Contract* mainly in his realistic awareness of its enormous influence over the mind of Europe: "It was the match which kindled revolutionary fire in generous breasts throughout Europe." [79]

Emile, Rousseau's educational novel of 1762, reversed the mechanical emphasis of the *Social Contract* by substituting the idea (and the metaphor) of growth for that of mechanism in education. It also reversed what had been for centuries the dominant philosophy of education, and Rousseau became the father of modern thought about education by substituting the ideal of cultivation for that of indoctrination. To the revolutionary spirit of the novel, though not to all of its doctrines, Morley responded, as we shall see, warmly.

Against the background of Rousseau's literary career, *Emile* may be seen as the attempt to define the role which education is to play in the restoration of nature to an artificial world. Against the background of the whole eighteenth century, the novel may be seen as an expression of the new, wider conceptions of education as something which commences not in adolescence but in infancy and which has to do with parents and children as much as with teachers and pupils. Against both these backgrounds, *Emile* is an expression of the new and unchristian idea of education as the development and strengthening, rather than the suppression or destruction, of the natural man.

Rousseau sought to depict a kind of upbringing in which liberty and nature would take the place of traditions, conventions, and the child's helpless dependence on the aid and approval of others. He argued that domestic (as opposed to public) education was the only way of rearing a child properly, or according to nature. The most brilliant tutor was never an adequate substitute for even the most ill-educated parent willing to educate his child. Love and the natural bond counted for more than intellect and disciplined training. Mothers should nurse their own children; the children should be given the utmost freedom of movement instead of being confined by bandages, swathings, and leading strings; and all children should be reared in the country even if destined to return to the accursed cities later in life.

According to Rousseau, early education should be purely negative. The heart was naturally good and the intelligence naturally true; if allowed to develop without interference, the one would remain free of vice, the other clear of error. Moral instruction prematurely given only prevents nature from performing her task of moralizing the youngster better than he ever can be moralized through preaching; it also rushes boys prematurely into manhood. At this point, Morley—speaking with the orthodox voice of Victorian culture—must demur to urge that the development of reason and a social conscience are tasks so difficult that they cannot begin too soon, especially given Rousseau's premise that the years from birth to twelve are the crucial ones.

Nevertheless, Morley goes on to say that the most valuable of all Rousseau's ideas about education was that example and actual circumstances speak far more persuasively to the child than explicit injunctions and prohibitions. Rousseau was the first to see the great importance of spontaneousness as a foundation of moral habits. Forsaking the mechanism of his political writings, he showed how the development of sympathy with, and the desire to please, others was a surer foundation of moral behavior than the adoption of rational formulas. The rational grounds of right conduct may, indeed must, be taught when the child's understanding is capable of receiving them; otherwise, he will grow up without respect for reason and without an open mind. But Morley—who must certainly have known of the way in which many of his fellow Victorian liberals had been paralyzed by inaction when the religious or philosophical bases of their moral convictions had been undermined—warns that unless the habit of moral conduct becomes a kind of second nature in youth, "a man grows up with a drifting unsettledness of will, that makes his life either vicious by quibbling sophistries, or helpless for want of ready conclusions." [80]

Agreeing as he does with Rousseau's emphasis on spontaneousness, Morley often dissents from Rousseau's definition of it. He finds Rousseau's prohibition of the idea and the experience of authority from education, lest the child become conscious of the pressure of another will on his own, merely foolish and wasteful. If Rousseau wished the child to form his moral habits on the basis of practical experience or the consequences of his actions, how could he narrow this experience more fatally than by so arranging it as to exclude all external interference? Morley rightly points out that, by protecting his ideal child from all knowledge and experience of the authority that he would encounter in later life, Rousseau was providing him not with the most natural but with the most artificial ambience in which to grow. And finally, Morley asks, what could be more unnatural than depriving the child—as many progressive educators have done since Morley's day, we might add, in the belief that they were thereby being faithful to nature—of the collective experience of the human race in this matter?

Before making a final estimate of *Emile,* Morley states what in his view are the three moral attributes which should be instilled in every human being by education. The first is respect for truth, the second "a deep feeling for things of the spirit which are unknown and incommensurable," the third a passion for justice. Where Morley finds Rousseau's regimen most lacking is in the third area —necessarily so, because Rousseau founded all morality upon self-interest. By doing so, Morley charges, Rousseau damaged the interests of society by weakening the individual's social conscience; and he also corrupted the individual by making of him an isolated personality. It is amusing to see the way in which Morley —who shared the common Victorian notion that children could be educated to be social reformers—forgets his own earlier approval of Rousseau's contempt for proselytizers who foist their creeds on youth in his enthusiasm for inculcating his own: "The good causes of enlightenment and justice in all lands,—here is the church militant in which we should early seek to enrol the young, and the true state to which they should be taught that they owe the duties of active and arduous citizenship." [81]

Morley's final word about *Emile* is that it is one of the seminal books in the history of literature. Like many such books—and like many of Rousseau's works—its value is not in its particular doctrines but in the spirit which permeated it:

It filled parents with a sense of the dignity and moment of their task. It cleared away the accumulation of clogging prejudices and obscure inveterate usage, which made education one of the dark formalistic arts. It admitted floods of light and air into the tightly closed nurseries and schoolrooms. It effected the substitution of growth for mechanism. A strong current of manliness, wholesomeness, simplicity, self-reliance, was sent by it through Europe, while its eloquence was the most powerful adjuration ever addressed to parental affection to cherish the young life in all love and considerate solicitude. It was the charter of youthful deliverance.[82]

To define the influence of *Emile* on France would be, says Morley, to write the history of the French Revolution.

To one section of *Emile*, the Savoyard Vicar's profession of his Deistic religious faith, Morley devotes a separate chapter. Rousseau, Morley reminds us, understood, as the Encyclopedists did not, that to weaken religious dogma and shake religious organization was not the same as to destroy religious sentiment and abolish the religious habit of respect for authority. The Savoyard Vicar appealed to this sentiment and this habit in his profession of faith, which became the convenient symbol of the religious reaction that Rousseau led. This reaction, however inadequate as a full expression of the religious spirit, Morley argues, served a crucial historical function. It kept the religious emotions alive in conjunction with "a tolerant, pure, lofty, and living set of articles of faith, instead of feeding them on the dead superstitions which were at that moment the only practical alternative." [83] The good that Rousseau did by keeping alive the religious spirit may not have equalled the damage he did by diverting the assault of the rationalists upon Christianity before they had completed their appointed task, but that it was a good no one should doubt.

Before Rousseau, French Deism had been of a mainly dry and negative character. It had been a product not of the religious but of the rationalizing and philosophic spirit. Often it was mere sentimentality, or a halfway house between dogmatic Christianity and atheism, the alternative to religion that had to be produced to meet the exigencies of controversy. But the Savoyard Vicar's Deism—that is to say, Rousseau's—is no mere philosophical counter; it is "the product not of reason, but of emotional expansion, as every fundamental article of a faith that touches the hearts of many men must always be." The Savoyard Vicar demonstrates no logical propositions about the creator of a smoothly running, mechanical universe; in fact, he can offer no proof of his faith in a God behind creation other than that which is inscribed in his heart and conscience. Such an emotional expression of faith had about it, in Morley's view, a reality notably absent from the writings of the more cool-headed Deists. It succeeded, moreover, in doing what the philosophical Deists could never have done: it gave credibility to the claims of the inner life of the individual and restored that life to "the centre of that imaginative and spiritual existence, without which we live in a universe that has no sun by day nor any stars by night." [84] It made the emotional and imaginative life once again the concern of reasonable men.

But the Deism of the Savoyard Vicar does not escape from the very criticisms which, as we have seen earlier, Morley made of Voltaire's Deism. Emotional Deism, like its rational counterpart, strikes Morley as a religion for fair weather only, a religion which can be acquiesced in only by those who are well off or by the tiny minority who can be aroused without gross stimulants and consoled without doctrinal extravagances. The God of Deism, whether his prophets be philosophers or emotionalists, is too remote, too mysterious, and too impalpable to become the God of the many.

Finally, Rousseau's emotionally based Deism was essentially subjective in character. If the Savoyard Vicar could "demonstrate" the existence of his God and the nature of His attributes by saying they were written in his heart, what was to prevent the Christian and the Mohammedan from saying that the truth of their books of scripture was inscribed in *their* hearts? This subjective principle was essentially anarchic, and it could be used to "prove" anything and therefore nothing. Here we might expect Morley to stop, but he is tempted by his own Comtist sectarianism to suggest that, in the future, the religious impulse will have to be bound up not with a Being whose nature must by definition be veiled in mystery but with "the long brotherhood of humanity." The "devout" contemplation of the experience of the human race will bring a man into closer and truer relations with his fellows, instead of enveloping him in the mists of controversy and metaphysics. [85]

However weak and misplaced Morley's importation of the notions of the Religion of Humanity into the discussion of Rousseau and the religious reaction he led may now seem to us, it is the best sort of indication of the immediacy with which Rousseau spoke to him. He could present Rousseau as a man committed to innumerable doctrines as pernicious as they were erroneous, as a man whose work and life were fatally marred by the exaltation of emotion over intelligence; but he could sympathize with him as a man whose very errors showed a keener awareness of the problems that were to bewilder succeeding generations than did the truths of his antagonists.

III   Diderot

Denis Diderot was the last of the three great names in the movement of thought that prepared the French Revolution. He was not so remarkable a personality as either Voltaire or Rousseau; he produced no great single work even comparable to the many which they produced. Yet he was an indispensable part of the movement because he was able to organize as well as express its spirit; and his *Encyclopédie* gave to the new spirit that appearance of unity and comprehensiveness without which it could not have offered itself as a practical alternative to the reigning philosophy of life and society.

Morley sets out to show how Diderot, more clearly than either of his more famous collaborators, illustrates the difference between all those intellectual rebels who had been easily subdued by the Catholic Church and the far more successful philosophical insurrectionists of the Enlightenment. Before Diderot's time, rebels had had the scientific idea but not the social idea; the movement represented by Diderot was far more formidable because it had both a conception of life as a whole and a comprehensive philosophy of society and morality. The great central moral of the movement was that human nature is good and that, since the evil in the world is wholly the result of bad education and bad institutions, man has the capacity greatly to improve the world he inhabits. Morley feels obliged to tell his readers—who no doubt shared his complacency more than we can today—that "this cheerful doctrine now strikes on the ear as a commonplace and a truism." [86] But in eighteenth-century France, where the opposite belief, one in man's inherent sinfulness, was the prevailing truism, this Victorian commonplace was a new and very radical gospel.

Diderot's *Encyclopedia* was to become the voice of the new spiritual power and of its provisional organization—provisional when contrasted with that of the dominant spiritual power, the Catholic Church, which was so intimately bound up with, and strongly supported by, the power of the French state. The new school of thought, Morley points out, had to, and did, win control over opinion by the only legitimate means: its own power of attraction. That power arose from its lucid vision of social needs and of the ways to satisfy them. The Encyclopedists, Morley asserts, sowed the seeds of all the great improvements that were later bestowed on France by the revolution. In his own day, moreover, the movement which they started is again in full swing: "Materialistic solutions in the science of man, humanitarian ends in legislation, naturalism in art, active faith in the improvableness of institutions—all these are once more the marks of speculation and the guiding ideas of practical energy." [87]

Morley regards Diderot as the type of the new kind of spiritual leader who arose in the eighteenth century and was known as the man of letters. The rise of this new class signified the transfer of the spiritual power from ecclesiastical hands. Morley incisively remarks of Voltaire and Diderot and of other renegade pupils of the Jesuits that "These men were not only the pupils of the Jesuits; they were also their immediate successors as the teachers, the guides, and the directors of society." The man of letters, according to Morley, was neither imaginative creator nor pure philosopher; he was something in between. His task was to propagate only some portions of a philosophic or poetic conception and the idea it suggests: "The characteristic of his activity is dispersiveness. Its distinction is to popularise such detached ideas as society is in a condition to assimilate; to interest men in these ideas by dressing them up in varied forms of the literary art; to guide men through them by judging, empirically and unconnectedly, each case of conduct, of policy, or of new opinion as it arises." [88] We may here recall that Morley was at this time busily planning and editing the "English Men of Letters Series" for Macmillan, a venture to which he devoted a great deal of care and time.

Diderot appealed to Morley, as did Voltaire, because, despite his incessant theorizing on every subject, he had a strong sense of practical life. More than this, he saw doing good as the only acceptable motive for seeking truth; books were never ends in themselves but always means to some end beyond. Perhaps that is why Diderot never produced a single masterpiece—too prone to temporary excitements and involvement in practical causes, he lost patience and capacity for large-scale construction in art or philosophy.

Far more than in the books on Voltaire and Rousseau, Morley is

here preoccupied with laboriously describing, transcribing, and
analyzing the innumerable productions of his author, from his
early *Philosophical Thoughts* (written as a materialistic pendent
to Pascal's *Pensées*) to his unsuccessful plays to his Encyclopedia
articles on such diverse subjects as Power of the Imagination in
Pregnant Women upon the Unborn Young; Theosophs; Genius;
Gallantry; Perfection; Melancholy; Prostitution; Pardon; Spinoza;
Academies; and Weaving. The subject matter is so impossibly
diffuse that it proves intractable for Morley. He was overly concerned with the fact that the English public knew little of Diderot's work; therefore, he felt obliged to describe much of it.

As a result, the image we finally get of Diderot and of his importance in the philosophical movement is far less clear than the
images Morley has already given us of Voltaire and Rousseau.
Morley, who became aware of the shortcomings of his approach,
tried desperately in the second volume to justify them by saying
that "a critic who has undertaken to give an account of Diderot,
finds himself advancing from digression to digression, through a
chain of all the subjects that are under the sun." [89] We may here
content ourselves with tracing what Morley takes to be the large
general outlines of Diderot's enterprise and his methods of executing it.

In dealing with Diderot, as with Voltaire, Morley seeks to remind his readers of the English roots of many of the strongest—
and, in Morley's view, healthiest—tendencies of the Enlightenment. In *The Letter on the Blind for the Use of those who See*
(1749), Diderot had sought to introduce to France some of the
ideas of the empirical school of Locke and his followers—the
school of English philosophy to which the Utilitarians and Morley
himself owed their allegiance. To substitute for the belief in innate ideas the principle that, as Morley puts it, "all knowledge is
relative to our intelligence, that thought is not the measure of existence, nor the conceivableness of a proposition the test of its
truth," [90] was, in France, to challenge the whole existing religious
organization as well as the reigning school of philosophic thought.
The method of Diderot's *Letter* was to ask, in a systematic way,
how the absence, from birth, of one of the five senses would modify the notions of a man. Diderot believed, and sought to prove,
that our metaphysics and our morality, far from being absolute,
are relative to the state and experience of our organs and senses.

Morley applauds Diderot's relativism but not the inferences he draws from it. He warns that a moral principle or practice does not lose its worth or its reason for existing once it is shown to be artificial, the product of human ingenuity rather than of divine commandment. For morality is relative not merely to the five senses but to our mental constitution and to the social conditions of every time and place. What may seem to us to be Morley's excessive caution in dealing with Diderot's principle of moral relativism is perfectly understandable when we remember that, in the '70s of the last century in England, relativism was widely looked upon as a dangerous radical doctrine which threatened the dissolution of all moral principle, if not of civilized society itself. Walter Houghton has shown that the idea of relativism, the view that things were good or true only for a particular society at a particular stage of its evolution, "did not reach general consciousness . . . until after 1870 when it came to be debated in the periodicals by men like John Morley, Edward Dowden, and Henry Sidgwick." [91] Aware of treading on new and dangerous ground, Morley took pains to show that the relativistic (or "historical," to use his favorite term) attitude did not necessarily issue in a corrosive, thoroughgoing skepticism.

The idea of the *Encyclopedia* occurred to Diderot in 1745, and for the next twenty years it was the main occupation of his life. According to Morley, Diderot's achievement in producing it, especially under conditions of harassment and persecution, makes him "one of the few true heroes of literature." The inspiration for the *Encyclopedia*, as for so many of the projects of the *philosophes*, came from an Englishman. It was from Francis Bacon that Diderot took the idea of a systematic classification of all existing knowledge; the *Encyclopedia* was to unify all the fragments of new knowledge as yet unsystematized and uninterpreted; to synthesize into a new philosophical system all those newly discovered facts, all those results of scientific analysis, that could not be incorporated into the old synthesis.

But, if the intellectual impulse of the *Encyclopedia* had an English source, even Morley must admit that the social impulse of Diderot in undertaking this awesome task was characteristically French. Diderot recognized, more clearly than any of his contemporaries, that scattered attacks upon the sacred books, miracles, and moral codes of Catholicism would not finally be effective in obliterating and supplanting old ways of thinking; it was his special merit to see that the attack had to be founded and begun in philosophy. Instead of undermining particular beliefs of people, it was necessary to shift their point of view so as to enable them to consider a much larger range of facts; more was to be gained by instilling the sense that all our ideas are relative than by denying the truth or asserting the credibility of individual ideas.

The publication of the *Encyclopedia* was, according to Morley, the result of a new consciousness in men of letters of their power and dignity; for the highest and most exciting moral ideas now belonged to them and not to the clergy. Diderot and his co-editor D'Alembert (who supervised work in the mathematical sciences) were "the first to assert the lawful authority of the new priesthood. They revolted deliberately and in set form against the old system of suitorship and protection." [92] And by a curious irony—Morley never tires of making this point in his French studies—the old priesthood itself, that is, Catholicism, was reformed intellectually and spiritually by the necessity it now lay under to respond to the attacks of formidable and learned opponents.

Morley shows why it was important for the *Encyclopedia* to give the appearance (even if it never attained the actuality) of philosophic unity. Diderot and D'Alembert presented it as the collection of all new truths into a united body of interconnected and interdependent doctrine. They doubted that they could win many converts unless they presented a common front, united behind a comprehensive doctrine and in pursuit of a single aim. Morley, although he knew that the actual relationship of the Encyclopedists to one another fell far short of the ideal one, always looked fondly upon ages and intellectual movements in which at least the ideal of intellect as a collective and social rather than individual and private pursuit existed.

The *Encyclopedia* impressed Morley as a massive effort to relate intellect to practical life. He agreed with Bacon that the wise man *uses* knowledge: "It was the characteristic note and signal glory of the French revolutionary school, to subordinate mere knowledge to the practical work of raising society up from the corruption and paralysis to which it had been brought by the double action of civil and ecclesiastical authority. The efforts of the Encyclopaedists were not disinterested in the sense of being vague blows in the air. Their aim was not theory but practice, not literature but life." [93] Yet Morley can also praise Diderot for not losing sight of the work that would remain to be done after the Encyclopedists had won their battle, for remembering that the ultimate goal was the perfection of man and not the accumulation of physical facts.

The publication of the first volume of the *Encyclopedia* in 1751 marked the transformation of the Enlightenment from a speculative and philosophical movement into a social and political one. In discussing the *Encyclopedia*, Morley defines the main features of the speculative revolution and tries to discover their practical tendencies and effects. Not surprisingly, Morley finds that the main speculative ideas of the French Enlightenment all come from England. First, the substitution of Newtonian physics (which Voltaire had helped to popularize) for the Cartesian system meant the substitution of observation for hypothesis in philosophic and scientific investigation. Second, the influence of Bacon led to a change from supernatural to empirical explanations of phenomena. Third, the acceptance of Locke's psychology (the application of which has been illustrated in Diderot's inquiry into the effects of blindness from birth) meant the reference of ideas to bodily sensations, and the identification of mind with the functions of matter.

As a result of these speculative changes, the universe was now seen by the philosopher to be susceptible of rational explanation based on observation of phenomena. Men in general were becoming more conscious of their power to control natural forces and more interested in objective, observable phenomena: Diderot therefore wisely sought to weaken religion and theology not by direct attack so much as by diverting men's minds from unknowable and uncontrollable matters to those which seemed to repay the expense of time and energy with ascertainable truths and tangible results. Having absorbed the sensational psychology, Diderot and his friends had a heightened idea of the power of education and institutions to mold character: the more we see how external impressions make men what they are, the more we seek to control and improve these impressions.

The great contribution of the *Encyclopedia* was not, Morley therefore asserts, the revelation of new methods, or the discovery of new ideas, but the transformation of ideas into instruments, especially into social and political ones. Thus the *Encyclopedia's*

glorification of work (an idea Morley had also noticed in *La Nouvelle Héloïse*) was used to increase the respect for, and the self-
respect of, the millions of people involved in productive industry.
(Morley, who had read Carlyle, knew that the doctrine of work
could be used for less respectable purposes.) Its attack on religion
was characterized not by materialism and atheism so much as by
the same *social* feeling that inspired the articles on economics: the
Encyclopedists were trying to undermine priestly power by promoting the principle of toleration, one celebrated throughout their
work.

It was precisely because the *Encyclopedia* succeeded so well in
its social aim that it failed, in Morley's view, to achieve philosophical completeness. Its greatest social achievement was to make its
readers "lose their interest, rather than their belief, in mysteries";[94]
for to replace the old ways of thinking and the old objects of
intellectual interest with new ones was to sap the power of the
church. But, in the course of realizing this object, Diderot lost
what Morley considers the truly encyclopedic point of view which
sees the beliefs and customs of the past, not as so many monuments (requiring to be shattered) to superstition and error, but as
integral parts of the whole forward movement of intellectual and
social history. In other words, Diderot was not relativistic enough;
he failed to see that the beliefs and institutions which he rightly
attacked as false and harmful had at one time in history been true
and beneficial. We note how Morley's final judgment of the *Encyclopedia* is presented to his readers as a model of this historical
and relativistic method of evaluation:

As I replace in my shelves this mountain of volumes, "dusky and huge,
enlarging on the sight," I have a presentiment that their pages will
seldom again be disturbed by me or by others. They served a great
purpose a hundred years ago. They are now a monumental ruin,
clothed with all the profuse associations of history. It is no Ozymandias
of Egypt . . . whose wrecked shape of stone and sterile memories we
contemplate. We think rather of the gray and crumbling walls of an
ancient stronghold, reared by the endeavour of stout hands and faithful, whence in its own day and generation a band once went forth
against barbarous hordes, to strike a blow for humanity and truth.[95]

The most interesting parts of Morley's book on Diderot, after
those dealing with the *Encyclopedia*, are those which assess his

work in literature and in criticism. Morley finds Diderot's theatrical writings and his dialogues and romances infused with the spirit of the Enlightenment movement, but also possessed of an intrinsic interest and value. Diderot's writings on drama formed a part of his larger campaign to return a corrupted and artificial world to "nature." Custom, in the eyes of Diderot and the Encyclopedists generally, was the antithesis to nature; and whatever was merely customary and traditional in art, as in life, was suspect. The other main purpose of Diderot's dramatic criticism (and of his sentimental, moralizing plays) was to glorify the private virtues as opposed to the public, and the domestic life as opposed to the martial or political.

Although Morley can acquiesce in Diderot's strictures on the wholly literary and artificial character of French classical drama, he is sharply (and intelligently) critical of Diderot's own ideal of drama and of stage representation. Diderot's plays, *The Natural Son* and *The Father of the Family*, were, as even their titles might suggest, propaganda for bourgeois virtues and ideals. They were intended by Diderot as illustrations of a new middle-class genre called "serious comedy"—comedy whose object is not to provoke laughter or ridicule but to inculcate virtue and duty, often by dissolving the audience in tears. Morley attributes the dismal failure of these plays to Diderot's theory of conscious didacticism: "The emphasizing moralists of Diderot's school never understood that virtue may be made attractive, without pulling the reader or the spectator by the sleeve, and urgently shouting in his ear how attractive virtue is." The earnest Victorian proves to be more reasonable in his didacticism than the eighteenth-century roué. Morley knows that a writer can hope to win his spectators or readers to the cause of virtue only by arousing their sympathy for it, not by commanding moral approval or disapproval. His job is to present character, not to talk about it. We shall have occasion, in the next chapter, to notice again Morley's sophisticated understanding of the moral function of literature.

In rejecting Diderot's crude didacticism, Morley is also defending the autonomy of the imagination. No mere reproduction of reality, even if we knew what that meant, can ever move us as a great work of imagination does. Furthermore, the insistence on moralizing about Duty is likely to check imagination, restrict fancy, and severely limit invention. Morley, political and practical

as his mind was, saw more clearly than did many of his contemporaries that the imagination cannot thrive in fetters and that imagination is the lifeblood of literature.

Morley is also critical of Diderot for impeding the arrival of a
new kind of drama by perpetuating in his plays and criticism the
major premise of the pseudoclassical drama he so disliked. According to Diderot's definition of domestic or bourgeois drama,
types of certain classes would be substituted for merely individual
characters. Morley rightly indicates that this was a strange manner of imitating nature in drama; in fact, it was a return to the
central premise of the French classical drama, which also dealt in
types, though of an ethical rather than a class character. Morley's
last word on Diderot's theatrical ideas is that the way through to
Romanticism and all it implied about the uniqueness of the individual was not open to an Encyclopedist wholly lacking in sympathy for that great storehouse of Romantic inspiration, the Middle
Ages.

Diderot, in Morley's view, attained far more success in his dialogues—"the most effective and masterly" since Plato—and in his
prose romances than in his plays. In both these forms, Diderot
discarded the didacticism of his drama and expressed the very
different impulse of scientific curiosity about human nature, in all
its vagaries and irregularities. The dialogue which is of most importance to Morley, as to the majority of twentieth-century readers of Diderot, is *Rameau's Nephew.* Here, says Morley, Diderot
depicts the type of the parasite in Rameau; yet he does not revile
his creation but studies him as the prodigious embodiment of
characteristics that are to be found in persons we would not think
of considering vile, of something despicable that usually remains
hidden in the depths of every man and woman. Morley sees Diderot's detached and restrained treatment of Rameau as the exem-
plification of a new and "scientific" attitude toward character:
"This assumption of the scientific point of view, this change from
mere praise and blame to scrutiny, this comprehension that mere
execration is not the last word, is a mark of the modern spirit." [96]
This indulgence of a curiosity about vice which came dangerously
close to sympathy with it, this new moral patience of judgment,
represented a far more genuine break with classicism than any of
Diderot's theatrical innovations.

The attitude of scientific curiosity exhibited in *Rameau's*

Nephew was eventually, in Morley's view, carried by Diderot to dangerous extremes. We have already seen how gingerly Morley must deal with Diderot's moral relativism as a highly valuable but also dangerous instrument of inquiry. "Diderot . . . was always very near to the position that there is no such thing as an absolute rule of right and wrong, defining classes of acts unconditionally, but each act must be judged on its merits with reference to all the circumstances of the given case." [97] In three dialogues of 1769— works not intended for the public, but the ones with which Diderot was most satisfied—Diderot seemed to Morley to have arrived at the unqualified relativist position. Morley finds the dialogues, of which the best known today is *D'Alembert's Dream*, to be disgusting in their physiological frankness and disturbing in their materialistic drift toward the idea that virtue and vice do not really exist and that will is a fantasy. But he refrains from discussing this idea, not because it is unworthy of serious discussion, but because in England (unlike Germany) one does not write to an audience of professors only!

Morley's remarks on Diderot's prose romances, brief as they are, make us sorry that he did not devote more effort to the criticism of fiction; for they show the talent for applying a knowledge of sociology to the phenomena of the novel that has been so brilliantly exploited in our own day by a writer like Ian Watt. Morley, in some ways anticipating Watt, connects the fact that the novel was born in England with certain social causes. The most important one was that England was the first European country to achieve even a partial overthrow of the feudal and aristocratic system. In consequence of this, English writers were the first to attach a large importance to the private lives of ordinary men and women. The triumph of Samuel Richardson as a novelist marked a great social as well as a great literary transition. In France, therefore, sympathy for Richardson (which was very strong in both Rousseau and Diderot) became a badge of social and political revolt. Morley reminds us that Voltaire, indifferent to political forms and to democratic and egalitarian sentiment, positively disliked Richardson. In eulogizing and imitating Richardson, Diderot became the prophet of the social aspirations that dominated the inner world of many ordinary Frenchmen of his time.

The Nun (*La Religieuse*) was Diderot's attempt to imitate the realism and the pathos of Richardson. The faithful account given by the narrator of her appalling and grotesque experience of conventual life was modeled upon the pathetic and sentimental accounts of their tribulations which Richardson's poor but virtuous heroines gave in their endless streams of letters. But, in addition to expressing the new cult of *sensibilité*, *The Nun* was also, Morley notes, a continuation of the mode of *Rameau's Nephew* in that it showed the same scientific curiosity about even the most shameful manifestations of human nature.

Of *Jacques le fataliste*, a story far more widely read today than *The Nun*, Morley has surprisingly little to say. He remarks that, as *The Nun* was inspired by the example of Richardson, Jacques was conceived after the manner of Laurence Sterne's *Sentimental Journey*. (Most critics think Diderot's tale more closely related to the incoherence and digressions of *Tristram Shandy*, from which Diderot even admitted copying a paragraph.) But Morley does not see, or at least does not mention, the revolutionary implications of the relations between Jacques and his master throughout the novel, which seemed to Marx and Engels a depiction of ideal management-labor relations. Jacques, his master's social and political inferior, is yet far superior to his master in wit and intellect. Is not the time soon to come, Diderot is in effect asking, when the social structure must be revolutionized so that the relations between human beings will reflect real and not artificial distinctions?

IV   *The Enlightenment and the French Revolution*

Morley's books on the three great intellectual precursors of the French Revolution do not, of course, constitute the whole of his work either on the intellectual preparation of the revolution or on the revolution itself. They do, however, express the views which rule his treatment, in a considerable number of short essays, of the lesser forerunners of the revolution, of the great actors of it, and of its consequences. These views, which have often been cited in the course of this chapter, may usefully be summarized here. They are that eighteenth-century France, despotic as it was, would have dissolved in anarchy if not for the French Revolution, which must therefore be accounted, with whatever qualifications, a great good; that the revolution was made possible by the spiritual and intellectual renovation of a sizable portion of the people and their leaders by Voltaire, Rousseau, Diderot, and their followers; that this great spiritual and intellectual movement was split by the defection of Rousseau; and that the split was reproduced, tragically, in the revolution itself.

We may take as an example of Morley's ability to see the ideas of the Enlightenment at work in the revolution the following account of the election to the Convention in 1792 of Condorcet, the follower of Voltaire and Diderot, and of Saint-Just, the follower of Rousseau:

[Condorcet] was elected . . . for the department of the Aisne, having among his colleagues in the deputation Tom Paine, and—a much more important personage—the youthful Saint-Just, who was so soon to stupefy the Convention by exclaiming, with mellow voice and face set immovable as bronze: "An individual has no right to be either virtuous or celebrated in your eyes. A free people and a national assembly are not made to admire anybody." The electors of the department of the Aisne had unconsciously sent two typical revolutionists: the man of intellectual ideas, and the man of passion heated as in the pit. In their persons the Encyclopaedia and the Guillotine met.[98]

But even though Morley found Rousseau's influence upon the revolution in many ways unfortunate, he steadfastly refused to acquiesce in imputations of guilt for the atrocities of the revolution to the Encyclopedists or to Rousseau. His reply, in the essay "France in the Eighteenth Century," to Hippolyte Taine's attack upon the great leaders of the eighteenth-century movement of thought is one of Morley's fullest statements of the relation between the ideas of Voltaire, Diderot, and Rousseau and the cataclysmic events which followed their death:

. . . we venture to put to M. Taine the following question. If the convulsions of 1789–1794 were due to the revolutionary doctrine, if that doctrine was the poison of the movement, how would he explain the firm, manly, steadfast, unhysterical quality of the American Revolution thirteen years before? It was theoretically based on exactly the same doctrine. Jefferson and Franklin were as well disciplined in the French philosophy of the eighteenth century as Mirabeau or Robespierre. The Declaration of Independence recites the same abstract and unhistoric propositions as the Declaration of the Rights of Man. Why are we to describe the draught which Rousseau and the others had brewed, as a harmless or wholesome prescription for the Americans, and as maddening poison to the French? The answer must be that the quality of the drug is relative to the condition of the patient, and that the vital question for the student of the old *régime* and the circumstances of its fall is what other drug, what better process, could have extricated France on more tranquil terms from her desperate case? [99]

CHAPTER 4

The Criticism of Life

> It has been very wisely said that the
> end and aim of all literature is, in
> truth, nothing but a criticism of life.
> The reason why so few novels have
> any place at all in literature proper is
> that so few of them exhibit even the
> feeblest sense of the need or possibil-
> ity of such criticism.
> —John Morley,
>   "George Eliot's Novels" (1866)

> John Morley, the editor of the *Fort-
> nightly*, . . . has several times at-
> tacked my things severely, but . . .
> has certainly learnt something from
> me, and knows it.
> —Matthew Arnold, Letter of 1871

A MONG nineteenth-century English men of letters, Matthew
Arnold seemed to Morley by far the most serious, the most
influential, and the most important. Because of his literary and his
social insight, he impressed Morley as "incomparable among Englishmen of his day." Morley saw Arnold as the English continuator
of the tradition of the Enlightenment, as a man who believed in
the power of reason to transform society, and who always saw
literature in intimate relation to life and the world: "In every page
of his literature you have the rare feel for life, and sincere living
care and interest in the world around us." Arnold had, moreover,
been justified in calling himself a Liberal; and "the debt of Liberalism to Arnold as a general critic of our needs will long deserve
grave commemoration." [1]

It was Arnold's notion of literature as a criticism of life that

mainly inspired Morley's own criticism of literature. To see literature as essentially a criticism of life was to insist that the greatness
of a literary work could only be measured by extraliterary standards, by an evaluation of the way in which the literary work im-
pinged upon life and society. Morley's first essays on contemporary writers—Hugo, Swinburne, George Eliot—appeared in 1866,
the year following the publication of Arnold's first series of *Essays
in Criticism*, and they everywhere show the influence of Arnold.

That great literature has to be involved with life and society
was to be as much an article of faith for Morley as for Arnold. In
an 1866 review of George Eliot's novels, Morley praised her for
remaining always in the human realm and, despite a clear vision
of the weaknesses and meannesses of humanity, for not seeking
solace in transcendental emotions or mystic visions.[2] In an 1873
review of *Studies in the Renaissance* by Pater—also a disciple of
Arnold—he praised the author for his "constant association of art
with the actual moods and purposes of men in life. He redeems
beautiful production in all its kinds from the arid bondage of their
technicalities, and unfolds its significance in relation to human
culture and the perplexities of human destiny." [3] In 1885, in an
interesting reversal of opinion, he censured George Eliot for having been aloof from life and thus of depriving her work of vitality.[4]

But to say that literature must be involved with, and criticize,
life was easier than to define the rules which such criticism must
follow. Others besides Arnold argued, though they used different
words, that literature must criticize life; but their meaning, as well
as their words, differed from his. Arnold knew that all kinds of
pitfalls awaited the insensitive critic who believed, with him, that
art should cater to morality, to truth, and to social well-being. In
the first instance, many people—Arnold called them "Philistines"
—would insist that literature enforce conventional morality by
preaching and by didacticism. A very different group of persons,
the Positivists, would say that literature ministers to truth best by
saying nothing whatever about it, for truth is discoverable only by
scientific methods and expressible only in terms of positive phenomena. Still a third group, the Utilitarians (or the less sensitive
of them) would argue that literature serves a social purpose only
by celebrating practical proposals for social and political reform.
Morley, like Arnold, tried through his criticism to show how litera-

ture might minister to morality, to truth, and to social well-being without ceasing to be literature. But being, as Arnold was not, both a Utilitarian and a Positivist, Morley had special obstacles to overcome. It is the purpose of this chapter to define the answers which Morley gave to the questions posed for literature and for men of letters by the moral, scientific, and political pressures of the second half of the nineteenth century.

Previous discussions of Morley's literary criticism have dealt with his more important critical essays as independent units, summarizing and analyzing each of them in their order of publication. The reason for this procedure is evident: Morley's criticism is little known, and the best way of making it better known is to convey to the reader a clear picture of those individual essays which make notable contributions to the critical assessment of important writers. Basil Willey is quite right to complain that, "although questions on Morley are never found in university examinations on Victorian literary criticism, his essays on Macaulay, Carlyle, Byron, Browning and Wordsworth . . . are quite as worthy of inclusion in the canon as some of Arnold's." [5] My own approach, however, is a thematic one which stresses the unifying principles of all Morley's criticism—but at the risk of fragmenting individual essays which are still less well known than they should be to students of Victorian literature. I hope, therefore, that the reader will keep in mind that the practical value of Morley's major critical essays exists independently of the critical theories I seek to discover in them.

I *Literature and Morality*

Morley gave a free and rich interpretation to the idea that literature should serve a moral purpose. Yet the piece of literary criticism by which he is best known to a great many students of Victorian poetry gives the impression that he was a dreadful and even hysterical Puritan. When Swinburne's second volume of poetry, entitled *Poems and Ballads,* was published in 1866, it expressed a distaste for Christianity and a love of sensuality that were intended to, and did, shock the respectable bourgeois; and they also shocked John Morley. His review of the book in the *Saturday Review* for August 4 of that year is nowadays used to illustrate the fact that not only the pious and conventional but also the liberal and enlightened in the Victorian period were horrified by sensual-

ity. Thus G. Robert Stange and Walter Houghton have remarked
that "the review . . . is characteristic [of Morley] in its extraliterary point of view, but not in its one-sided and emotional judgment. . . . There is no evaluation of Swinburne's poetry as poetry, but only a scream of moral condemnation. Indeed, the essay
may stand as a supreme example of the Victorian conscience horrified by any 'fleshly' expression of sensual emotion." [6]

The review's main criticisms of Swinburne's poems can be enumerated briefly. Swinburne always subordinates reason to sense;
he openly celebrates sensuality and values nothing else; he lacks
the tone of mind as well as the quality of thought of the Greek
poets with whom he has (wrongly) been associated, being incapable of meditation or moderation and always trying to substitute
for the steady flow of thought the mere swing of words. But the
tone of the review reveals far more than any restatement of its
main criticisms can do; and the tone is best conveyed by the flavor
of the epithets: Swinburne is a poet "tuning his lyre in a stye"; he
depicts "the spurious passion of a putrescent imagination, the un-
named lusts of sated wantons"; and he is entitled to be "the libidinous laureate of a pack of satyrs." [7]

It would be wrong to say that the horror of sensuality eventually disappeared from Morley's criticism. We have already mentioned, in the previous chapter, that it appears frequently in the
French studies, and especially in the volume on Rousseau. As late
(in his development as a literary critic) as 1876, he could contrast
Macaulay's healthy sensuousness with that of his own contemporaries: "Let it be said that if Macaulay exults in the details that go
to our five senses, his sensuousness is always clean, manly, and fit
for honest daylight and the summer sun. There is none of that
curious odour of autumnal decay that clings to the passion of a
more modern school for colour and flavour and the enumerated
treasures of subtle indulgence." [8] Morley continued to describe
favored writers as "manly" and "wholesome" with a frequency
that twentieth-century readers (perhaps wrongly) find suspicious.
Yet there is no other example, after this very early one, of Morley
making his disapproval of a writer's sensuality or sensuousness a
substitute for a rounded judgment of either the writer's work or
his character.

In fact, almost everywhere that he touches on moral questions
as they relate to literature his utterances are characterized by tol-

erance and flexibility rather than by rigidity. In the Swinburne essay itself he took pains to distinguish his position from that of "fat-headed Philistines and poor-blooded Puritans who insist that all poetry should be such as may be wisely placed in the hands of girls of eighteen, and is fit for the use of Sunday schools." [9] Seven years later, in his discussion of Rousseau's *La Nouvelle Héloïse,* he defended the author from the attacks of those who argue that no books ought to be written which cannot be put into the hands of children. Such a theory is nothing but "a puerile and contemptible doctrine that must emasculate all literature and all art, by excluding the most interesting of human relations and the most powerful of human passions. There is not a single composition of the first rank outside of science, from the Bible downwards, that could undergo the test." [10] In writing of Victor Hugo's *Ninety-Three,* he reminded his countrymen that "the tragedy of the parlour and the frockcoat," though it has its uses, hardly exhausts the possibilities of life or of art, however soothing it may be to a certain class of readers: "Art is nothing if not catholic and many-sided, and it is certainly not exhausted by mere domestic possibilities." [11]

Again, in the Swinburne review itself, we find Morley stating a principle of critical tolerance to which he would adhere in later years. This is simply that "an artist, at all events an artist of such power and individuality as Mr. Swinburne, works as his character compels him" and must therefore be allowed a free choice of subject matter. We may regret that Swinburne's genius "drives him pretty exclusively in the direction of libidinous song," "but it is of no use to advise him and to preach to him." [12] Lest we think Morley is being facetious here, we should refer to his review, three years later, of Browning's *The Ring and the Book.* Many strictures had been made on the poem's lurid subject matter (adultery and murder), but Morley defended it by saying that "wisdom is justified of her children, that the poet must be trusted to judge of the capacity of his own theme, and that it is his conception and treatment of it that ultimately justify or discredit his choice." [13]

Morley repeatedly spoke out against the moral narrowness of English literary criticism. The tendency of English critics to mistake a moral for a comprehensive literary judgment is censured by him in the essays on Carlyle, Byron, and Macaulay. One of the few aspects of Carlyle's work which Morley found exemplary was his "constant contempt for excessive nicety in moral distinctions, and an aversion to the monotonous attitude of praise and blame." For all Carlyle's other faults—and Morley's essay on Carlyle is a shrewd analysis of his characteristic maladies—he escaped from Puritanism and its habit of assuming that the moral aspect of behavior is the only one worthy of consideration. In a passage that I suspect owes much to Mill's remarks on the same subject in his "Bentham" essay of 1838, Morley writes:

One might suppose, from the tone of opinion among us, not only that the difference between right and wrong marks the most important aspect of conduct, which would be true; but that it marks the only aspect of it that exists, or that is worth considering, which is most profoundly false. Nowhere has Puritanism done us more harm than in thus leading us to take all breadth, and colour, and diversity, and fine discrimination, out of our judgments of men, reducing them to thin, narrow, and superficial pronouncements upon the letter of their morality, or the precise conformity of their opinions to accepted standards of truth, religious or other.[14]

The Puritanism which narrowed English judgments of men also warped English judgments of intellectual and artistic productions. Nowhere in English criticism was the tendency to narrow criticism into a moral judgment more clearly expressed than by Macaulay, for whom, says Morley, "criticism was only a tribunal before which men were brought to be decisively tried by one or two inflexible tests, and then sent to join the sheep on the one hand, or the goats on the other." Nowhere was this tendency more triumphantly flouted than in the criticism of Carlyle. Sharing Macaulay's view that Dr. Johnson's Tory creed was a blind and stupid one, Carlyle was yet able to see that there was more to the man than his creed. In dealing with Robert Burns, he was able to see that, beyond the drunkenness and unchastity and thriftlessness, lay something genuine; and he did justice to that. Carlyle offers to modern literary criticism the example of a "broad and poetic temper" which can see that Johnson's Toryism and Burns's drunkenness are the least important things about them; "and if we see in modern literature an increasing tendency to mount to this higher point of view, this humaner prospect, there is no living writer to whom we owe more for it than Mr. Carlyle." [15]

Later in the same year (1870), Morley tried to practice Carlyle's broad and poetic brand of criticism on Byron, who, in his work as well as his life, had flouted the moral laws which the Victorians held sacred. How should criticism deal with this transgression? The most important and general way in which Morley answers the question about Byron's moral character is to pay it very little attention. Far from looking upon it as the main question to be asked about the poet, he relegates it to a very minor position in the essay and fixes his attention, as we shall see below, upon the political nature of Byron's poetry. When he does come, near the end of the essay, to comment on the scant respect paid by Byron's poetry to the principles of moral duty and social obligation, he does not excuse this dereliction of moral duty but does extenuate it by reminding his readers of the time and place in which Byron wrote:

If we accept what seems to be the fatal law of progress, that excess on one side is only moderated by a nearly corresponding excess of an opposite kind, the Byronic dissolution of domestic feeling was not entirely without justification. There is probably no uglier growth of time than that mean and poor form of domesticity, which has always been too apt to fascinate the English imagination, ever since the last great effort of the Rebellion, and which rose to the climax of its popularity when George III. won all hearts by living like a farmer.[16]

Byron, though he eventually led people too far in the opposite direction, had the salutary effect of drawing men's minds away from the selfish ideal of family comfort and prosperity to a loftier outlook which encompassed romance, politics, and great national causes.

Connected with the English and more particularly Victorian habit of confusing an artistic with a moral judgment was a widespread hostility to literary works that, although not immoral in tendency, seemed to carry no message applicable to conduct. They might be works of pure imagination or introspective and subjective poems that seemed to do nothing more useful than express the personal despair of the writer. Literate and articulate reviewers often expressed this Philistine point of view. We can see it in Charles Kingsley's 1850 essay on Tennyson's poetry as the antidote to Wertherism, and in a more sophisticated form we find it in Arthur Hugh Clough's 1853 review of a volume of poems by

Alexander Smith and of the first two volumes of Matthew Arnold's
poetry. Clough found Smith, a mechanic-poet, full of righteous
purpose; and he contrasted him with the "reflecting, pondering,
hesitating, musing, complaining" Arnold, who forgot that, "for the
present age, the lessons of reflectiveness and the maxims of caution do not appear to be more needful or more appropriate than
exhortations to steady courage and calls to action." [17]

In Morley's earliest criticism, we find echoes, though faint ones,
of this kind of criticism. In his 1866 review of George Eliot's
novels, he chides contemporary novelists and dramatists for their
morbid interpretation of realism. Unlike the majority of them,
George Eliot is a novelist who "steers clear of the Charybdis of
depraved realism, without falling into the Scylla of sentimental-
ism." What Morley means by "depraved realism" can only be
guessed at; it seems to involve an excessive concern with the influences of money and sex upon human behavior, and George Eliot
avoids it:

Emphatically realist in her style, yet she is realist in a sense to which
not many other novelists and dramatists can lay claim, and in which
there are none of those characteristics that have made realism in contemporary fiction only another name for a steady and exclusive devotion to a study of all the meanest or nastiest elements in character and
conduct. There is no blinking of the eyes to the part which debts and
want of money, and uncontrolled impure desires, . . . play in life:
only, on the other hand, these lurking ugly things which pluck back
the feet of men and women in the path, are not painted from under
the microscope, while better things are left in their bare unmagnified
dimensions. [18]

A related kind of dissatisfaction with literature that dwells on
the darker side of nineteenth-century life can be found in Morley's
1868 review of William Morris' *The Earthly Paradise*. Morris'
Chaucer-like series of tales, we should remember, pay no attention to the problems of Victorian society and say, in effect, that, if
there is such a thing as an earthly paradise, it is found in the
world of art. Morley, nevertheless, has nothing but praise for the
poem. He finds it an antidote to "excess of purely subjective verse,
some of it deep and admirable and sincere, much of it mere hollow echo and imitation, and most of it essentially sterile in its
solutions. . . ." It is not Morris' exclusion of social and political

questions from his poetry that attracts Morley so much as his apparent freedom from the psychological and spiritual dilemmas of the age:

His mind seems to have travelled in paths remote from the turgid perplexities of a day of spiritual transition. Either the extraordinary directness and brightness of his temperament have made him unconscious of them, or else they have presented themselves to him for a space just long enough to reveal their own futility and flat unprofitableness. . . . We nowhere see in his work the enfeebling influences of the little doubtings, and little believings, and little wonderings, whose thin wail sounds in a conventional manner through so much of our current writing, whether in prose or verse, weakening life and distorting art.[19]

The best qualities of Morris' work are precisely those lacking in Morley's age of spiritual transition: serenity, purity, freshness, and objectivity.

But Morley came gradually to look upon the absence of inward turmoil, of morbid subjectivity, of the signs of spiritual upheaval —all, after all, adequate reflections of the spirit of the age—as a weakness rather than as a virtue. By 1876, he could chastise Macaulay for his inflexibility and for his unconsciousness of infirmity; and he could contrast him both as man and critic with those Romantics, like William Hazlitt, Charles Lamb, and Thomas De Quincey, whose more elastic sensibilities made them more tolerant as men and more flexible as critics. They had what all great writers must have, and what Macaulay lacked: some "inward agitation" which humanizes the soul.[20] Again in "Emerson" Morley asserted that all great writers experience some upheaval in their lives, and "return upon themselves" instead of progressing in an unbroken line forward.[21] When he came once again, in 1885, to write of George Eliot, he found her fiction too moralized.[22] The more Morley became involved in practical, political affairs the more he saw the need to extend literary sensibility beyond what morality and utility require; and in 1917 he recounted a conversation he had once had with an even more political character, Gladstone himself: "I trotted out my favorite proposition that *Measure for Measure* is one of the most modern of all the plays: the profound analysis of Angelo, the strange figure of the duke, the deep irony of our modern time in it all. But I do not think he well knew what I meant. He is too healthy, too objective, too simple for all the complexities of morbid analysis, and knows not the very rudiment of *Weltschmerz.*" [23]

For this seemingly un-Utilitarian sympathy for the expression of *Weltschmerz*, Morley had an important precedent in Utilitarianism itself. John Stuart Mill had complained of Bentham, in his 1838 essay, that "He knew no dejection, no heaviness of heart. He never felt life a sore and a weary burthen. . . . Self-consciousness, that daemon of the men of genius of our time, from Wordsworth to Byron, from Goethe to Chateaubriand, and to which this age owes so much both of its cheerful and its mournful wisdom, never was awakened in him." [24]

Still another problem which the moralizing bent of the Victorian reading public posed for the literary critic was that of separating judgment of an author's work from that of his life. Most Victorian critics solved the problem in the easiest way—by ignoring the distinction between an author's life and his work; and they had a long and respectable tradition which supported them in so doing. M. H. Abrams has shown that the idea of a correspondence between the nature of the artist and the nature of his product is an old one: "That a writer reveals his moral character in his art continued to be generally maintained through the eighteenth century and (with sharply divergent interpretations of the nature of morality and the mode of its artistic expression) by Goethe, Coleridge, Shelley, Carlyle, Ruskin, Arnold, and others in the nineteenth century." [25] To this particular version of the tradition Morley had no strong objection; he himself sometimes, as in the essay on Macaulay,[26] uses style as an indicator of morality and of personality. The more dangerous Victorian application of the idea of unity between a man's life and his work, and the one to which Morley vigorously objected, was that biography was the certain key to criticism and that knowledge of an author's life provided the critic with the main, indeed the all-important, clue to his work.

In an early *Saturday Review* essay entitled "Authors and Books," Morley challenged this assumption of the importance of biography. While admitting that biography is often helpful, and sometimes indispensable, in throwing light on an author's work, he maintains that we may nevertheless think the book excellent and the life dreadful. The functions of the critic and of the biographer must not, therefore, overlap: "It is the business of two men, or at least of one man in two quite different capacities, to point out whatever may be worth pointing out in the conduct and character of an author, and to show us what is good and bad, lofty and mean, in his writings. The moralist, or the moralizing biographer, does the first, the genuine critic the second." [27] Morley goes on to say that Carlyle's essays (which we know Morley to have thought admirable in some respects) were not criticism because they used literature to assess the honesty and sincerity of the author's nature. Francis Jeffrey, therefore, despite his errors of judgment, was a more genuine literary critic than Carlyle. In fact, Morley contends, the whole tradition which flows from C. A. Sainte-Beuve tends to extinguish criticism and to put in its place either biographical gossip or an endless stream of sermonizing.

The distinction between biography and criticism is frequently drawn in Morley's literary essays. In the essay on Byron, he complains that more attention is now paid to Byron's life than to his poetry and that "criticism and morality are equally injured by the confusion between the worth of the verse he wrote, and the virtue or wickedness of the life he lived." Those who like Byron's poetry are continually tempted into irrelevant defenses of his conduct, and those who have felt it worth their while to collect the details of his conduct have always felt obliged to express their doubt that good poetry could be written by so bad a man. But what purpose is served, so far as criticism is concerned, by minute investigations of Byron's private life? Were we choosing Byron for our friend or our prime minister, we should be justified in seeking guarantees of his conduct and manners; but "art knows nothing of guarantees. The work is before us, its own warranty. What is it to us whether Turner had coarse orgies with the trulls of Wapping? We can judge his art without knowing or thinking of the artist. And in the same way, what are the stories of Byron's libertinism to us?" [28]

So keenly aware of the tendency of his contemporaries to confuse a literary with a moral judgment was Morley that in the essay on Macaulay he feels obliged to tell his readers at the beginning that he will refrain from reading G. O. Trevelyan's biography, just published, until he has formed his opinion of Macaulay's place in English literature and written his essay. The opinion was a low one. The essay was written, Morley read the biography, and then added a note explaining the distinction between the estimate of a man's work and that of his character. Trevelyan's biography

showed Macaulay to be "irresistibly attractive" as a man; and
Morley sees no contradiction between this portrait and the denigrations of his own essay: "On reading my criticism over again, I
am well pleased to find that not an epithet needs to be altered,—so
independent is opinion as to this strong man's work, of our esteem
for his loyal and upright character." [29] Some years later, when he
reviewed J. W. Cross's "life" of George Eliot, Morley took satisfaction in finding that, for once, "the woman and the writer were
one." [30]

Morley's view of the relation between criticism and biography
was an "advanced" one in the Victorian period. But we must not
make the mistake of equating it with the extreme view, held by
certain influential recent schools of criticism, that biography can
never be a help to criticism. Morley thought biography could aid
criticism if the critic, instead of being a narrow moralizer, could
recognize that a man is just as much himself in his capacity of
author as in any of the other roles he plays in life:

There is a sense in which biographical detail gives light to criticism,
but not the sense in which the prurient moralist uses or seeks it. The
life of the poet may help to explain the growth and prominence of a
characteristic sentiment or peculiar idea. Knowledge of this or that fact
in his life may uncover the roots of something that strikes, or unravel
something that perplexes us. Considering the relations between a man's
character and circumstance, and what he produces, we can from this
point of view hardly know too much as to the personality of a great
writer. Only let us recollect that this personality manifests itself out-
wardly in two separate forms, in conduct, and in literary production,
and that each of these manifestations is to be judged independently of
the other. If one of them is wholly censurable, the other may still be
the outcome of the better mind; and even from the purely biographical
aspect, it is a plain injustice to insist on identifying a character with its
worse expression only.[31]

We have so far seen the ways in which Morley tried to loosen
the constrictions and to correct the distortions that resulted from
the moralizing bent of Victorian literary criticism. Morley con-
demned an exclusively moralistic criticism which denigrated the
imagination, presumed to prescribe subjects to the writer, demanded that literature be optimistic and avoid subjects that might
cause a young lady to blush, and confused biographical sermoniz-

ing with literary analysis. But Morley himself believed that literature had a moral dimension and a moral purpose. We must now
look at the positive side of his definition of the relation between
literature and morality.

In 1863, Matthew Arnold, in his Oxford lecture on Joseph
Joubert, had said that the end and aim of all literature is *"a criticism of life."* [32] Morley was attracted by the expression and gave to
it something like the application which Lionel Trilling has suggested: "what Arnold meant is that literature—although it does
indeed, in one of its activities, say specifically what is wrong with
life—characteristically discharges its critical function by possess-
ing in a high degree the qualities we may properly look for in life
but which we are likely to find there in all too small an amount—
such qualities as coherence, energy, and brightness; and in its
possession of these qualities literature stands as the mute measure
of what life may be and is not." [33]

In 1866, Morley was already employing the idea of "a criticism
of life" as a touchstone of value in fiction. In writing of George
Eliot's novels, he complained that novels could not generally be
admitted as literature because most of them failed to exhibit
"even the feeblest sense of the need or possibility of such criticism." George Eliot's fiction is a welcome exception because it
does rise to such a criticism. Morley's attempt to define the moral
use of fiction as a vehicle of the criticism of life is less clear than it
might be, but we can see him not only as aware that literature has
a moral purpose but also as growing into the awareness that that
purpose is not properly fulfilled by means of didacticism: "If a
novel has any use at all apart from the idlest diversion and time-
killing, it must be as a repertory of vivid texts, by which I certainly do not mean merely texts of morals, pointing only to the
right and wrong of conduct, though this is the first standard, but
those reflections also which lead people to work out for themselves a more exquisite intellectual sensibility, and to enlarge their
own scope of affection and intensity of passion." [34]

If he is inexpert in defining the moral awareness which he calls
the criticism of life, Morley is nevertheless highly sensitive to its
presence or absence. He could censure even writers whom he
greatly admired for their inadequate awareness of evil (and in
the Victorian period such censure was not the merely automatic
response that it so often is in literary critics of the mid-twentieth

century). Writing in 1883, Morley found Emerson, for example, in many ways exemplary as a moral teacher and reformer. Yet he was irritated by Emerson's stoical indifference to evil and by the consequent absence from his writings of moral indignation. Emerson's Transcendentalism seemed to Morley, as did Rousseau's Deism, too much a fair-weather philosophy of comforting abstractions: "Emerson has little to say of that horrid burden and impediment on the soul, which the churches call Sin, and which, by whatever name we call it, is a very real catastrophe in the moral nature of man. He had no eye, like Dante's, for the vileness, the cruelty, the utter despicableness to which humanity may be moulded. If he saw them at all, it was through the softening and illusive medium of generalised phrases." [35]

Just as Matthew Arnold had charged that "Wordsworth's eyes avert their ken/From half of human fate," [36] so Morley accused Emerson of "sealing his eyes to at least one half of the actualities of nature and the gruesome possibilities of things." [37] Five years later, in 1888, he himself repeated Arnold's criticism of Wordsworth. In almost the last part of a laudatory essay, Morley remarked upon the poet's relative blindness to the harsh side of nature and to the evil of the world in general. Wordsworth's failure to recognize that there is nothing beneficient in the workings of nature's "laws," that their moral content is zero, had led him into optimism and complacency.[38]

It is plain, then, that despite his quarrel with the moralizing bent of much Victorian criticism, Morley believed that literature was obliged to enlist in the great war against evil, natural and man-made. Literature could serve its moral purpose, however, only by legitimate, esthetic means—by cultivating sensibility and by widening and heightening imagination. This view of literature's moral action informed Morley's literary criticism from its beginning in the early 1860's until the late 1880's when his interests became more exclusively political.

In an early *Saturday Review* essay, "Imagination and Conduct," Morley argued that good conduct is largely dependent upon the quality of a man's imagination. "The immense power of imagination as a moral agent," he complains, "is almost invariably overlooked in the current domestic theories of moral education." These theories too frequently demand the severe repression of imagination in favor of a purely scientific training. The proponents of such theories forget that a cultivated imagination is perfectly compatible with the strictest philosophic disipline and that, even if it were not, "it will be an exceedingly evil day when little boys and girls are regaled with mathematical puzzles, and experiments with the lever and the pulley, to the detriment of fairy tales and romances." Fairy tales and romances, by cultivating the imagination, aid morality as scientific knowledge can never do. For actions hurtful to others arise not from innate malevolence (original sin) but from defective imagination. Intellectual knowledge of the suffering our actions cause others is less likely to deter us from such actions than is the imaginative capacity to put ourselves in the place of those who suffer and to feel what they feel: "Persons with blunt sensibilities and sluggish imaginations know that this or that thing is sure to be disagreeable to others, because they can tell the outward signs of pain and mortification. Only, their conception of pain is so dull, and corresponds so imperfectly and scantily with the reality, as to have no restraining power over their conduct." [39]

Morley rightly saw George Eliot as the great novelistic practitioner of this ideal of sympathy through imagination. In a letter of 1859, she herself had written that "if Art does not enlarge men's sympathies, it does nothing morally. I have had heart-cutting experience that opinions are a poor cement between human souls; and the only effect I ardently long to produce by my writings, is that those who read them should be better able to *imagine* and to *feel* the pains and the joys of those who differ from themselves in everything but the broad fact of being struggling erring human creatures." [40] Morley, in his 1866 review of her novels, congratulated George Eliot for having humanized the popular concept of religious belief and for having shown that tolerance and religious devotion are not incompatible. She had performed an immense moral service by showing her readers that humanity is not the exclusive property of any set of religious devotees or of their opponents, and "there cannot be much higher praise for a book than that it tends to bring men nearer to one another. . . ." [41] When Morley wrote about George Eliot in 1885 after her death, he could still praise her for having been true to the function of the "aesthetic" teacher who rouses the noble emotions which make mankind desire the social right instead of preaching her particular version of that right in the form of social and political measures.[42]

Morley's most detailed treatment of the relation between literature and morality is his excellent essay of 1869 about Browning's
The Ring and the Book. Browning tended to unnerve many Victorian readers by his profoundly relativistic conceptions of morals,
by his refusal to issue definite moral dicta in his own voice, and by
what André Gide called his "elastic soul" by which he could "put
himself momentarily into someone else." [43] *The Ring and the Book*
contained all of these provocations plus that of a lurid subject
matter. When the poem was attacked in many quarters, Morley
came to its defense; he recognized in it a new freshness and range
of experience which readers should welcome rather than flee:

We have for long been so debilitated by pastorals, by graceful presentation of the Arthurian legend for drawing-rooms, by idylls, not robust
and Theocritean, by verse directly didactic, that a rude blast of air
from the outside welter of human realities is apt to give a shock, that
might well show in what simpleton's paradise we have been living. The
ethics of the rectory parlour set to sweet music, the respectable aspirations of the sentimental curate married to exquisite verse, the ever-
lasting glorification of domestic sentiment in blameless princes and
others, as if that were the poet's single province and the divinely-
appointed end of all art, as if domestic sentiment included and summed
up the whole throng of passions, emotions, strife, and desire; all this
might seem to be making valetudinarians of us all. Our public is beginning to measure the right and possible in art by the superficial
probabilities of life and manners within a ten-mile radius of Charing
Cross.[44]

No wonder, then, that such a public, when confronted with something like the tragedy of Pompilia, finds itself adrift in a large,
uncharted moral universe.

Precisely this sense of exuberance and plenty attracted Morley
to the poem. In Browning's presentation of an infinite number and
variety of human beings he finds a "Shakespearian fulness, vivid-
ness, directness." As if to defy both Puritan and Utilitarian fore-
bears, Morley expresses delight in Browning's amoral creation of
life for its own sake and warmly responds to this free exercise of
an abundant creative power that is "absolutely uninterfered with
by the artificial exigencies of ethical or philosophic purpose." [45]

It was no surprise to Morley that his contemporaries felt themselves cheated by a poem of "some twenty-one thousand and

seventy-five lines, which do not seem to have any direct tendency to make us better or to improve mankind." After all, he points out, "the crude and incessant application of a narrow moral standard, thoroughly misunderstood, is one of the intellectual dangers of our time." Yet, Morley patiently explains to his readers, it seems strange that people should cling to their belief in the efficacy of the direct inculcation of morals, in literature and elsewhere, when it has always proved so futile an approach to the moral question. Art does serve a moral function but not by being didactic:

The truth is that nothing can be more powerfully efficacious from the moral point of view than the exercise of an exalted creative art, stirring within the intelligence of the spectator active thought and curiosity about many types of character and many changeful issues of conduct and fortune, at once enlarging and elevating the range of his reflections on mankind, ever kindling his sympathies into the warm and continuous glow which purifies and strengthens nature, and fills men with that love of humanity which is the best inspirer of virtue.[46]

Poetry like Browning's, then, even though it espouses no clearly defined moral position, can be morally inspiring by exercising the powers of imagination and sympathy. But Morley admits that poetry can only work upon raw materials already present; it cannot create them: "Given a certain rectitude as well as vigour of intelligence, then whatever stimulates the fancy, expands the imagination, enlivens meditation upon the great human drama, is essentially moral." [47] This is something of a retreat from Morley's earliest position, sanguinely set forth in "Imagination and Conduct," that morality depends entirely on the health and strength of the imagination and that the only alternative theory of morality is the belief in innate evil or original sin. But the qualification to which Morley admitted is not fatal to the notion that poetry is morally useful. For religious morality has never succeeded in proving that it can produce a moral being out of one in whom "a certain rectitude" is not inherent. The men of religion, if they admitted this fact in the Victorian period, were inclined to say (as John Henry Newman often did) that if religion had failed to produce a moral society, nothing—least of all poetry—could succeed. But any honest recognition of the diversity of human nature would seem to suggest the advisability of trying all possibilities without falling into the error of supposing any single one of them to be a universally effective nostrum for the human condition.

In 1873, Morley transferred his justification of the morality of Browning's poetry to drama—not inappropriately, since Browning's poetry was the product of a man who had given ten years of his life to playwriting and who was essentially dramatic in principle. Morley replies to Rousseau's charge, made in the famous *Letter to D'Alembert on Stage Plays,* that the moral effect of the stage is never good in itself, and is often very harmful, by saying that the drama does not, any more than other forms of art, work in the sphere of direct morality. The moral aspect of drama has nothing to do with attempts to inculcate practical moral lessons but everything to do with "producing a stir in all our sympathetic emotions, quickening the imagination, and so communicating a wider life to the character of the spectator." [48] At this point, Morley is careful once again not to claim too much for literature's moral power. Literature can never guarantee that the interest and sympathy which it awakens will lead to right action; it is a necessary moral agency, but it is not the only one.

If we jump ahead ten years to examine some of Morley's literary essays of the 1880's, we find his views on the moral function of literature essentially unchanged, except that he takes more pains to distinguish the several ways in which different authors perform that moral function, and the several objects to which different authors direct the sympathies of their readers.

Morley praises Emerson, in his essay of 1883, for being one of the very few moral reformers "whose mission lay in calming men rather than in rousing them, and in the inculcation of serenity rather than in the spread of excitement." Emerson was rare too in that his "inculcation" of morality proceeded "without the formality of dogma and the deadly tedium of didactics." Understanding that the poet's function was to extend human sympathies, Emerson wisely gave an essentially democratic application to the idea by finding joy in the commonest objects and influences of life. Most important, perhaps, Emerson understood that it was poetic emotion more than intellectual assent that drew men to the moral life. Therefore, he was unsystematic on principle; and "to complain that Emerson is no systematic reasoner is to miss the secret of most of those who have given powerful impulses to the spiritual ethics of an age. It is not a syllogism that turns the heart towards purification of life and aim; it is not the logically enchained propositions of a *sorites*, but the flash of illumination, the indefinable accent, that attracts masses of men to a new teacher and a high doctrine." [49]

On February 26, 1887, Morley addressed the students of the London Society for the Extension of University Teaching "On the Study of Literature" and again stressed literature's function in forming character. He tells his audience that literature gives a kind of knowledge neither scientific nor commercial (practical) but one at least as important as either of these. The function of literature is "the cultivation of the sympathies and imagination, the quickening of the moral sensibilities, and the enlargement of the moral vision." It is, therefore, not less but more necessary than ever before because "the great need in modern culture, which is scientific in method, rationalistic in spirit, and utilitarian in purpose, is to find some effective agency for cherishing within us the ideal. That is the business and function of literature." At this point, Morley, as usual, hastens to define the limits of his argument for literature's moral efficacy. Literature by itself can make neither the good man nor the good citizen; it can interpret and vivify for us the ideas of justice and perfection, but it cannot create them. Near the end of his lecture, Morley recalls his audience to the main point by warning them against mistaking the technicalities of literary scholarship—such as the study of style, form, and changes in taste—for its true purpose, which is to convey the force of literature as "one of the most powerful instruments, for forming character." [50]

Morley's last important treatment of the subject of literature as an instrument of morality appears in his 1888 essay on Wordsworth. He wrote the essay in full awareness of how many Victorians—including men whom he knew and revered, such as Mill, Arnold, and Leslie Stephen—had written moving testimonials to Wordsworth's "healing power," one which had restored them from aridity and despair to spiritual health. Where did the secret of Wordsworth's healing power lie? Wordsworth himself had said that "Every great poet is a teacher; I wish to be considered as a teacher or as nothing." The first half of Wordsworth's statement, in Morley's view, is certainly false; for it is no more the essential business of poets than of musicians to be teachers: "They attune the soul to high states of feeling; the direct lesson is often as nought." [51] But the second half of the statement is, in a special sense, perfectly true.

Wordsworth is certainly not among those poets who delight us purely by appealing to our fancy and imagination. His peculiar eminence as a poet lies in his appeal to will and conduct. His genius is essentially moral and therefore realizes the ideal aim of poetry, which is—we are here particularly reminded of the Emerson essay—"not intoxication, but . . . a search from the wide regions of imagination and feeling for elements of composure deep and pure, and of self-government in a far loftier sense than the merely prudential. . . ." Thus Morley finds that even a poet the most different from Browning in his positive desire to work on the will and conduct can only work through the methods proper to poetry—through an exploration of the "wide regions of imagination and feeling" for those elements lacking in the spiritual composition of his contemporaries. Wordsworth taught not the mind but the heart; and he "went higher and further, striving not only to move the sympathies of the heart, but to enlarge the understanding, and exalt and widen the spiritual vision all with the aim of leading us towards firmer and austerer self-control." [52]

It is interesting to note that in those essays, like the "Emerson" and "Wordsworth," where Morley takes the trouble to describe the ideal with which we are imaginatively to sympathize, it is a somewhat Stoical ideal of quiet contemplativeness and acquiescence in our individual fate. But we must not suppose that Morley is himself falling into the characteristic error of those Victorian critics he had censured for subordinating literature to their own moral prejudices and programs. He always remains true to the conviction that literature best serves morality when the imagination is given perfect autonomy to explore all the possibilities of life and to convey a true sense of them to people—that is to say, most of us—whose possibilities of life would otherwise be limited by the narrow round of daily experience.

II   *Literature and Truth*

The second major concern of Morley's literary criticism was the relation between literature and truth. It was also a major concern of the Victorian period, preoccupying poets as well as critics. The Romantic poets had still been able to believe that the imagination was capable of grasping, perhaps even of creating, truth. By the Victorian period, the incursions of science and of what after 1854 (the date, according to the Oxford English Dictionary, of the first English use of the term) came to be called "Positivism," had forced most poets to retreat from the Romantic position.

Among Victorian poets, it was Matthew Arnold who felt and grasped the problem most acutely. Arnold could not believe what Keats had so blithely accepted: that "what the imagination seizes as Beauty must be truth—whether it existed before or not." [53] Thus, in his 1862 Oxford lecture on Maurice de Guérin, Arnold distinguished a poetic from a scientific interpretation of the natural world in the following way:

The grand power of poetry is its interpretative power; by which I mean, not a power of drawing out in black and white an explanation of the mystery of the universe, but the power of so dealing with things as to awaken in us a wonderfully full, new, and intimate sense of them, and of our relations with them. When this sense is awakened in us, as to objects without us, we feel ourselves to be in contact with the essential nature of those objects, to be no longer bewildered and oppressed by them, but to have their secret, and to be in harmony with them; and this feeling calms and satisfies us as no other can. . . . I will not now inquire whether this sense is illusive, whether it can be proved not to be illusive, whether it does absolutely make us possess the real nature of things; all I say is, that poetry can awaken it in us, and that to awaken it is one of the highest powers of poetry.[54]

Those writers who judge all Victorian literature from the point of view of Romanticism naturally regard Arnold's reluctance to assert that the poetic imagination mediates a scientifically true image of reality as a lamentable retreat from the true faith of poets.[55] But others see that Arnold consciously rejects the Romantic faith as an illusion, both because it is blind to the tragic side of human experience, and because it denies the primacy of scientific method in the discovery of truth.[56]

Morley, as we saw in our discussion of his editorship of the *Fortnightly Review*, was one of the leaders of a campaign to propagate the scientific attitude and to apply it in all areas of life and thought. He endeavored to carry the standard of science and rationalism into the study of nature, of man, and of society. At times, he could go so far as to indulge in the wishful thinking

which supposes that science fosters cosmopolitanism by obliterating in its devotees all traces of political and national prejudice and
by unifying them by a common ideal.[57] James D. McCallum, in a
doctoral dissertation on Morley's literary criticism, even argues
that Morley's rationalistic philosophy dominates his discussion of
literature, so that when he is dealing with the Romantics, for example, he has "wherever possible . . . fitted their aspirations into
the rationalistic program." [58]

To me, Morley's literary criticism is in most ways not much
more "scientific" or "rationalistic" than Arnold's. Like Arnold, he
tried to be a mediator between the literary tradition and the
newer schools of Positivistic and of scientific thought. He was like
Arnold in seeing that the epistemological question of whether literature gives us genuine knowledge or truth cannot be settled
without reference to the relatively new mode of seeking truth
through formulating and empirically testing hypotheses which is
called "science." He was also like Arnold in stressing the obligation of the modern writer, whether creative or critical, to emulate
the "objective" spirit of science by seeing the object as it really is
and by being a "disinterested" observer. Most important, he resembled Arnold in seeing the need for the modern writer to join
his feelings to his intellect, to attach his emotions to a scientifically
valid explanation of the world.

But, if Morley arrived at something like Arnold's position about
the relationship between literature and truth, we must remember
that he started from the opposite extreme. He was no poet; he was
a rationalist and a Positivist. Consequently, his criticism is an important complement to Arnold's because, although it is not simply
rationalistic or Positivistic criticism, it is the criticism of a rationalist and a Positivist who is accommodating the claims of his tradition to those of an opposing one; and the compromise reached
often has a concreteness and particularity lacking to Arnold's rap-
prochement between literature, which he knew well, and science,
of which he had only the vaguest sense.

Although Morley dissociated himself from the harsh and crude
antagonism which many Victorian rationalists and Positivists
evinced toward literature, he defined some of the ways in which
he thought that literature could satisfy the demands of scientific
thinkers for an objective criticism of life based on fact rather than
on illusion and desire. If a Victorian thinker's opinion of the rela-

tive merits of science and literature as modes of finding truth was to be determined by his opinion in the famous controversy over the relative importance of science and literature in education, we should be in no doubt about Morley's. He was squarely on the side of literature in this debate, as we see from remarks scattered throughout his writings from "Imagination and Conduct" of 1867 to the "Science and Literature" address to the English Association in 1911, but we may use his 1887 lecture "On the Study of Literature" as a representative statement of his views on this subject.

In this lecture, Morley says that he can understand why the representatives of science, because of the contempt (and worse) with which their discipline has for centuries been treated by the representatives of literature, are tempted to make exaggerated claims for science and to insist that literature take second place to it. Nevertheless,

I only have to say on the relative claims of science and literature what Dr Arnold said:—"If one might wish for impossibilities, I might then wish that my children might be well versed in physical science, but in due subordination to the fulness and freshness of their knowledge on moral subjects. This, however, I believe cannot be; wherefore, rather than have it the principal thing in my son's mind, I would gladly have him think that the sun went round the earth, and that the stars were so many spangles set in the bright blue firmament" (Stanley's *Life of Arnold*, ii.31). It is satisfactory that one may know something of these matters, and yet not believe that the sun goes round the earth. But if there is to be exclusion, I, for one, am not prepared to accept the rather enormous pretensions that are nowadays sometimes made for physical science as the be-all and end-all of education.[59]

In judging particular writers, Morley never based his evaluations exclusively (or even primarily) on the writer's degree of interest in, and comprehension of, science; but he could be very severe with writers who openly flouted the scientific spirit. He could prefer—other things being equal—writers who were abreast of the scientific spirit to those who were not. In a lecture before the English Association on "Science and Literature" he remarked that Tennyson, unlike Browning, had been a serious and conscientious follower of scientific developments, especially in evolution, and yet Morley concluded that "Tennyson has hardly shown that the scientific ideas of an age are soluble in musical words." He found that the work of George Eliot, the one major writer of fiction who had been "saturated with the spirit of science," was "impaired, and at last worse than impaired, by her daily associations with science." And he could recall, without appearing at all chagrined by the fact, that Dante Gabriel Rossetti, "a true poet, if not a great one," was fond of declaring that he was not at all sure that the earth revolved around the sun and did not in any case think it mattered one way or the other.[60]

On the other hand, Morley definitely believed that the relations between literature and science had been transformed during the nineteenth century and that writers and critics had to recognize the fact. One of the two great changes of the previous two generations, he said in 1911, had been "the rise of physical science and invention into reigning power through the whole field of intellectual activity and interest"; the spirit of the time was unquestionably "the spirit of science, and fact, and ordered knowledge." [61] Darwin's ideas on evolution, natural selection, environment, heredity, and survival of the fittest had quickly passed from being heresies in 1859 to being blindly accepted superstitions in the last quarter of the century. Some writers benefited because they were attuned to the new *Zeitgeist*. It was, for example, Emerson's "good fortune that some of his strongest propositions harmonise with the scientific theory of the survival of the fittest in the struggle for material existence." Carlyle, on the other hand, did not merely set himself against those currents of thought which led to and were impelled by Darwin, but "chose to fling himself headlong and blindfold athwart the great currents of things, against all the forces and elements that are pushing modern societies forward." [62]

Morley correctly considered Carlyle to be the key figure in any attempt to resolve the question of how science and rationalism had affected literature's claim to give knowledge and to reveal truth. For Carlyle loudly and consistently asserted the unity between his feelings and the facts of nature, the harmony between his imagination and ultimate truth, and the alliance between his instincts and the moral law. He looked upon science and rationalism as purely destructive enterprises which had transformed the world from an organism, instinct with life and mystery, into a machine, one easily understood yet the bearer of death. "The beginning of Inquiry," he charged, "is Disease: all Science, if we consider well, as it must have originated in the feeling of something being wrong, so it is and continues to be but Division, Dismemberment, and partial healing of the wrong." [63]

In his 1870 essay on Carlyle, Morley carefully sets forth his view of the relation between poetry and science in the search for truth before he analyzes Carlyle's antiscientific bias. The distinction between the poetic and the scientific temper is, he says, a familiar one. "The one fuses or crystallizes external objects and circumstances in the medium of human feeling or passion; the other is concerned with the relations of objects and circumstances among themselves . . . and with the discovery and classification of these relations." All phenomena have two aspects: a scientific and a poetic. In other words, Morley does not subscribe to the "two-truths" theory that Kathleen Nott has ascribed to T. E. Hulme, C. S. Lewis, Cleanth Brooks, and others; instead, Morley maintains that the poetic and the scientific aspects of a phenomenon complement each other: "The starry heavens have one side for the astronomer, as astronomer, and another for the poet, as poet." [64]

Though the distinction between the scientific and the poetic apprehension of an object seems clear enough when we are dealing with natural phenomena, says Morley, many furiously object to applying the same distinction to our apprehension of man and society. Man, one school of thinkers persistently maintains, is not a proper object of scientific study—at least not of the scientific study of moralists and historians. Consequently, the proponents of moral and historical science have had to spend more time in answering their prejudiced opponents than in applying their ideas. As a result,

poetic persons have rushed in where scientific persons ought not to have feared to tread. That human character and the order of events have their poetic aspect, and that their poetic treatment demands the rarest and most valuable qualities of mind, is a truth which none but narrow and superficial men of the world are rash enough to deny. But that there is a scientific aspect of these things, an order among them that can only be understood and criticised and effectually modified scientifically, by using all the caution and precision and infinite patience of the truly scientific spirit, is a truth that is constantly ignored even by men and women of the loftiest and most humane nature.[65]

Just as Rousseau had been the chief spokesman for anti-intellec-
tual sophistry in eighteenth-century France, so was Carlyle for
England in the nineteenth century. Carlyle, like his Swiss precursor, searched no further than his own bosom for truth and right,
made reason everywhere subservient to feeling, referred to introspection problems that can only be resolved by external observation, and looked upon human society as a falling-away fron the
state of nature. With Carlyle, as with Rousseau, primitivism led to
anti-intellectualism and to the celebration of will and passion at
the expense of disciplined intelligence.[66]

For Morley, it is the irony of Carlyle's career that, while inspir-
iting his readers and listeners with an overriding passion for truth
and for its application to social problems, he simultaneously
sought to discredit "the only instruments by which we can make
sure what right is, and that our social action is wise and effective." [67] Impatient to arrive at his destination, Carlyle recklessly
cast away the instruments of reason and observation necessary to
navigate his course by denying the role of scientific inquiry and
rational thought in social questions.

The disparity between the genuineness of Carlyle's desire for
social transformation and the foolish irrelevance, and often worse,
of the means by which he would realize that transformation
proved to Morley the urgency of scotching the notion that society
is "the one field of thought in which a man of genius is at liberty to
assume all his major premisses, and swear all his conclusions."
Many applauded the radical reactionaries—Cobbett, Carlyle,
Dickens, and Ruskin—for their attacks on the Dismal Science of
political economy; but fervid denunciation of the conditions of a
problem was surely not the way to solve it. One might excoriate
the immorality of a market economy regulated solely by supply
and demand without thereby gaining a glimpse of some more
moral regulator: "Granting the absolute and entire inadequate-
ness of political economy to sum up the laws and conditions of a
healthy social state—and no one more than the present writer deplores the mischief which the application of the maxims of political economy by ignorant and selfish spirits has effected in confirm-
ing the worst tendencies of the commercial character—yet is it not
a first condition of our being able to substitute better machinery
for the ordinary rules of self-interest, that we know scientifically
how those rules do and must operate?" [68]

Morley rightly saw Carlyle as a victim of those pitfalls against which Arnold had warned critics in "The Function of Criticism at the Present Time" and in the first chapter of *Culture and Anarchy*. Carlyle had forgotten that, to use Arnold's terms, the critic of a culture needs to have the "scientific passion" as well as the "social passion"—the ability to see things as they are as well as the desire to make them better. Carlyle not only lacked the scientific impulse and method, he ridiculed them. Morley applauds and shares Carlyle's revulsion from

a community where political forms . . . are mainly hollow shams disguising the coarse supremacy of wealth, where religion is mainly official and political, . . . and where literature does not as a rule permit itself to discuss serious subjects frankly and worthily—a community, in short, where the great aim of all classes and orders with power is by dint of rigorous silence, fast shutting of the eyes, and stern stopping of the ears, somehow to keep the social pyramid on its apex, with the fatal result of preserving for England its glorious fame as a paradise for the well-to-do, a purgatory for the able, and a hell for the poor. . . .[69]

But Morley knew that the solutions Carlyle proffered were impotent. Carlyle ordered men to do their duty, yet he warned them away from all rational methods of ascertaining what duty was—other than the mindless act of renouncing happiness and doing the work which lies nearest to hand. By a cruel irony, which Morley lucidly defines, the people who responded most warmly to Carlyle's creed were the very industrialists who had turned England into the hell of dirt and slavery that Carlyle denounced: "When trade is brisk, . . . the books that enjoin silence and self-annihilation have a wonderful popularity in the manufacturing districts. This circumstance . . . furnishes some reason for suspecting that our most vigorous moral reformer, so far from propelling us in new grooves, has in truth only given new firmness and coherency to tendencies that were strongly marked enough in the national character before." [70]

Morley considers Carlyle's failure to renovate his society to be symptomatic of those whose exclusive appeal is to emotion. An emotional appeal that is not allied to a rationally communicable set of principles and precepts can never have more than a negative effect. Carlyle's creed of self-renunciation was a useful anti-

dote to Byronism, but no more. England, of all nations, now
needed intelligence more than earnestness, understanding more
than silent work, light more than heat. But too many modern men
of genius lacked the moral patience to encounter the morass of
new social difficulties in a scientific way; and, as a result, they
emerged as prophets with nothing but themselves to announce
and profess. Carlyle, and many like him since the time of Rousseau, complained that the poison of modern life was "not intellectual dimness chiefly, but torpid unveracity of heart." Morley, believing that literature would have to adopt the spirit of science if
it would continue to be a vehicle of truth, answers that "to refuse
to use the intellect patiently and with system, to decline to seek
scientific truth, to prefer effusive indulgence of emotion to the
laborious and disciplined and candid exploration of new ideas, is
not this, too, a torpid unveracity? And has not Mr. Carlyle, by the
impatience of his method, done somewhat to deepen it?" [71]

Later in the year (1870) in which Morley published his essay
on Carlyle, he brought out a companion piece on Byron. Although
the primary concern of this essay is the relation between poetry
and politics, it also shows Morley dealing with an additional aspect
of the relations between literature, science, and truth. He seeks to
illuminate these relations by asking how the idea of "positivity"
enters the realm of esthetics. Once we have grasped the theory of
a "Positivistic" literature that Morley sets forth in this essay, we
shall have no trouble in illustrating its application elsewhere in his
literary criticism.

The poet, according to Morley, may envision "a certain form of
the truth, which the rest of men laboriously discover and prove by
the tardier methods of meditation and science." It is not extrava-
gant to assert that the historical and relativistic mode of viewing
men and society which "scientific" Positivists practice was fore-
shadowed in Shakespeare. Shakespeare's unequalled capacity for
putting himself into the skins of the most varied characters, for
sympathizing with all positions, even antithetical ones, meant that
he had had recourse to whatever was the nearest possible
approach to a historical method in the Elizabethan era: "Shakespeare did not walk in imagination with the great warriors, mon-
archs, churchmen, and rulers of history, nor conceive their conduct, ideas, schemes, and throw himself into their words and
actions, without strengthening that original taste which must have

first drawn him to historical subjects, and without deepening both his feeling for the great progression of human affairs, and his sympathy for those relative moods of surveying and dealing with them, which are not more positive, scientific, and political, than they may be made truly poetic." [72]

Later in the essay, Morley reproaches Byron for having taken Freedom rather than Truth as his byword. It had, of course, been the byword of the revolutionary spirit which Byron's poetry sought to express. But Morley is certain that both poetry and revolutions would be greatly improved if truth were their first concern and if it were the only one they deemed "divine and sacrosanct." [73] Freedom and spaciousness are, to be sure, among the chief characteristics of the modern spirit—and well did Byron express them. Yet he failed to grasp what for Morley is the "crowning glory" of the modern spirit: "In a word, there was no science. Byron was a warm admirer of the genius and art of Goethe, yet he never found out the central secret of Goethe's greatness, his luminous and coherent positivity." [74]

Morley had already broached the idea of "positivity" in literature in the Carlyle essay, where it was also presented as almost the peculiar possession of Goethe. The German poet's "positivity" consisted in his accepting all things as part of a natural or historic order, in his insisting on recognition of the conditions of this order as indispensable to intellectual seriousness, and yet in his celebrating all forms of beauty in art and of nobleness in moral aspiration.[75] In the Byron essay, Morley describes "positivity," in rather orthodox Comtist terms, as "the cardinal condition of strength for times when theology lies in decay, and the abstractions which gradually replaced the older gods have in their turn ceased to satisfy the intelligence and mould the will." It is already generally recognized as the precondition for the attainment of scientific truth, but its power in the esthetic realm is just beginning to be noticed—even though "great work enough has been done in past ages by men whose recognition was informal and inexpress." [76]

It is of the first importance to be conscious of what Morley is here trying to do, and of how few Positivists tried to do the same. He is saying that just as there was a form of art appropriate to the "Theological" stage of knowledge and one appropriate to the later "Metaphysical" stage, so there is also a form of art appropriate to the "Positive" stage, when a phenomenon is explained not by a god or by an abstract force but by another phenomenon. Whereas most Positivists, from Morley's time to the present, have argued that the habitual association of truth with scientific method must relegate imaginative literature to the realm of amusing distortions of reality, Morley seeks to define the conditions in which literature may survive and flourish in a Positivistic age.

Morley argues that works of art created under the aegis of a Positivistic intellectual outlook will differ from one another according to the material out of which they are made, "but the critic may expect to find in all a profound unity of subjective impression, and that, the impression of a self-sustaining order and a self-sufficing harmony among all those faculties and parts and energies of universal life, which come within the idealising range of art." Not only will all works of art attuned to the Positivistic intellectual era express the idea of a self-sustaining universe moving according to unalterable scientific laws; that idea will actually inspire them: for "the characteristically modern inspiration is the inspiration of law. The regulated play of forces shows itself as fit to stir those profound emotional impulses which wake the artistic soul, as ever did the gracious or terrible gods of antique or middle times." [77] Turner's depictions of nature are, in Morley's view, so many glorious celebrations of the new scientific idea of nature in that they idealize the energies of matter in isolation not only from the divine but also from the human realm. The idea of a harmonious natural universe moved Turner as powerfully as the idea of nature as the handiwork of God had moved painters of earlier ages.

The often-expressed view that the Positivist idea of a self-sustained order in the universe must chill the emotions and thus be fatal to art is a mere prejudice, according to Morley. Why should the withdrawal of nature from the realms of Theology and Metaphysics stimulate scientific curiosity about it and yet deaden esthetic response to it? Never was Morley closer to entering the Comtist "church" than when he made this plea for an art celebrating the Positivist universe and the religion of humanity:

Why should all that part of our mental composition which responds to the beautiful and imaginative expression of real truths, be at once inflamed and satisfied by the thought that our whole lives, and all the movements of the universe, are the objects of the inexplicable caprice of Makers who are also Destroyers, and yet grow cold, apathetic, and unproductive, in the shadow of the belief that we can only know ourselves as part of the stupendous and inexorable succession of phenomenal conditions, moving according to laws that may be formulated positively, but not interpreted morally, to new destinies that are eternally unfathomable? Why should this conception of a coherent order, free from the arbitrary and presumptuous stamp of certain final causes, be less favourable, either to the ethical or the aesthetic side of human nature, than the older conception of the regulation of the course of the great series by a multitude of intrinsically meaningless and purposeless volitions? The alertness of our sensations for all sources of outer beauty remains unimpaired. The old and lovely attitude of devout service does not pass away to leave vacancy, but is transformed into a yet more devout obligation and service towards creatures that have only their own fellowship and mutual ministry to lean upon. . . .[78]

The literary form which Morley thought best suited to expressing the scientific, or Positivist, view of the universe, was the drama. We have already seen how he looked upon Shakespeare as a sort of unconscious Positivist because of his capacity for objectivity. Byron, lamentably deficient as he was in the spirit of Positivism, partly redeemed himself in Morley's eyes by his devotion to dramatic composition; for "Dramatic art, in its purest modern conception, is genuinely positive; that is, it is the presentation of action, character, and motive in a self-sufficing and self-evolving order. There are no final causes, and the first moving elements are taken for granted to begin with. The dramatist creates, but it is the climax of his work to appear to stand absolutely apart and unseen, while the play unfolds itself to the spectator, just as the greater drama of physical phenomena unfolds itself to the scientific observer. . . ." [79] We may notice in this exalted view of the drama a similarity to the view of James Joyce, as expressed by Stephen Dedalus in *Portrait of the Artist as a Young Man,* that literature progresses through three stages, from lyric to epic to drama: "The personality of the artist, at first a cry or a cadence or a mood and then a fluid and lambent narrative, finally refines itself out of existence, impersonalises itself, so to speak. The esthetic image in the dramatic form is life purified in, and reprojected from the human imagination. The artist, like the God of creation, remains within or beyond or above his handiwork, invisible, refined out of existence, indifferent, paring his fingernails." [80]

The "Byron" essay contains Morley's fullest exposition of the idea of a literature that meets the intellectual requirements of a Positivist age. But the idea also appears in many of his literary essays, including some written after 1874, when his Comtist fervor had begun to cool. If we trace the appearance of the idea through his literary essays, we shall see that Morley introduces it whenever he is dealing with an author who expresses a relativistic conception of morals, or a strong sense of a universe governed by law, or an objective view of character, or any combination of these.

One of Morley's earliest pieces of criticism was a favorable review of Victor Hugo's *Les Travailleurs de la Mer* which had appeared in the *Saturday Review* in April, 1866. Morley found that the force of Hugo's novel came from the way in which it conveyed the sense that the works and laws of nature are far more impressive and significant than the interests and actions of the human beings who inhabit it. The disproportion between the world of nature and that of man that is depicted in the book serves to remind us that "the vastness of the unmeasured forces which labour and rage in the universe outside the minds of mortals is what the self-importance of mortals pleasingly blinds them to." [81] That man is not the measure of all things and that the harmony and order of the natural universe are regulated by laws not made by gods or by men are orthodox Positivist homilies designed to lessen man's pride; and Hugo has done well to enforce them through art.

In a review of George Eliot's novels published in August, 1866, Morley was glad to extend a hand of welcome to a novelist whose main premise was the Positivist idea that all human fates are interconnected in a vast network of cause and effect. George Eliot everywhere demonstrated her grasp of the truth that "life moves from a thousand complicated and changing springs, and works into infinitely diversified results, which it is the highest interest of men to meditate upon." All fiction which pretended to a criticism of life would have to possess this comprehensive and unified view of the world. The novelist's task resembled that of the scientific investigator in that he too had to discover uniform laws and principles: "the criticism of life traces the working of the more momentous laws of circumstance and character and conduct." The "laws of circumstance" became for a modern novelist like George Eliot what fate had been to the ancient tragedian; and, just as the latter had shown the conflict between divinely ordained fate and the free exercise of human will, so she sought to find the right proportion "between the power of the individual and the might of circumstance." [82] Morley's insights into the "scientific" premises and procedures of George Eliot five years before she began to publish *Middlemarch* make us regret that he did not review that great novel, which is so filled with scientific imagery, so informed by the metaphors of scientific investigation and the habit of comparing people and actions with scientific processes. But we should not forget that it was Morley who first pointed out that George Eliot was looking at nature and the world in a way that was closer to the scientist's than to the painter's or the poet's.

In March, 1869, Morley published his favorable review of Browning's *The Ring and the Book.* We have already noticed the way in which the review defended Browning against charges of indifference, or even hostility, to morality by saying that even poetry which espouses no clear moral position can be morally useful by exercising the imaginative and sympathetic emotions. But Morley was at least as interested in the intellectual implications of Browning's relativistic conception of morals. In 1852, Browning had published an essay on Shelley which distinguished between the objective poet, the type of whom would be Shakespeare, and the subjective poet typified by Shelley. The objective poet reproduces the things of the external world—"whether the phenomena of the scenic universe, or the manifested action of the human heart and brain"—which are the common property of the race; but the subjective poet, whose main study has been himself, transforms the external world into a reflection of his inner light, which he believes to be a reflection of the divine in man.

Browning, who had begun his poetic career as a follower of Shelley but had then adopted the "objective" or Shakespearean mode, says in this essay that "the objective poet, in his appeal to the aggregate human mind, chooses to deal with the doings of men, (the result of which dealing, in its pure form, when even description, as suggesting a describer, is dispensed with, is what we call dramatic poetry). . . ." [83] We do not know whether Morley ever read this essay, but its notion of the objectivity which the dramatic form achieves by separating the creator in some mysterious way from his creation plays an important part in Morley's criticism of Browning and in his criticism generally. In writing of *The Ring and the Book,* he says that the dramatic form of poetry is the "highest expression and measure of the creative power of the poet" because it is the form best suited for depicting the struggle of the individual with his circumstances, or with the "given" of his character.[84]

What Morley finds most interesting in the poem, aside from its method of presenting and developing character, is its relativistic conception of action and morality. Browning wished to demonstrate how elusive and fragmented truth is in the actual world; and he did so by showing how a single action has as many sides as it has witnesses. The truth, if obtainable at all, is to be gained only by a balancing of all points of view, no two of them identical. The dramatic monologue form could give only the points of view of so many different characters, never that of their creator. Morley's belief that Browning's use of the dramatic monologue perfectly suited the intellectual conditions of an age addicted to the historical method, relativistic in morals, and scientifically objective in its general view of life has been borne out by the fact that the dramatic monologue has, since Browning's time, become the dominant form of modern poetry.

In responding to the intellectual and scientific qualities of Browning's poem, Morley responded as Browning would have wished. For Browning liked to think of his investigations of evil as clinical in their studied avoidance of moral condemnation, and he chided his wife for lacking "a scientific interest in evil." [85] Morley thought of *The Ring and the Book* as having been intellectually rather than emotionally conceived, and therefore as appealing to judgment rather than to sensibility. Browning seemed to him to search for truth in the way that a scientist or a Positivist historian would, and he saw the poem as analogous to "a scientific essay on history, or a treatise on the errors of the human understanding and the inaccuracy of human opinion and judgment." Great as was Browning's exuberant creative power, it was not more remarkable than "the scientific attitude of his intelligence." [86]

Another writer of the period who often praised Browning for being the most "modern" of poets was Walter Pater. Indeed, several of Pater's literary views are informed by the scientific and Positivist premises of Morley. The 1867 essay on Johann Winckelmann, for example, expresses ideas about the relation between scientific laws and modern literature which closely resemble those Morley had begun to express in his 1866 essays on Victor Hugo and George Eliot. What modern art, according to Pater, is obliged to do in the service of culture is to keep alive the sense of freedom. Yet "the chief factor in the thoughts of the modern mind concerning itself is the intricacy, the universality of natural law, even in the moral order." This is the modern version of necessity —no longer a mythological personage but a magical web which runs through all the world, including our own minds. It is too early, says Pater, to know whether art can "represent men and women in these bewildering toils so as to give the spirit at least an equivalent for the sense of freedom." Yet the romances of Goethe and of Victor Hugo—Morley's exemplars of "positivity," we recall —are examples of modern art "dealing thus with modern life, *regarding that life as the modern mind must regard it,* yet reflecting upon it blitheness and repose" (my italics). Modern writers who see the world as modern science obliges men of intellectual integrity to see it may yet find in the idea of unalterable scientific laws of nature the basis of a new conception of tragedy: "In those romances of Goethe and Victor Hugo, in some excellent work done *after* them, this entanglement, this network of law, becomes the tragic situation, in which certain groups of noble men and women work out for themselves a supreme *Dénouement.*" [87]

Without asking whether it was Pater who was indebted to Morley, or Morley to Pater, we may readily remind ourselves of how similar were their ideas of the new, "scientific" setting for tragedy by placing alongside the remarks of Pater just quoted the words of Morley in his explanation, given in 1874, of the reason why Hugo reminds him of Aeschylus: "Because Hugo makes us conscious of that tragedy of temperament, that sterner Necessity of character, that resistless compulsion of circumstance, which is the modern and positive expression for the old Destiny of the Greeks, and which in some expression or other is now an essential element in the highest presentation of human life. Here is not the Unknown. On the contrary, we are in the very heart of science; tragedy of the modern is not $\tau\acute{v}\chi\eta$ [chance], but a thing of cause and effect, invariable antecedent and invariable consequent." [88]

When we are aware of the important critical ideas which Morley and Pater shared, we can turn again to Morley's very favorable notice of Pater's *The Renaissance* in 1873 and see that it is something more than a generous welcome to a young writer. For what Morley applauds in Pater is the Positivist bent of his criti-

cism, which shows scholarly solidity, and a concrete and positive
(as opposed to metaphysical) quality.[89] Morley did not, of course,
persuade himself that Pater was really a Positivist; but he saw that
Pater, like himself, recognized the changed intellectual circumstances within which the artist now had to function; and Pater,
like the Positivists, although for very different ends, used the historical method to show that all institutions and beliefs were only
"right" and "true" for their particular periods, not absolutely and
eternally.

I have stressed the way in which writers like Browning and
Pater not only served to illustrate Morley's theory of the new relationship between literature and science but, to some extent,
shared it themselves. For it is important to see that Morley formulated his theory of a modern literature in harmony with the assumptions of a scientific age not as an abstract intellectual position but in relation to a living tradition of literature. He did not
merely say that literature could, if writers were intellectually serious, continue to provide truthful interpretations of a changed
world; he pointed to particular literary works which did so. To his
credit, the works which he did select for this honor now seem to
us the forerunners of that kind of twentieth-century literature
which carries the honorific label "modern."

III   *Literature and Society*

The last of the three principal questions which Morley's criticism asks about literature is, what is its social function? Proceed-
ing from the premise that the greatest literature inevitably impinges upon social and political concerns, Morley seeks in much of
his literary criticism to define the relations between particular literary works and the historical situation from which they emerge,
and also to ascertain whether, or when, the writer has a positive
duty, as writer, to enter the realm of practical politics. To answer
this question, we shall see, first, what Morley's views of the writer's duty to society were, and second, how his criticism makes use
of the idea that great works of literature are the expression of a
particular historical ethos.

Most of Morley's literary criticism was written and published
before he entered Parliament in 1883, although so distinguished
an essay as the "Wordsworth" dates from 1888. It is touching to

see him, as when he writes in 1897, trying to sustain his former interests after he has definitely transformed himself from the man of letters to the practical politician: "I banished politics and spent most of the day sauntering on the shore, with Wordsworth and Arnold in my pocket." [90] But it would be wrong to suppose that Morley's change in roles meant a radical change in attitudes, any more than Arnold's or Ruskin's movement from the criticism of art to that of society meant a radical transformation of attitude. Morley was from the start an eminently political mind with a strong taste for literature and with a keen sense for discovering the crossroads where literature and politics meet.

Involved as Morley was, both intellectually and practically, with politics, we might expect him to have been more prone than most Victorians to the belief, widely held by Victorian radicals, that literature had a positive duty to forward the great works of reform in a definite, practical way. Harriet Martineau, the Victorian radical who wrote short stories to teach the precepts of political economy and to prove that all economic misfortunes arose from acts inconsistent with those precepts, epitomized the widespread Victorian conviction that art proved its utility by becoming propaganda. She insisted that "if the office of casting new lights into philosophy, and adding new exemplifications and sanctions to morals, be not the 'business' of literary genius, we know not what is." She was a severe critic of the coarseness and immorality of George Eliot's novels, and her biographer tells us how "when George Eliot told her that true delineation was good art—they were standing before a disagreeable picture of a stork killing a toad . . . —Miss Martineau replied by asking whether it would also be good art to show men on a raft eating a comrade, and Miss Evans was silent." [91] But Morley, as we have often noted before, was a humanist as well as a radical; and, when he wrote of George Eliot in 1885, while serving in Parliament, he stated explicitly that it was "not the business of an artist to form judgments in the sphere of practical politics." [92]

In fact, Morley had dissociated himself from the crude utilitarianism of such views as those of Miss Martineau or of many of the writers of the *Westminster Review* long before this time. He had once gone so far as to criticize the greatest Utilitarian of all, his master Mill, for counting it a drawback to Victor Hugo's worth that he had not brought forward a single practical proposal for the improvement of the society he was always criticizing. "I ventured to urge that it is unreasonable to ask a poet to draft acts of parliament; and that by bringing all the strength of his imagination and all the majestic fulness of his sympathy to bear on the social horrors and injustices which still lie so thick about us, he kindled an inextinguishable fire in the hearts of men of weaker initiative and less imperial gifts alike of imagination and sympathy, and so prepared the forces out of which practical proposals and specific improvements may be expected to issue." [93] We can here see Morley applying to the relation between literature and society precisely the argument that he had applied to the relation between literature and morality. Literature, as such, does not deal either in moral or social doctrine, does not define the good life or the good society; but it works, in the only way proper to it, to enlarge imagination and to purify emotion and so to enable men to recognize the good life or the good society when they see it, or are told about it.

When he praised Pater, in 1873, Morley must have shocked many *Fortnightly* readers by arguing that Pater's creed of "art for art's sake" was not at odds with the work of social reconstruction but was its necessary precursor and also by censuring Ruskin for deserting his proper realm and plunging into "the difficult career of the social reconstructor, . . . hardly with a success that any man can call considerable." Morley saw the esthetic creed of Pater —which said that the end of life is not action but esthetic contemplation, "*being* as distinct from *doing*"—as a continuation of the Oxford Movement's protest against the mechanical and ugly qualities of modern life. While Morley did not acquiesce in Pater's assertion that the true wisdom of life is to be found in cultivating beautiful impressions, he found the doctrine

pregnant with intellectual play and expansion, and it is intellectual play and expansion that we require, before the social changes craved by so many can fully ripen. . . . We have suffered more from the excessive absorption of national interest in theological strife and the futilities of political faction, than we are at all likely to suffer from the devotion of a few men of special impulses to the subjects where those impulses will tell with most effect. The prodigious block of our philistinism needs to have wedges driven in at many points, and even then they will be all too few.[94]

Five years later, Morley wrote that it was the great bane not only of Diderot's but of all theatrical criticism to impute ethical or social purpose to the dramatist and to demand "direct and combined ethical or social effect from the drama." [95]

It seems clear, then, that Morley firmly rejected the idea that it is an author's duty consciously and directly to set about instructing and improving society by means of literature. But there is another side to his position on the relation between literature and society, a side which may seem contradictory to the first but is really complementary: his belief that the critic, unlike the creative author, always has the duty to relate literature to society. Morley saw literature as the embodiment of ideas—"about religion, conduct, society, history, government, and all the other great heads and departments of a complete social doctrine." [96] Not all literary works which engaged themselves with important and comprehensive ideas were equally successful, for the ideas had to be transformed, by the alchemy of art, into their emotional equivalents, things which were felt upon the pulses as well as communicated to the brain. Morley found that George Eliot had succeeded in her early novels in giving imaginative shapes to the new ideas of biology, sociology, and anthropology; yet parts of the later *Daniel Deronda* seemed to him "simply hopeless: as difficult as Hegel." [97] Nor were all ideas of equal value, either in themselves or as materials for art. Many writers, like Macaulay, gained immense popularity by the imaginative handling of very commonplace ideas. [98]

Declaring himself indifferent to the "metaphysics" of poetry in particular and of literature in general, Morley set himself to discovering the historical, philosophical, and moral relevance of the works he criticized. [99] In his book on Rousseau, he defined the business of criticism as the process of separating what is merely accidental, transitory, and local in a particular work from the large, general ideas which inform it. "We are only encouraging poverty of spirit, when we insist on fixing our eyes on a few of the minutiae of construction, instead of patiently seizing larger impressions and more durable meanings; when we stop at the fortuitous incidents of composition, instead of advancing to the central elements of the writer's character." [100] Those central elements are the writer's ideas—or rather, those of his ideas which have been incarnated as *literary* ideas. To understand them, one had to do more than read the particular work under consideration. One had to understand the age in which it was written, for "there are causes and relations between great compositions and the societies in which they have emerged." [101]

The best example of Morley's historical method of criticism (apart from his book-length studies of Voltaire, Rousseau, and Diderot) is his 1870 essay on Byron. In it, Morley starts from the premise that each historical period impresses a certain character upon those of its writers great enough to be conscious of the spirit of their age. He then asks how an epoch of transition, one which by definition lacks fixed beliefs and accepted conventions, will be celebrated in poetry. Admitting that such an epoch cannot give so powerful or so lasting an impulse to a writer as can a settled, organic epoch, he asserts that Byron came closest to expressing the spirit of an era characterized by "elements so intrinsically un-favourable to high poetry as doubt, denial, antagonism, and wea-riness." [102] Byron, in short, epitomized the spirit of the revolution.

Before telling us just how Byron did so, Morley offers a defini-tion of literature and of literary criticism. Literature (as, indeed, every branch of art) is "the transformation into ideal and imagi-native shapes of a predominant system and philosophy of life." Writers who express no philosophy of life are by definition "minor" and may be relegated to the outer darknesses of the mere literature of taste. Criticism of such works will share their trivial-ity, for they will inevitably be an enumeration of fine lines or ex-pressions, of new turns of speech, and of the success or failure of these little graces in conforming to the traditions of poetry. Seri-ous criticism rivets its attention upon the "loftier masters," who "come to us with the size and quality of great historic forces, for they represent the hope and energies, the dreams and the con-summation, of the human intelligence in its most enormous move-ments." The critic who would rightly appreciate such writers must do more than analyze their works into idea, form, and treatment; he must synthesize the materials which his analysis has revealed in order to reconstruct the mind of the poet and to relate the poet's ideas to the ideas and tendencies of his age.[103]

In regarding Byron as an essentially political poet, Morley is placing him in what he sees as the central tradition of English poetry. In English poetry, according to Morley, more than in that of any other nation, great spiritual force is mingled with a strong sympathy for social and political affairs. We have only to read the two greatest of English poets—Shakespeare and Milton—and to set them alongside the consumingly spiritual Dante or the exclusively intellectual Goethe to see that this is so. Byron, like his greater predecessors, combined a sense of the highest and purest spiritual aspirations with an ability to view man as a social and political animal rather than as a high abstraction.

Shelley, Morley admits, was Byron's superior in purely poetic attributes; and he had too a genuine passion for social justice. Yet he was far less effective as a political poet than Byron because he lacked Byron's worldliness of spirit in poetry and in life. Byron, unlike Shelley, did not allow his impassioned flights of lyricism to transport him to an ethereal realm where human actualities were either forgotten or transformed. Byron's ability to keep his passion and his imagination always in touch with the earth and with men made him "a social force" and enabled him to become "the genuine exponent of that immense social movement which we sum up as the Revolution." [104]

The aspect of Byron's poetry which, in Morley's opinion, most clearly expresses the view of things peculiar to the revolution is his treatment of nature. Byron never so lost himself in ecstasies over the mightiness and wonder of nature that he neglected to use her to express the idea of the unsatisfactoriness of man's life in society. Nature, in other words, was always used by him as a background for the great human drama. Byron, like other revolutionary writers since the time of Rousseau, did not celebrate nature for her own sake but used the solitude and seeming freedom of nature as a mute criticism of the clutter and slavery of civilized society.

The antisocial side of revolutionary sentiment was glorified by Byron's long series of individualistic heroes—his Laras, Conrads, Manfreds, and Harolds. Byron was able to express through them his sense of the upheaval of the revolutionary period, when men had lost faith in existing institutions and beliefs and were subjectively searching within themselves for new ones, or at least for the basis for them. What attuned Byron so well to the revolutionary mood was his "full-blooded" temperament even more than his intellect: "It was this temperament which . . . gave Byron the amazing copiousness and force that makes him the dazzling master of revolutionary emotion, because it fills his work with such variety of figures, such free change of incident, such diversity of passion, such a constant movement and agitation. It was this never-ceasing stir, coupled with a striking concreteness and an unfailing directness, which rather than any markedly correct or wide intellectual apprehension of things, made him so much more than any one else an effective interpreter of the moral tumult of the epoch." [105]

Byron voiced the revolutionary protest against a society which was more concerned with the rights of property than with the spirit and dignity of men. He was the spokesman for a whole generation which repudiated the foundations of a social order which clung to the outward forms of convictions long discredited, and whose temporal and spiritual institutions were therefore permeated by falsehood and duplicity. Byron became the great poet of the revolutionary movement by elaborating this common emotion, "as the earliest modern poets elaborated the common speech. He gave it inflections, and distinguished its moods, and threw over it an air of system and coherency, and a certain goodly and far-reaching sonorousness." [106] In other words, Byron did not himself originate political ideas; he articulated and vivified the ideas of his most advanced contemporaries.

Even in his intellectual shortcomings, Morley argues, Byron adequately reflected the revolutionary movement of his time. Like the chief revolutionary ideologists descending from Rousseau, he espoused the crude and unscientific idea of nature as a benign state from which civilized society was a lamentable departure. These false intellectual conceptions were transformed in Byron's poetry into the form of passionate and willful outbreaks. Here was the evil side of revolutionary sentiment—the fact that it was too exclusively sentiment undisciplined by scientific intelligence and self-control. By indulging their passionate disgust with existing society without taking the trouble to acquire a historical understanding of the antecedents of that society and of the necessary conditions of every civil society, Byron and the propagandists of the revolution destroyed all faith in order, potential as well as actual, and encouraged an anarchic individualism.

This individualism, in which each man who was ready to make large claims on life erected his own passions, ambitions, and beliefs into moral laws, was the moral state which Byron expressed and interpreted:

His relation to it was a relation of exact sympathy. He felt the force of each of the many currents that united in one destructive stream. . . . The list of his poems is the catalogue of the elements of the revolutionary spirit. For of what manner is this spirit? Is it not a masterful and impatient yearning after many good things, unsubdued and uninformed either by a just knowledge of the time, and the means which are needed to bring to men the fruits of their hope, or by a fit appreciation of orderly and tranquil activity for the common service, as the normal type of the individual life? And this is precisely the temper and spirit of Byron.

Readers who are puzzled by the frenzied search of Byron's heroes after freedom and by the frequency with which their fiery energies end only in melancholy and despondency, may find their explanation, following Morley's mode of criticism, in the peculiar characteristics of the revolutionary movement itself. Its leading spirits had, to revert once more to Arnold's terms, the social passion but lacked the scientific; they hoped to seize freedom without paying due regard to truth, "which means science in the intellectual order, and justice in the social order." In literature, this desire for freedom in isolation from all other good things was expressed as the passionate—and futile—longing of the individual for an unconditioned life, the life of the free spirit whose will is untrammeled by circumstances or impossibilities. Seeking, and not finding, this unconditioned life, the Byronic hero "fills the world with stormy complaint." The combination of spiritual emptiness and energetic activity which we find in Byron's heroes was the result of Byron's having come onto the scene when he did, when the revolutionary spirit had run into plenty of impossibilities, when plenty of circumstantial limitations on the freedom of the spirit had arisen, and when the social faith of 1789 had declined into Napoleonism.[107]

The "Byron" essay is the most detailed example of Morley's historical method of criticism applied to English literature. It shows how Morley relates an author to a historical movement when he believes that movement to have given the author's work its most characteristic qualities. The chief virtue of the method is that it endows a literary work with the kind of magnitude that comes from an involvement with the life of its time and is the best guarantee that it will do effective work in the life of later times.

Morley would have understood what Shaw meant when he said that the work that is written not for an age but for all time has its reward by going unread in all ages; and he never fell into the modern critical error, or pretense, of supposing that the purity of an author's work or a reader's response to it depends on achieving an almost Olympian detachment from worldly concerns.

Morley had not the slightest hesitation in asserting that Byron had been an important and even a great poet because of his experience of a particular world; or that the ninth, tenth, and eleventh books of Wordsworth's *Prelude* gained much of their immense truth and power from the fact that they were inspired by the French Revolution, and that Wordsworth's poetry began to decline when, after Waterloo, he lost his interest in progress and his grasp of social fact.[108] The main vice of the historical method is its determinism, its habit of reducing a work of literature to the product of a particular historical moment, forgetting that all kinds of historical moments have gone uncelebrated by a major work of literature because their call for attention has not been answered by the right man.

After "Byron," the essay of Morley's which contains the most interesting statements and applications of the historical method of criticism, is "Emerson," published in 1883. Morley praises Emerson not only for a kind of "sanity" that was lacking in his friend Carlyle and that made him move with, not against, the currents of the modern age but also for propagating ethical doctrines which were in harmony with the new scientific and social doctrines. But Morley is severely critical of Emerson for not following the historical method in his criticism—"he introduces the great names of literature without regard for true historical perspective in their place, either in relation to one another, or to the special phases of social change and shifting time," [109]—and, as if to teach that method by example, Morley gives very historical and circumstantial explanations of two of Emerson's weaknesses.

Morley explains what he considers the two main weaknesses in Emerson's thought by the conditions of American society in Emerson's time. Of all the nineteenth-century writers who were in reaction against the philosophy of the Enlightenment, none, according to Morley, went to such extremes of reaction as Emerson, who remained blind to all that was of value in the leading speculations of the *philosophes*. Unlike them, he was entirely indifferent to the role of reformed institutions in the regeneration of mankind; and the reason he was so is readily explained by the difference between his historical circumstances and those of the *philosophes.* "Institutions needed regeneration in France, and so those thinkers came into vogue and power who laid most stress on the efficacy of good institutions. In Emerson's America, the fortunes of the country made external circumstances safe for a man, and his chance was assured; so a philosophy was welcomed which turned the individual inwards upon himself, and taught him to consider his own character and spiritual faculty as something higher than anything external could ever be." [110]

Emerson's optimism, his closing his eyes to the evil half of nature and of life, is also to be explained by his historical situation. Emerson was born and reared in a country that had cut itself free from "old history" or, at any rate, from the history of Europe. His unconsciousness of evil, Morley argues, is but the reflection of a condition of national innocence: "The black and devious ways through which the race has marched are not real in North America, as they are to us in old Europe, who live on the very site of secular iniquities, are surrounded by monuments of historic crime, and find present and future entangled, embittered, inextricably loaded both in blood and in institutions with desperate inheritances from the past." [111] Once again, Morley showed a remarkable capacity for discovering the fruitful themes of a truly modern literature; when he wrote this passage, Henry James was already dealing, in book after book, with this contrast between American innocence and European experience of evil.

I have tried to show how, in defining the relation between literature and society, as in defining literature's relation to morality and to truth, Morley tries to keep a balance between the demand that literature be a useful, proper, and truthful criticism of life, and the integrity of literature as a liberal pursuit, subservient to no end. He rejects the Utilitarian theory of literature as political and social propaganda; but he also insists upon viewing literature at those points where it impinges on society and politics. If, in pursuing the latter purpose, he seems to some modern readers to have narrowed, if not distorted, the nature of literature, they should remember that, political man though he was, he paid literature the honor of looking on it as a potent social force which had important work to do in the modern world. He saw it as a neces-

sary accompaniment to democracy and as a remedy for some of
the defects peculiar to democratic societies. In a lecture of 1887,
when already embarked upon a political career, he praised the
movement to bring the literary education that had hitherto been
the privilege of Oxford and Cambridge students within the reach
of all classes of the community. Such a movement was eminently
democratic, for "nothing . . . is more calculated to remedy defects that are incident to democracy, more thoroughly calculated
to raise modern democracy to heights which other forms of government and older orderings of society have never yet attained."

The new attempts to diffuse the best education, the new trans-
lations of the classics by Benjamin Jowett and others which enabled those without a Classical education to read them—all these
were laudable efforts "to connect learning with the living forces of
society, and to make industrial England a sharer in the classic
tradition of the lettered world." The notion that education beyond
the merely practical will unfit manual laborers and their like for
the jobs they are assigned by the social order to do is alien not
merely to the spirit of democracy but also to the spirit of literature
itself. Morley, like his masters Mill and Arnold, urges his countrymen to take Periclean Athens as the Platonic ideal of modern England, which had the opportunity "to bring the Periclean ideas of
beauty and simplicity and cultivation of the mind within the
reach of those who do the drudgery and the service and rude
work of the world."

As for the companion prejudice which said that literary men
were unfitted for practical affairs, Morley had only to point to the
considerable number of men of letters who had in recent years
exhibited the highest form of practical energy—in running the
government of England. Morley had in mind such men as Gladstone, Salisbury, Disraeli, and Balfour;[112] but, having already
served a brief term as chief secretary for Ireland, he might justi-
fiably have included himself among those who took seriously and
very literally the idea that literature was a criticism of life and
therefore the best preparation for the art of government.

CHAPTER 5

Conclusion

JOHN Morley's influence upon literature and ideas during the Victorian period was exercised through his own writing, through his promotion of new writers and ideas in the *Fortnightly Review,* and through his long tenure as senior literary adviser to the Macmillan publishing house. His studies of the great intellectual precursors of the French Revolution enabled the English reading public, virtually for the first time, to view that upheaval, "that object," as Matthew Arnold had called it, "of so much blind love and so much blind hatred," [1] with some degree of intellectual detachment. He succeeded in demonstrating that the ideas which lay behind the French Revolution had not been discredited by the English victory over France on the battlefield, and that these ideas were, both in origin and in essence, by no means alien to Englishmen. Morley's fifteen years as editor of the *Fortnightly Review* have rightly been called "as distinguished an editorial term of office as any in the nineteenth century." [2] During those fifteen years the *Fortnightly* carried the spirit of liberalism and rationalism into considerations of religion, politics, and even literature, although the hand of welcome that Morley extended to some of the most promising young writers of the day was not withdrawn if they seemed lacking in progressive virtue. His talents as a literary entrepreneur flourished at Macmillan's publishing house, where he was able to combine his literary acumen with his zeal for carrying culture to the uninstructed in such projects as "Twelve English Statesmen" and the "English Men of Letters" series. The latter series was one of Morley's greatest editorial successes, for he recruited some of the best critics of his day (Leslie Stephen for *Johnson,* Henry James for *Hawthorne,* Thomas Huxley for *Hume,* Anthony Trollope for *Thackeray*), and the first series of thirty-nine volumes became virtually a British educational institution in itself.

If much that Morley wrote has been engulfed by the time spirit, much also retains its value today. *On Compromise* may not quite rank, as Basil Willey asserts, with *On Liberty* and *Culture and Anarchy*, but it is an articulate defense of certain qualities of intellectual integrity and moral courage that are even more deeply threatened today than they were a hundred years ago. Many of the critical studies—especially the essays on Macaulay, Byron, Carlyle, Mill, and Emerson—still deserve to be read by students of English literature.[3] They not only shed light on their subjects but afford to modern critics who are now seeking ways of going beyond formalism in assessing literary works excellent examples of the intelligent and tactful application of social and historical standards to literature.

The reasons for the neglect of Morley today are both literary and political. Like many Victorians, he appears to modern readers to have lived too long. The image of Morley as a superannuated relic of the nineteenth century who tried to keep the twentieth century from being born can be confirmed by such evidence as his notorious reader's report, in 1900, to Macmillan's on the work of a young Irish poet:

I would not read a page of it again for worlds, and I care not how many good judges swear that "Yeats is the only man who counts." Talk of Meredith, Browning, Tennyson, etc. being found obscure when they were new, and therefore Yeats ought to have his chance! To measure the weight and force of that, just take down *Maud* or *Lotus-Eaters,* or any volume of selections from Browning, and then read (if you can) a few pages of *The Wind among the Reeds.* There is no saying in these rather demented days what an industrious band of admirers may not succeed in foisting into an ephemeral popularity.[4]

John Gross acidly comments about this report that although *The Wind Among the Reeds* is not yet Yeats at his most powerful, it is, "by comparison with anything that Morley ever wrote, enough to burn a hole in the page." [5] The avant-garde editor of the *Fortnightly Review* had by the twentieth century come to see the progeny of Walter Pater, whom he had himself promoted, as the characteristic offspring of "these rather demented days."

It is Morley's response, as an active politician, to "these rather demented days" that is the major cause of indifference or downright hostility to him today. Modern social critics have assumed

Morley to be an easy and inviting target primarily for two reasons. One is that, as what is condescendingly called "a nineteenth-century liberal," he placed individual liberty, as defined by Mill, before social justice. The other is that, when he held positions of political power, in Ireland and in India, he betrayed his own liberal principles. Our response to the first charge against Morley will depend in part upon whether we see the terrible moral debacles of our own time as caused primarily by an indifference to the social evils wrought by laissez-faire industrialism or by the willingness of social reformers confident of their rectitude and good intentions to sacrifice the safeguards of personal liberty that have been developed slowly and painstakingly in democratic countries to the realization of their ideals. Our response to the second charge will depend upon whether or not we can live comfortably with the awareness that the great ideas of liberalism were conceived by men, not by angels, and that Morley's weakness was that he did not always reach the perfection of his own ideal.

Notes and References

Chapter One

1. *Great Contemporaries* (London, 1937), pp. 103, 106.
2. *Recollections*, 2 vols. (New York, 1917), II, 86; I, 6. It should be noted that most Evangelicals remained in the State Church, but Morley uses the term *Evangelical* to identify a kind of religious life rather than a religious group with a particular church affiliation.
3. *On Compromise* (London and New York, 1903), p. 38. Frederic Harrison, however, always saw the preacher in Morley and called him a combination of "Diderot *plus* John Wesley."—F. W. Hirst, *Early Life and Letters of John Morley*, 2 vols. (London: Macmillan, 1927), I, 162.
4. Matthew Arnold, *Lectures and Essays in Criticism*, ed. R. H. Super (Ann Arbor, 1962), p. 290; John Henry Newman, *Apologia pro Vita Sua*, ed. C. F. Harrold (New York, 1947), p. 237.
5. *Recollections*, I, 14, 19. Morley is paraphrasing Leslie Stephen in the second quotation.
6. Warren Staebler, *The Liberal Mind of John Morley* (Princeton, 1943), p. 38.
7. *Recollections*, I, 86.
8. *Edmund Burke: A Historical Study* (London, 1867), pp. 255–256.
9. *Ibid.*, pp. 20, 150.
10. *Burke* (London, 1902), p. 116.
11. *Edmund Burke*, p. 281.
12. *Recollections*, II, 104, 106.
13. "Joseph de Maistre," *Critical Miscellanies*, 3 vols. (London, 1886), II, 282.
14. Hirst, I, 188.
15. *Recollections*, I, 187–88.
16. *Ibid.*, I, 56.
17. *Ibid.*, I, 55–56.
18. "Coleridge," *Dissertations and Discussions*, 4 vols. (London, 1859–74), I, 398.

19. "Mr. Mill's Autobiography," *Critical Miscellanies,* III, 54, 56.

20. "The Death of Mr. Mill," *Critical Miscellanies,* III, 47, 42, 44. See also "John Stuart Mill: An Anniversary," in *Miscellanies: Fourth Series* (London, 1908), pp. 162–65.

21. "The Death of Mr. Mill," pp. 40–41.

22. "Mr. Mill's Autobiography," p. 73.

23. *Recollections,* I, 60.

24. *Ibid.,* I, 62.

25. *On Liberty,* ed. C. V. Shields (Indianapolis, 1956), p. 72. See Walter E. Houghton's discussion of Mill's "Romantic" ideal in *The Victorian Frame of Mind* (New Haven, 1957), pp. 290–91.

26. *Recollections,* I, 61.

27. See Mill, *Autobiography* (New York, 1924), p. 76, and Morley, *Recollections,* I, 99.

28. *Recollections,* I, 106.

29. Hirst, I, 316.

30. Bertrand Russell, "John Stuart Mill," *Proceedings of the British Academy,* XLI (1955), 46.

31. "Mr. Lecky's First Chapter," *Fortnightly Review,* V (May, 1869), 538.

32. *Recollections,* I, 84.

33. "Turgot," *Critical Miscellanies,* II, 56–57, 118.

34. *Ibid.,* p. 97.

35. *Ibid.,* p. 101.

36. *Ibid.,* p. 107.

37. See Shelley's *A Defence of Poetry,* in *Prose of the Romantic Period,* ed. Carl R. Woodring (Boston, 1961), pp. 507–8.

38. "Condorcet," *Critical Miscellanies,* II, 181.

39. Carl L. Becker, *The Heavenly City of the Eighteenth-Century Philosophers* (New Haven, 1932).

40. "Condorcet," pp. 212–13.

41. *Ibid.,* pp. 213–15.

42. *Ibid.,* p. 255.

43. Hirst, I, 198, 242; *Recollections,* I, 69.

44. Hirst, I, 300. See Morley's review of Harrison's *The New Calendar of Great Men,* in *Miscellanies: Fourth Series,* pp. 109–42.

45. "Auguste Comte," *Critical Miscellanies,* II, 376–77.

46. *Auguste Comte and Positivism* (Ann Arbor, 1961), pp. 119–20.

47. "Auguste Comte," pp. 378–80.

48. Hirst, II, 67.

49. *Ibid.,* II, 161.

50. *Ibid.,* II, 177.

51. *Ibid.,* II, 121. For a good indication of the strength of Morley's moral fiber, see his letter about Forster written on December 13,

190

JOHN MORLEY

1882, to Mrs. Humphry Ward, Forster's niece.—Hirst, II, 179–80. See also Mrs. Ward's remarks on Morley in Chapter 1, volume II of *A Writer's Recollections* (London, 1918).

52. Hirst, II, 244; *Recollections*, I, 204. Morley's position on Ireland caused him to break with an old friend, Joseph Chamberlain, who resigned from the Gladstone government in 1886 rather than support Home Rule. He went on to become a leading advocate of imperial expansion.

53. Elizabeth Longford, *Queen Victoria: Born to Succeed* (New York, 1964), p. 487.

54. *Recollections*, I, 267.

55. *Ibid.*, I, 328.

56. *Ibid.*, I, 317.

57. *Ibid.*, I, 354.

58. *Ibid.*, I, 338–40, 333, 346; II, 45.

59. *Ibid.*, II, 45–46.

60. "Turgot," p. 148.

61. *Speeches on Indian Affairs* (Madras, 1908), p. 198.

62. *The Life of William Ewart Gladstone*, 3 vols. (London and New York, 1903), I, 190, 198, 200, 204.

63. Yet he foresaw a great problem in the condition of the American Negro: "The future of the Negro in the U.S.A. has always profoundly interested and excited me, as well it might. What will the numbers amount to, twenty or fifty years hence? Terrible to think of!! Talk of India and other 'insoluble problems' of great States, I declare the American Negro often strikes me as the hardest of them all."— *Recollections*, II, 336–37.

64. See "The Analogy of Ireland," in *Speeches on Indian Affairs*, pp. 88–90.

65. *Recollections*, II, 278–79, 174, 186. See also II, 282.

66. *Ibid.*, II, 212. See also II, 318, 327.

67. See, e.g., *Recollections*, II, 263–65, where Morley politely but firmly puts down Minto's impatient request for a "Free Hand" in India; and also II, 269, 273, 282.

68. *Ibid.*, II, 251.

69. "Viscount Morley," *A New England Group and Others* (Boston and New York, 1921), p. 218.

70. See George M. Harper, *John Morley and Other Essays* (Princeton, 1920), p. 4.

71. *Recollections*, II, 343.

72. *Memorandum on Resignation* (New York, 1928), p. 4. Even a cursory examination of Morley's published work and private letters will show that he had very strong, and often quite irrational, German partialities. One may trace from 1870 an unbroken record of intellec-

tual flabbiness and something very close to servility in his attitude toward German power. The dangers of political relativism appear in his view that although militarism was undesirable for England, it was both natural and necessary for Germany. In the 1870's he approved Bismarck's anti-Catholic legislation but attacked the French government for trying to get rid of clerical control over education through legislation. For other illustrations of Morley's strange infatuation with Germany, see Hirst, I, 172, 178, 183, 208–9, 286–87, 297–98; II, 40, 53, 77; and *Recollections*, II, 346.

73. *Memorandum on Resignation*, p. 13.

74. *The Liberal Mind of John Morley*, pp. 124–25.

75. "Bernard Shaw at Eighty," *Eight Essays* (Garden City, New York, 1954), p. 139.

76. *Recollections*, I, vii.

77. *Memorandum on Resignation*, p. 28.

78. Tom A. Cullen, *When London Walked in Terror* (Boston, 1965), p. 267.

79. Hirst, I, xxii.

80. *Recollections*, I, viii.

Chapter Two

1. *Lectures and Essays in Criticism*, pp. 270–71.

2. Anthony Trollope, *An Autobiography* (London: Oxford University Press, 1947), pp. 172–73.

3. *Ibid.*, p. 174.

4. *Fortnightly Review*, V (February, 1869), 141. Morley was somewhat miffed at Huxley's epithet and suggested that Huxley insert the adjective *religious* before *philosophy* because "Comte's philosophy contains so much that has no Catholic or Christian bearings. . . ." Huxley finally placated Morley by referring to Comte's "philosophy in practice."—MS Letters of January 12 and January 13, 1869 in the Huxley Papers. 23.11 and 23.12.

5. T. H. Huxley, "The Scientific Aspects of Positivism," *Fortnightly Review*, V (June, 1869), 653–70.

6. *Recollections*, I, 86.

7. "Miracles and Special Providences," *Fortnightly Review*, I June, 1867), 660.

8. "The Political Prelude," *Fortnightly Review*, IV (July, 1868), 103.

9. *Recollections*, I, 86.

10. "The Liberal Programme," *Fortnightly Review*, I (September, 1867), 359.

11. *Ibid.*, p. 361.

12. *Ibid.*, p. 362.

13. *Ibid.*, pp. 363–64.

14. *Ibid.*, p. 368.

15. See Morley, "England and the War," *Fortnightly Review*, VIII (October, 1870), 479–88, and "A Note to Colonel Chesney's Letter," *Fortnightly Review*, VIII (November, 1870), 588–91; Goldwin Smith, "The Aim of Reform," *Fortnightly Review*, XI (March, 1872), 243–64; E. S. Beesly, "The Social Future of the Working Class," *Fortnightly Review*, V (March, 1869), 344–63.

16. See Chamberlain's "The Liberal Party and Its Leaders," *Fortnightly Review*, XIV (September, 1873), 287–302.

17. Hirst, I, 296.

18. The five sections originally published under this title in the *Fortnightly* were afterward combined with an appendix on Mill's *Liberty* to form the book we now read.

19. Basil Willey, *More Nineteenth-Century Studies: A Group of Honest Doubters* (London, 1956), p. 276.

20. *On Compromise*, pp. 3–4.

21. *The Portable Matthew Arnold* (New York, 1949), p. 4.

22. *On Compromise*, p. 16.

23. *Ibid.*, p. 34.

24. *Ibid.*, pp. 36–37.

25. *Lectures and Essays in Criticism*, pp. 43–44.

26. *On Compromise*, p. 56.

27. *Ibid.*, p. 65.

28. *Ibid.*, p. 74.

29. *Ibid.*, pp. 80–81.

30. *Ibid.*, p. 104.

31. *Lectures and Essays in Criticism*, p. 268.

32. *On Compromise*, p. 104.

33. *Ibid.*, p. 117.

34. *Ibid.*, p. 121.

35. *Ibid.*, p. 143.

36. *Ibid.*, p. 154.

37. *Ibid.*, p. 156.

38. *Ibid.*, p. 166.

39. *Ibid.*, p. 192.

40. *Ibid.*, p. 188.

41. *Ibid.*, p. 218.

42. *Ibid.*, pp. 237–38.

43. *Ibid.*, p. 198.

44. "Notes of New Books," *Fortnightly Review*, I (July 15, 1865), 633.

45. See the chapter "Literary Insignificancies," pp. 96–129 of G. L. Nesbitt, *Benthamite Reviewing* (New York, 1934).

46. "Mr. Pater's Essays," *Fortnightly Review*, XIII (April, 1873), 470.

47. Hirst, I, 240.

48. Morley himself, in the pages of the *Saturday Review*, had been one of the most hysterical attackers. At some time between his viperish review of August 4, 1866, and Swinburne's appearance in the January, 1867, issue of the *Fortnightly*, Morley made the acquaintance of Swinburne and underwent a partial change of heart.

49. Walter E. Houghton and G. Robert Stange, *Victorian Poetry and Poetics* (Boston, 1959), p. 558.

50. "Memorials of a Man of Letters," *Studies in Literature* (London, 1891), p. 286.

51. *Ibid.*, p. 287.

52. *Ibid.*, pp. 303–5.

53. "Valedictory," *Studies in Literature*, p. 328.

54. Hirst, I, 288.

55. "Valedictory," p. 342.

56. *Ibid.*, pp. 343–45.

57. E. M. Everett, *The Party of Humanity* (Chapel Hill, 1939), p. 322.

58. "Valedictory," pp. 346–47.

Chapter Three

1. In a letter of 1872, Frederic Harrison replied in this way to Morley's latest fulmination against the French people: "I am amused at your tirade against the poor French. Your literary spleen drives you into droll contradictions. You say they are worthless children, etc. . . . If what you say of the French is true your whole life has been a mistake. It has been devoted to popularising the French social and political ideas. . . . What is it that is about to place you in the first rank of living writers—your *Voltaire*, your Voltairean estimate and conception of the most typical of Frenchmen. Why is your *Review* flowing over with French ideas, French history, and French systems?" —Hirst, I, 207.

2. "A Few French Models," *Studies in Literature*, p. 157.

3. *Ibid.*, pp. 158–61.

4. *Ibid.*, pp. 179, 181. Morley quotes the passage on the *Social Contract* from his book on Rousseau.

5. *Autobiography*, p. 76.

6. "A Few French Models," p. 182. See *Burke*, pp. 244–45.

7. *Recollections*, I, 91.

8. Hirst, I, 196. When working on *Rousseau*, Morley felt sure he "was meant for a novelist."—Hirst, I, 219.

9. "Condorcet," p. 179.

10. *Ibid.*, p. 171.

11. *Voltaire* (New York, 1872), p. 5. Morley could not know that Voltaire's correspondence, assiduously collected in the twentieth century by Theodore Besterman, would itself fill 104 volumes, containing 18,000 letters. It would appear that no one who received a letter from Voltaire ever threw it away.

12. *On the Classical Tradition,* ed. R. H. Super (Ann Arbor, 1960), p. 48.

13. *Voltaire*, p. 12.

14. *Ibid.*, p. 34.

15. *Ibid.*, pp. 37–38.

16. Peter Gay, *Voltaire's Politics* (Princeton, 1959), p. 11n.

17. *Voltaire*, p. 57.

18. *Lettres Philosophiques ou Lettres sur les Anglais* (Paris, 1956), pp. 36, 53.

19. *Voltaire*, p. 69.

20. *Lettres Philosophiques*, pp. 43–44.

21. *Voltaire*, pp. 75, 78. For a very different view of Voltaire's attitude toward politics from that of Morley, see Gay, p. 11n. and *passim*.

22. *Voltaire*, p. 89.

23. John Henry Newman, *The Tamworth Reading Room* (London, 1841), p. 18.

24. *Voltaire*, p. 70.

25. *Ibid.*, p. 95.

26. *Ibid.*, pp. 113–14.

27. *Ibid.*, pp. 125–26.

28. *Ibid.*, p. 139.

29. *Ibid.*, pp. 143, 119.

30. *Ibid.*, pp. 142–47, 32. In one of his maxims for revolutionists in *Man and Superman*, George Bernard Shaw says: "Do not give your children moral and religious instruction unless you are quite sure they will not take it too seriously. Better be the mother of Henri Quatre and Nell Gwynne than of Robespierre and Queen Mary Tudor."

31. *Ibid.*, p. 156.

32. *Ibid.*, pp. 168–69.

33. *Ibid.*, pp. 182–83.

34. *Ibid.*, p. 210.

35. *Ibid.*, pp. 214, 216.

36. *Ibid.*, p. 242.

37. *Ibid.*, p. 244.

38. This seems to me highly disputable, for the general idea of the

miraculous is often subjected to criticism by Voltaire. See, e.g., "Miracles" in the *Dictionnaire Philosophique,* and the *Dialogues d'Évhémère.*

39. *Voltaire,* pp. 278–79, 283.
40. *Ibid.,* p. 287.
41. *Ibid.,* p. 316.
42. *Ibid.,* pp. 335–36.
43. *Ibid.,* p. 353. Morley quotes from Voltaire's letter to Chauvelin of April 2, 1764.
44. *Rousseau,* 2 vols. (London, 1896), I, 5. Cf. "Wordsworth," *Studies in Literature,* pp. 35–36.
45. *Rousseau,* I, 3.
46. *Ibid.,* I, 63.
47. *Ibid.,* I, 64.
48. Quoted *ibid.,* I, 83.
49. Quoted *ibid.,* I, 77.
50. *Ibid.,* I, 15–16.
51. *Ibid.,* I, 112.
52. *Ibid.,* I, 127.
53. *Ibid.,* I, 131.
54. Quoted *ibid.,* I, 133–34.
55. *Ibid.,* I, 138.
56. *Ibid.,* I, 148–49.
57. *Ibid.,* I, 150.
58. *Ibid.,* I, 153.
59. *Ibid.,* I, 154–55.
60. Quoted *ibid.,* I, 167–68.
61. *Ibid.,* I, 177.
62. *Ibid.,* I, 184.
63. *Edmund Burke,* p. vi.
64. *Rousseau,* I, 194.
65. *Ibid.,* I, 199.
66. *Ibid.,* I, 304.
67. *Ibid.,* I, 311.
68. *Ibid.,* I, 337.
69. *Ibid.,* II, 21.
70. *Ibid.,* II, 33.
71. *Ibid.,* II, 42.
72. *Ibid.,* II, 55.
73. *Ibid.,* II, 124.
74. *Ibid.,* II, 137–38.
75. *Ibid.,* II, 144.
76. *Ibid.,* II, 156–57.

77. *Ibid.*, II, 191.

78. *Ibid.*, II, 194.

79. *Ibid.*, II, 187, 192. For Halévy's analysis of Burke's Utilitarian and empirical arguments against the doctrine of the rights of man, see *The Growth of Philosophic Radicalism*, trans. M. Morris (London, 1934), pp. 155–64.

80. *Rousseau*, II, 211–12.

81. *Ibid.*, II, 230, 235.

82. *Ibid.*, II, 250.

83. *Ibid.*, II, 258.

84. *Ibid.*, II, 264, 267.

85. *Ibid.*, II, 276–78.

86. *Diderot and the Encyclopaedists*, 2 vols. (London, 1886), I, 5.

87. *Ibid.*, I, 8.

88. *Ibid.*, I, 18.

89. *Ibid.*, II, 24.

90. *Ibid.*, I, 84.

91. *The Victorian Frame of Mind*, p. 15.

92. *Diderot*, I, 129.

93. *Ibid.*, I, 144.

94. *Ibid.*, I, 200.

95. *Ibid.*, I, 247.

96. *Ibid.*, I, 355.

97. *Ibid.*, II, 238.

98. "Condorcet," pp. 200–201. See also, in the essay "Robespierre," Morley's analysis of the struggle between the faction of Robespierre and that of Chaumette as the reproduction, under the shadow of the guillotine, of the earlier literary struggle between Rousseau and the Encyclopedists.—*Critical Miscellanies*, I, 72.

99. "France in the Eighteenth Century," *Critical Miscellanies*, III, 288.

Chapter Four

1. *Recollections*, I, 125–31. See also Hirst, II, 82.

2. "George Eliot's Novels," *Macmillan's Magazine* (August, 1866). pp. 274–75.

3. "Mr. Pater's Essays." p. 474.

4. "The Life of George Eliot," *Critical Miscellanies*, III, 105–7.

5. *More Nineteenth-Century Studies: A Group of Honest Doubters*, p. 249.

6. *Victorian Poetry and Poetics*, p. 831.

7. "Mr. Swinburne's New Poems," *Saturday Review*, August 4, 1866, pp. 145, 147.

8. "Macaulay," *Critical Miscellanies*, I, 263.

9. "Mr. Swinburne's New Poems," p. 145.

10. *Rousseau*, II, 25.

11. "Victor Hugo's 'Ninety-Three,' " *Studies in Literature*, pp. 252–253.

12. "Mr. Swinburne's New Poems," p. 145.

13. "On 'The Ring and the Book,' " *Studies in Literature*, p. 255.

14. "Carlyle," *Critical Miscellanies*, I, 182. See Mill's "Bentham," *Dissertations and Discussions*, I, 386–87.

15. "Carlyle," pp. 184–86.

16. "Byron," *Critical Miscellanies*, I, 242.

17. "Recent English Poetry," *North American Review*, LXXVII (July, 1853), 20, 22. For Kingsley's essay, see his *Literary and General Lectures and Essays* (London, 1880), pp. 114–15.

18. "George Eliot's Novels," p. 276.

19. "The Earthly Paradise," *Fortnightly Review*, III (May, 1868), 714.

20. "Macaulay," pp. 278–80.

21. "Emerson," *Critical Miscellanies*, I, 322.

22. "The Life of George Eliot," pp. 131–32.

23. *Recollections*, I, 288. Shaw once remarked that with this play Shakespeare was ready to begin the twentieth century if only the seventeenth had let him.

24. *Dissertations and Discussions*, I, 354–55.

25. *The Mirror and the Lamp* (New York, 1953), p. 229.

26. See "Macaulay," pp. 260–62, 274, 277–79, 286, 288.

27. *Modern Characteristics* (London, 1865), pp. 211–12.

28. "Byron," p. 208.

29. "Macaulay," p. 254n.

30. "The Life of George Eliot," p. 99.

31. "Byron," p. 209.

32. *Lectures and Essays in Criticism*, p. 209.

33. *The Portable Matthew Arnold*, p. 23.

34. "George Eliot's Novels," p. 273. For other comments by Morley on the novel as a genre, see "On the Study of Literature," *Studies in Literature*, pp. 202–4, and "Aphorisms," *Studies in Literature*, p. 73.

35. "Emerson," p. 344.

36. "Stanzas in Memory of the Author of 'Obermann,' " ll. 53–54.

37. "Emerson," p. 346.

38. "Wordsworth," pp. 49–50.

39. *Studies in Conduct* (London, 1867), pp. 229–33.

40. *The George Eliot Letters*, ed. G. S. Haight, 7 vols. (London, 1954), III, 111.

41. "George Eliot's Novels," p. 279.

42. "The Life of George Eliot," p. 126.

43. *The Journals of André Gide*, 4 vols., trans. J. O'Brien (New York, 1947), III, 107.

44. "On 'The Ring and the Book,' " pp. 256–57.

45. *Ibid.*, pp. 259, 272.

46. *Ibid.*, pp. 268–69.

47. *Ibid.*, p. 269.

48. *Rousseau*, I, 326.

49. "Emerson," pp. 327–29, 335–36.

50. "On the Study of Literature," pp. 200–2, 226–27.

51. "Wordsworth," pp. 34–35.

52. *Ibid.*, pp. 43–45.

53. Letter of November 22, 1817.

54. *Lectures and Essays in Criticism*, pp. 12–13.

55. For a forceful and intelligent expression of this view, see Leon Gottfried, *Matthew Arnold and the Romantics* (Lincoln, 1963), pp. 139–40.

56. For the best exposition of the view that Arnold was not an unsuccessful Romantic poet but an altogether new *kind* of poet, see A. Dwight Culler, *Imaginative Reason: The Poetry of Matthew Arnold* (New Haven, 1966), pp. 19–43.

57. *Notes on Politics and History* (London, 1914), pp. 145, 147.

58. *Lord Morley's Criticism of English Poetry and Prose* (Princeton, n.d.), pp. 25, 30.

59. "On the Study of Literature," p. 200.

60. *Science and Literature* (London, 1911), p. 5.

61. *Ibid.*, pp. 3–4.

62. "Emerson," pp. 338, 339.

63. "Characteristics," *Critical and Miscellaneous Essays* (New York, 1904), III, 2.

64. "Carlyle," pp. 145–46. See Kathleen Nott, *The Emperor's Clothes* (London, 1953), pp. 58–61.

65. "Carlyle," p. 146.

66. *Ibid.*, p. 148.

67. *Ibid.*, p. 149.

68. *Ibid.*, pp. 150, 152. Cf. Mill, *Autobiography*, p. 166.

69. "Carlyle," p. 152.

70. *Ibid.*, p. 155.

71. *Ibid.*, pp. 156, 188.

72. "Byron," p. 211. Morley, as the essay on Byron illustrates, could readily fall into the unfortunate habit of using the terms *positive* and *scientific* interchangeably; yet in a letter of January 13, 1869 to Huxley

he sympathized with the scientist's vexation over the public's habit of supposing every scientifically minded person a Comtist.—MS in Huxley Papers. 23.12.

73. *Ibid.*, p. 227.

74. *Ibid.*, p. 235.

75. "Carlyle," p. 165.

76. "Byron," p. 236.

77. *Ibid.*

78. *Ibid.*, pp. 237–38.

79. *Ibid.*, pp. 240–41.

80. James Joyce, *A Portrait of the Artist as a Young Man* (London, 1958), p. 219.

81. "The Toilers of the Sea," *Saturday Review*, April 7, 1866, p. 415.

82. "George Eliot's Novels," pp. 272, 273, 277.

83. Introductory Essay in *Letters of Percy Bysshe Shelley* (London, 1852). pp. 2, 9.

84. "On 'The Ring and the Book,'" p. 260.

85. *The Letters of Robert Browning and Elizabeth Barrett: 1845–1846*, 2 vols. (New York, 1898), I, 379.

86. "On 'The Ring and the Book,'" pp. 271–73. Note that, in Morley's view, the scientific attitude of Browning's intelligence could coexist with his indifference, mentioned earlier in this chapter, to scientific developments.

87. *The Renaissance* (New York, 1899), pp. 244–45.

88. "Victor Hugo's 'Ninety-Three,'" pp. 241–42.

89. "Mr. Pater's Essays," p. 472.

90. *Recollections*, II, 75.

91. Robert K. Webb, *Harriet Martineau: A Radical Victorian* (New York, 1960), pp. 38–39.

92. "The Life of George Eliot," p. 127.

93. "Mr. Mill's Autobiography," p. 69.

94. "Mr. Pater's Essays," pp. 476–77. Three years earlier, in "Byron," p. 207, Morley had referred to the "Aesthetic Movement" in far less favorable terms. Much later, in 1917, he expressed a far more favorable view, not of Ruskin's doctrine, but of his influence.—*Recollections*, I, 16.

95. *Diderot*, I, 340–41.

96. "Carlyle," p. 141.

97. "The Life of George Eliot," pp. 126–27; Hirst, II, 9.

98. "Macaulay," pp. 267, 271–72.

99. Hirst, II, 174.

100. *Rousseau*, II, 20.

101. "On the Study of Literature," p. 219.

102. "Byron," p. 207.
103. *Ibid.*, pp. 209–10.
104. *Ibid.*, pp. 216–17.
105. *Ibid.*, p. 222.
106. *Ibid.*, p. 225.
107. *Ibid.*, pp. 227–32.
108. "Wordsworth," pp. 9, 26.
109. "Emerson," p. 318.
110. *Ibid.*, p. 333.
111. *Ibid.*, p. 346.
112. "On the Study of Literature," pp. 191–94.

Chapter Five

1. *Lectures and Essays in Criticism,* p. 264.

2. John Gross, *The Rise and Fall of the Man of Letters* (London, 1969), p. 99.

3. Several of the best essays have recently been returned to print in *Nineteenth Century Essays,* by John Morley, ed. Peter Stansky (Chicago, 1970).

4. Charles Morgan, *The House of Macmillan* (New York, 1944), p. 221.

5. *The Rise and Fall of the Man of Letters,* p. 111.

Selected Bibliography

PRIMARY SOURCES

Burke. London and New York: The Macmillan Company, 1902.

Critical Miscellanies. 3 vols. London: Macmillan and Company, 1886.

Diderot and the Encyclopaedists. 2 vols. London: Macmillan and Company, 1886.

"The Earthly Paradise," *Fortnightly Review,* III (June, 1868), 713–715.

Edmund Burke: A Historical Study. London: Macmillan and Company, 1867.

"George Eliot's Novels," *Macmillan's Magazine,* XIV (August, 1866), 272–79.

"The Liberal Programme," *Fortnightly Review,* I (September, 1867), 359–69.

The Life of Richard Cobden. London: Chapman and Hall, 1881.

The Life of William Ewart Gladstone. 3 vols. New York and London: Macmillan and Company, 1903.

Memorandum on Resignation. New York: The Macmillan Company, 1928.

Miscellanies: Fourth Series. London: Macmillan and Company, 1908.

"Mr. Pater's Essays," *Fortnightly Review,* XIII (April, 1873), 469–77.

"Mr. Swinburne's New Poems," *Saturday Review,* August 4, 1866, pp. 145–47.

Modern Characteristics. London: Tinsley Brothers, 1865.

Notes on Politics and History. London: Macmillan and Company, 1914.

Oliver Cromwell. London: Macmillan and Company, 1900.

On Compromise. London and New York: The Macmillan Company, 1903.

"The Political Prelude," *Fortnightly Review,* IV (July, 1868), 103–114.

Recollections. 2 vols. New York: The Macmillan Company, 1917.

Rousseau. 2 vols. London and New York: The Macmillan Company, 1896.

Science and Literature. London: The English Association, 1911.
Speeches on Indian Affairs. Madras: G. A. Natesan and Company, 1908.
Studies in Conduct. London: Chapman and Hall, 1867.
Studies in Literature. London: Macmillan and Company, 1891.
"The Toilers of the Sea," *Saturday Review,* April 7, 1866, pp. 414–16.
Voltaire. New York: D. Appleton and Company, 1872.
Walpole. London: Macmillan and Company, 1889.

SECONDARY SOURCES

CECIL, ALGERNON. "Lord Morley of Blackburn." *Six Oxford Thinkers.* London: John Murray, 1909. Contentious, often tasteless essay written from the antiliberal point of view.
CHURCHILL, WINSTON. "John Morley." *Great Contemporaries.* London: Thornton Butterworth Ltd., 1937. Delightful, intelligent, and revealing essay by a fellow member of the 1914 Cabinet from which Morley resigned.
EVERETT, EDWIN M. *The Party of Humanity.* Chapel Hill: University of North Carolina Press, 1939. Describes the founding of the *Fortnightly Review,* and its contents and policies during Morley's editorship.
GROSS, JOHN. *The Rise and Fall of the Man of Letters.* London: Weidenfeld and Nicolson, 1969. Includes an astute and amusing essay about how Morley helped shape the Victorian literary outlook as writer, editor, and senior literary adviser for the Macmillan firm.
HAMER, D. A. *John Morley: Liberal Intellectual in Politics.* Oxford: Clarendon Press, 1968. Very informative and very unsympathetic, this book blames Morley for failing to achieve the perfection of his own ideals.
HARPER, GEORGE MCLEAN. "John Morley." *John Morley and Other Essays.* Princeton: Princeton University Press, 1920. Sympathetic and incisive essay on the relation between Morley's liberal principles and his political actions.
HIRST, F. W. *Early Life and Letters of John Morley.* 2 vols. London: Macmillan and Company, 1927. Follows Morley's career up to 1885; an indispensable source of information.
KNICKERBOCKER, FRANCES W. *Free Minds: John Morley and His Friends.* Cambridge: Harvard University Press, 1943. Comprehensive general introduction to Morley's writings.
KOSS, STEPHEN E. *John Morley at the India Office, 1905–1910.* New Haven: Yale University Press, 1969. Absolves Morley of charges of ideological betrayal by arguing that he was a consistent disci-

ple of Gladstonian liberalism, not for exportation to non-European societies.

McCallum, James Dow. "Lord Morley's Criticism of English Poetry and Prose." Princeton University doctoral dissertation of 1921. This earliest discussion of Morley as a literary critic argues that he furnishes the model of a rigorously rationalistic literary criticism.

More, Paul Elmer. "Viscount Morley." *A New England Group and Others*. Boston and New York: Houghton Mifflin, 1921. A hostile essay which reveals more about its author and the "humanism" for which he spoke than about Morley.

Morgan, John H. *John, Viscount Morley: An Appreciation and Some Reminiscences*. London: John Murray, 1924. Written by a close friend; useful for its reproduction of many conversations with Morley on public questions.

Poulter, Molly C. *A Catalogue of the Morley Collection*. India Office Library: Commonwealth Relations Office, 1965. Essential guide for those interested in Morley's activities from 1905 to 1910 and March–May, 1911, when Morley was secretary of state for India.

Sardar Ali Khan, Saiyid. *The Life of Lord Morley*. London: Sir I. Pitman and Sons, 1923. Biography written by an Indian out of a feeling of gratitude for what Morley had done for his country.

Staebler, Warren. *The Liberal Mind of John Morley*. Princeton: Princeton University Press, 1943. Like Knickerbocker's book of the same year, a comprehensive survey of Morley's writings, but more critical in its approach.

Willey, Basil. "John Morley." *More Nineteenth-Century Studies: A Group of Honest Doubters*. London: Chatto & Windus, 1956. Makes a forceful case for including Morley among the major Victorian critics.

Index

(The works of John Morley are listed under his name)